English Sentence Constructions

English
Sentence
Constructions

Marjolijn H. Verspoor
University of Pannonia, Hungary

Tim Kassenberg
Merel Keijzer
Gregory J. Poarch
University of Groningen, the Netherlands

John Benjamins Publishing Company
Amsterdam / Philadelphia

The paper used in this publication meets the minimum requirements of the American National Standard for Information Sciences – Permanence of Paper for Printed Library Materials, ANSI Z39.48-1984.

doi 10.1075/z.240

Cataloging-in-Publication Data available from Library of Congress:
LCCN 2022024638 (PRINT) / 2022024639 (E-BOOK)

ISBN 978 90 272 1150 7 (HB) / ISBN 978 90 272 1149 1 (PB)
ISBN 978 90 272 5749 9 (E-BOOK)

© 2022 – John Benjamins B.V.
No part of this book may be reproduced in any form, by print, photoprint, microfilm, or any other means, without written permission from the publisher.

John Benjamins Publishing Company · https://benjamins.com

Table of contents

List of tables   11

Acknowledgements   12

Introduction   13

Chapter 1
Sentences: Communicative functions and typical patterns

1.1   Introduction   15
1.2   Declarative, interrogative, imperative and exclamatory sentence patterns   15
1.3   Participants, process, attributes, and setting   17
1.4   Subject, predicator, object, attribute, and adverbial   20
1.5   Typical sentence patterns   22
    1   The running pattern (intransitive verbs)   24
    2   The being pattern (copula verbs)   24
    3   The doing/seeing pattern (monotransitive verbs)   25
    4   The giving/buying pattern (ditransitive verbs)   25
    5   The making/considering pattern (complex-transitive verbs)   27
1.6   Same verb, different patterns   27
1.7   English word order   29
1.8   Summary   31

Chapter 2
Sentences: Simple, compound, and complex

- 2.1 Introduction 32
- 2.2 Sentences versus clauses 33
- 2.3 Sentence types 34
    - 1 Simple sentences 34
    - 2 Compound sentences 34
    - 3 Complex sentences 36
    - 4 Compound-complex sentences 41
- 2.4 Phrases 43
- 2.5 Summary 44

Chapter 3
Verbs I

- 3.1 Introduction 45
- 3.2 Simple versus complex verb phrases 46
- 3.3 Lexical versus auxiliary verbs 47
- 3.4 Finite versus non-finite verb forms 47
    - 1 Finite verb forms 48
    - 2 Non-finite verb forms 50
- 3.5 Auxiliary verbs 53
    - 1 Progressive *be* + present participle 53
    - 2 Perfect *have* + past participle 54
    - 3 Modals + (*to*) infinitives 54
    - 4 Passive *be* + past participle 56
    - 5 *Do* for questions, negation and emphasis 57
    - 6 Ordering of auxiliary verbs 58
- 3.6 One form, several senses: *Be*, *have* and *do* 60
- 3.7 Summary 61

Chapter 4
Verbs II

- 4.1 Introduction 64
- 4.2 Subtypes of lexical verbs 64
  - 1 Intransitive verbs (the running pattern) 65
  - 2 Copula verbs (the being pattern) 65
  - 3 Transitive verbs (the doing/seeing pattern) 65
- 4.3 Subtypes of transitive verbs 67
  - 1 Monotransitive verbs (the doing/seeing pattern) 67
  - 2 Ditransitive verbs (the giving/buying pattern) 67
  - 3 Complex-transitive verbs (the making/considering pattern) 67
- 4.4 Direct object forms 69
- 4.5 Passive constructions 72
  - 1 Monotransitive verbs and passive constructions 73
  - 2 Ditransitive verbs and passive constructions 73
  - 3 Complex-transitive verbs and passive constructions 73
  - 4 Non-finite clauses and passive constructions 74
  - 5 Past participles as adjectives 77
- 4.6 Identifying type of lexical verbs in complex sentences 78
- 4.7 Multi-word verbs 80
- 4.8 Summary 83

Chapter 5
Word classes

- 5.1 Introduction 86
- 5.2 Nouns 88
- 5.3 Verbs 91
- 5.4 Adjectives 92
- 5.5 Adverbs 92

5.6   Pronouns   95
        1   Personal pronouns   96
        2   Possessive pronouns   96
        3   Relative pronouns   96
        4   Interrogative pronouns   97
        5   Demonstrative pronouns   97
        6   Reflexive pronouns   98
        7   Reciprocal pronouns   98
        8   Indefinite pronouns   98
        9   So   99
5.7   Numerals and articles   99
5.8   Connectors   101
        1   Coordinators   101
        2   Subordinators   104
        3   Prepositions   108
5.9   Interjections   111
5.10 Summary   112

**Chapter 6
Phrases**

6.1   Introduction   117
6.2   Noun phrases   119
        1   Determiners   121
        2   Specifying versus classifying genitives   122
6.3   Postmodifiers of nouns   124
        1   Restrictive versus non-restrictive postmodifiers   125
        2   Relative pronouns and adverbs   129
        3   Ellipsis in relative clauses   132
6.4   Verb phrases   135
6.5   Adjective phrase   136
6.6   Adverb phrase   138

6.7	Prepositional phrase 140	
6.8	Functions of phrases 142	
6.9	Summary 146	

Chapter 7
Sentence constituents realized as clauses and non-canonical constructions

- 7.1 Introduction 150
- 7.2 Subjects, objects, and attributes 153
  1. Finite clauses 153
  2. Non-finite clauses 155
  3. Extraposed subject or object clauses 160
- 7.3 Adverbials 161
- 7.4 How to analyze non-canonical constructions 164
  1. Passive constructions 164
  2. Extraposed constructions 166
  3. Ellipsis 167
  4. Existential sentences with *there* 169
  5. Cleft constructions 170
- 7.5 Summary 172

Chapter 8
How to analyze sentences at all levels

- 8.1 Introduction 175
- 8.2 How to go about analyzing long and complex sentences 175
- 8.3 How to go about analyzing long and complex noun phrases 177
- 8.4 How to go about analyzing sentences at different levels 184
- 8.5 Analyzing sentences at different levels on your own 191
- 8.6 Summary 197

Chapter 9
How to apply sentence construction knowledge to writing

- 9.1 Introduction 198
- 9.2 How to avoid sentence and clause errors 199
  - 1 Fragment 199
  - 2 Run-on sentence 199
  - 3 Comma splice 200
  - 4 Dangling modifier 201
- 9.3 How to use commas 203
  - 1 Adverbials 203
  - 2 Restrictive and non-restrictive elements 204
  - 3 Coordinate constructions 207
- 9.4 How to make sure each sentence is effective 210
  - 1 Use simple sentences effectively 210
  - 2 Avoid redundancy 210
  - 3 Avoid front-weighted sentences 211
  - 4 Avoid awkward and vague passive constructions 213
  - 5 Make sure constructions are parallel 214
- 9.5 How to create coherence with sentence constructions 215
- 9.6 Summary 218

Key to the exercises 219

Index 258

Companion website

Exercises can be found on the book's companion website:

https://doi.org/10.1075/z.240.website

List of tables

Table 1 Sentence constituents 20
2 Copula verbs (possible verbs used in the being pattern) 25
3 Sentence constituents: A complete overview 31
4 Coordinators 35
5 Finite verb forms 48
6 Non-finite verb forms 50
7 Basic verb forms of regular and irregular verbs 51
8 Auxiliary versus lexical verbs 61
9 Verb forms: A complete overview 61
10 Auxiliary verbs: A complete overview 62
11 Ordering of auxiliaries and lexical verb in the verb phrase 63
12 Multi-word verbs 81
13 Types of lexical verbs 83
14 Passive constructions 84
15 Analyzing conventionalized passive constructions 85
16 'Open' versus 'closed' word classes 88
17 Open word classes 112
18 Pronouns, articles, and numerals 113
19 Connectors 114
20 Lists of prepositions, subordinators, coordinators, and conjunctive adverbs 115
21 Types of phrases 118
22 Noun phrase 146
23 Adjective phrase 147
24 Adverb phrase 147
25 Prepositional phrase 148
26 Verb phrase 148
27 Functions and realizations at sentence or clause level 152
28 Review of typical sentence patterns 164
29 Distinguishing sentences, clauses and phrases 173

Acknowledgements

To our students — past, present and future.

The current book is an adapted version of *English Sentence Analysis: An introductory course*. We decided to rename it to make our theoretical perspective — usage based linguistics and construction grammar — more clear to our colleagues and students.

The book has benefited a great deal from all the remarks our students have made over the course of many years. It is from their many questions and remarks that we have learned what they find so confusing but interesting about English Constructions. We thank them for their insights and hope this book can continue to serve as an introduction to English sentence constructions but also a constant companion book to return to, during their studies and beyond.

Introduction

Subject, predicate, head, premodifier....all these terms are used to denote English sentence constituents. *English Sentence Constructions* introduces English syntax to students at tertiary level majoring in English literature or linguistics or another language-related field of study. It departs from a usage-based theoretical perspective in which all language units — which we refer to as constructions — have both a meaning and form within a given context. It also takes a prototype view of categories, such as nouns or verbs, that have core members (best examples) and peripheral members (weak examples).

 This book is meant to provide a starting-level module to make students aware of different levels of analysis at the sentence, clause, and phrase level. It is also meant to make students familiar with terminology, and to provide hands-on experience analyzing English sentence constructions. As such, it forms a solid basis for theoretical courses in syntactic analysis but also aids practical courses such as grammar and writing. Moreover, the skills gained in this course can be applied to the analysis of literary works in English, for example in close reading. Finally, the book can serve as a reference for definitions in terminology in English as a Second language developmental research, to denote what a learner can do at any given point in forming English sentence constructions.

 The material in this book is primarily intended as a classroom-taught introductory course spanning approximately 10 weeks, with instructors elaborating on the constructs introduced in each chapter and providing essential hands-on practice sessions. However, students may also use the book as a self-study guide. The index provides a quick route to relevant sections of the book and each chapter contains exercises (with answers at the back of the book) for students to check their own understanding of the subject matter. The book's companion website contains a final knowledge test for each chapter. Because the chapters are incrementally ordered, they are meant to be dealt with in sequence.

Whether the book is used as part of a classroom-based course or as a self-study guide, the best results are reached when students work through the chapters incrementally, reading the text and doing the exercises. The exercises are scattered throughout the chapters by way of helping students engage with the material. The answers for each exercise should be checked with the key to the exercises only after they have been completed. The exercises are meant to check understanding and the answers in the back of the book therefore also occasionally provide additional explanations. We would like to stress that we fully understand that terminology and constructs may be hard to grasp at first. Mistakes will be — and should be! — made. This book can help with familiarization and consolidation of English sentence constructions. It is meant as a resource and a constant reminder of the complexity and beauty of English sentence constructions that never cease to be a discovery process.

1 Sentences
Communicative functions and typical patterns

1.1 Introduction

If you want to describe the English language, the first thing you need to do is decide on your focus as to the type of language. Not only are there hundreds of different English dialects all over the world, but even within dialects there are varieties, ranging from substandard and slang to informal and formal ones, which in turn may be spoken or written. In this book, we will concentrate mainly on a rather formal, standard, written variety, not only because this is the variety that we will come across most in academic books and articles, but especially because it has been most carefully thought about before being put on paper and therefore does not show the kinds of gaps and unfinished sentences that may occur in spoken language. Another reason is that a more formal written variety often contains sentences that are longer and are therefore more complex than spoken sentences. Actually, many of the exercises in this book contain passages from famous authors, who are known to be especially creative in their sentence use.

In this first chapter, we will start by taking a look at sentences in general to narrow down our object of analysis, then we will introduce you to the basic constituents of a sentence, and finally we will show you how these may or may not be combined in typical sentence patterns.

1.2 Declarative, interrogative, imperative, and exclamatory sentence patterns

When people communicate, they do so for various reasons; the four main reasons are:

> to inform someone of something
> to get information from someone
> to get someone to do something
> to express one's attitude about something

Each of these communicative functions has a typical sentence pattern:

> John is leaving.
> Is John leaving?
> Leave!
> How sad that John is leaving! What a shock that John is leaving!

These patterns have the following syntactic characteristics. You can look at this as a given construction with open slots:

> subject — whole verb
> part of verb — subject — rest of verb
> verb by itself
> *How..* or *What a ...* followed by remainder of sentence

We use different terms to denote each of these sentence types:

> *declarative*
> *interrogative*
> *imperative*
> *exclamatory*

If you were to look at any large body of written text, you would find that most sentences are informative and will constitute a declarative sentence pattern. That is why we will concentrate mostly on those, but note that almost any linguistic sign (including a typical sentence pattern) may have more than one sense or communicative function. For sentence types this means that in the right context, with the right intonation, a given sentence type may very well be used to express a different communicative function.

EXERCISE 1   Try to come up with one sentence that can be declarative, interrogative, imperative and exclamatory all at the same time. To get you started, say the words "*John is leaving*" in such a way that it expresses the following communicative functions:

1. informing
2. asking for information
3. getting someone to do something
4. expressing feeling/attitude

Exercise 1 is based on the fact that the same declarative pattern can have different communicative functions. In this book we will take the position that we will analyze the forms of the sentences as they are presented to us; so even though "*John is leaving*" when pronounced with surprise and a rising intonation ("*John is leaving?*") has the function of a question, its form still has the declarative pattern. In this course, we will name such a sentence by its form, not its communicative function. In other words, we describe the pattern of a sentence and not its intention.

1.3 Participants, process, attributes, and setting

In a *declarative* sentence, a speaker or writer gives information about situations or events. When different people describe the same event or situation, it is likely that they use different words to describe it because they may find different aspects of the scene important or interesting. The words the speaker uses shows which of the aspects of the scene they find most appropriate, relevant or effective at the moment of speaking. Consider the following cartoon* and quickly jot down about three simple sentences you might use to describe what is happening. (We will get back to these later.)

* From *Go to your room!* by Bill Keane, (1982) New York: Ballantine Books

From *Go to your room!* by Bill Keane, (1982) New York: Ballantine Books

Out of all the details in an event or situation, a speaker can name the following aspects: one or more participants (who is involved?), attributes of these participants (what can be said about these participants?), and information about the setting of the event or situation.

In other words, the speaker names at least one person or thing and says something about them or it. That same speaker may also choose to add additional information about the where, why, when or how in relation to the person or thing. In this cartoon, there are a few things that stand out: the little boy, the balloon, and the cactus. In a typical sentence, the person or thing that stands out the most (for us humans, that is usually a person doing something) is named first. We will call this person or thing the *first participant*.

Then the speaker names the *process*, such as *is, is holding, is walking*, which describes the act, deed, state of being or becoming that the first participant is involved in. The speaker may then say something about the first participant or name one or two more participants. As you can see in the following examples, if the speaker says something about the first participant, it will be an attribute describing a quality or characteristic, or one or more words identifying the participant or giving details as to the class the participant is a member of.

The little boy	is	**happy**	a quality
He	appears	**three years old**.	a characteristic
He	must be	**Annie's little brother**.	identification
He	was	**a toddler**.	class membership

But the speaker may also choose to mention a second participant, which is another thing, person, event, or situation that stands out in the scene.

| The little boy | is holding | **a balloon**. |

And, in some cases, it is possible to name an attribute of the second participant. In the following sentences, *unpoppable* and *his treasure* describe the second participant.

| The little boy | considered | the balloon | **unpoppable**. |
| The little boy | made | the balloon | **his treasure**. |

It is also possible for the speaker to name three participants. In such cases, something is transferred from one participant to another. In the following sentences, *the mother* is the first participant, *the balloon*, the second one, and *the boy*, the third one.

| The mother | had given | **the boy** | a balloon. |
| The mother | had bought | **the boy** | a balloon. |

Besides naming participants and attributes of these participants, the speaker may choose to give information about the *setting*, so the how, where, when, why, or under what condition(s), in the process or the event or situation takes place. The term 'setting' is to be taken very broadly. It may refer to time, reason, condition, cause and so on. Basically it refers to anything that is not a participant, an attribute of a participant or a process. In the following examples, *yesterday* tells us something about **when** the event took place. *Up high* relates **how** the balloon was held, *for his birthday* **why** the event took place and *when he walked through the hallway* says something about **when** the event took place.

The little boy was very proud **yesterday**.
He was holding his balloon **up high**.
The mother had given him the balloon **for his birthday**.
When he walked through the hallway, he considered it unpoppable.

EXERCISE 2 Go back to the sentences you jotted down about the cartoon and identify the elements you named (e.g. can you now identify first participant, second participant, process, attribute, and so on?).

1.4 Subject, predicator, object, attribute, and adverbial

So far we have talked about the roles different sentence parts may play in a sentence. A group of words used to name a particular role has a technical *function* in the sentence. The group of words themselves we call a sentence constituent. The technical terms and the abbreviations we will use for these are shown in Table 1.

Table 1 Sentence constituents

Roles	Function	Abbreviation
first participant	*subject*	S
process	*predicator*	P
something about the first participant	*subject attribute*	S A
a second participant	*direct object*	D O
something about the second participant	*object attribute*	O A
a third participant	*indirect object* *benefactive object*	I O B O
the setting	*adverbial*	A

Sentences: Communicative functions and typical patterns

To summarize, main participants, which tell us who or what, are *subjects*, *direct objects*, or *indirect objects*. The part that names the process is called the *predicator*, and characteristics of one of the participants are called *attributes*. Finally, those parts of the sentence that tell us when, why, how, and so on are called *adverbials*.

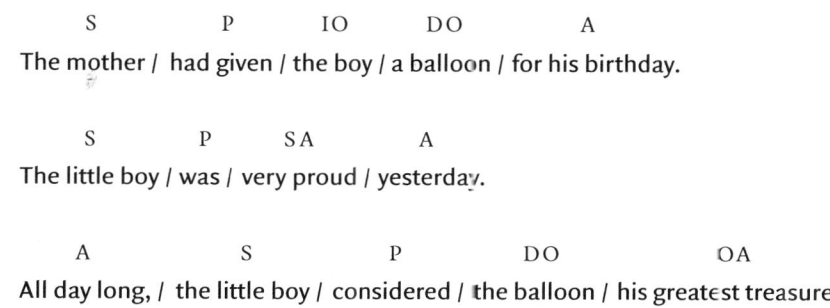

| S | P | IO | DO | A |

The mother / had given / the boy / a balloon / for his birthday.

| S | P | SA | A |

The little boy / was / very proud / yesterday.

| A | S | P | DO | OA |

All day long, / the little boy / considered / the balloon / his greatest treasure.

EXERCISE 3   In the following passage adapted from *True Trash* by Margaret Atwood, some sentence constituents have been set off with square brackets. Try to identify the functions of those constituents.

> [The waitresses] [are basking] [in the sun] like a herd of skinned seals, their pinky-brown bodies shining with oil. [They] [are wearing] [their bathing suits] [because it's the afternoon]. [In the early dawn and the dusk] [they] [sometimes] go skinny-dipping, which makes this itchy crouching in the mosquito-infested bushes across from their small private dock a great deal more worthwhile.
>
> [Donny] [has] [the binoculars, which are not his own but Monty's]. [Monty's dad] [gave] [them] [to him] [for bird-watching] but [Monty] isn't interested in birds. [He] [has found] [a better use for the binoculars]: [he] rents [them] out to the other boys, five minutes maximum, a nickel a look or else a chocolate bar from the tuck shop, though he prefers the money.

21   1.4   Subject, predicator, object, attribute, and adverbial

1.5 Typical sentence patterns

You will have noticed in Exercise 3 that the ordering of the sentence constituents is rather predictable: the subject comes before the predicator, objects and attributes. The only sentence constituent that may occur before the subject is the adverbial. In this section, we will take a closer look at typical sentence orders.

When a speaker describes an event or situation, they must organize the words according to a recognizable sentence pattern (or schema); otherwise, the listener cannot make sense of the stream of words. For example, the following two utterances will not make much sense because there are no recognizable patterns. In the first one, there are just words in alphabetical order and in the second one, phrases in alphabetical order.

>also but expresses ideas language not only our shapes the thinking use we
>expresses ideas not only… but also our thinking shapes the language we use

To make sense of words, a listener must recognize a pattern. First of all, words that make up one constituent (a subject, a predicator) are put together in a certain order. For example, we say *the language*, not *language the*. As a next step, the sentence constituents are arranged according to a recognizable pattern. The most common pattern in English is that the *subject* is named first, then the *predicate*, which is the remainder of the sentence, naming the process, other participants, attributes and setting. It is important here to note the distinction between the predicate and the predicator, the latter of which only denotes a process. While some grammar books use the terms interchangeably, we thus clearly distinguish between the two. English does not have a rich morphological system and therefore necessarily relies on word order to show who did what to whom. Languages that do have richer morphology have more freedom when it comes to the order of sentence constituents.

Now let's look at the previous utterances in a recognizable pattern. The subject and predicate have been separated with a slash.

>   subject   predicate
>The language we use / not only expresses ideas but also shapes our thinking.

The predicate, in turn, contains the *predicator*, consisting of one or more words denoting the process. The predicator may be followed by a *complement*, which is a term for the objects or attributes, which name other participants or attributes of participants that are necessary to complete the meaning of the predicator.

In the following example, the correlative conjunction *not only...but also** is set off with parentheses because it does not have a function in the sentence. It merely connects the two predicates.

subject	predicator	complement
The language we use /	(not only) expresses /	ideas
	/ (but also) shapes /	our thinking.

The complements *ideas* and *our thinking* are both direct objects. Therefore, this pattern is very similar to a very basic S — P — DO pattern. The main difference is that it contains two predicates joined by the words *not only* and *but also*.

In English there are five such basic, prototypical sentence patterns. That does not mean that you can never deviate from those prototypical sentence patterns, but most sentences you will come across, no matter how complex, will be somewhat similar to one of these. However, they are usually much more complex because often the constituents that make up the sentence are very complex and long. And as you will see in Chapter 7, there are some variations to these basic patterns.

Because the pattern that can be used is very much dependent on the meaning of the verb in the predicate, the patterns are named after very typical verbs for that pattern. The first three patterns are most common in everyday language; the last two occur much less frequently.

---

* These types of conjunctions (more commonly known as linking words) will be discussed in the next chapter.

1. **The <u>running</u> pattern (intransitive verbs)**
   Sentences with the *running* pattern consist of a subject and predicator, often (but by no means always) followed by an adverbial. For this pattern you need a verb that expresses an action involving only one main participant. There are many verbs like *run* that express a pure action, for example, *swimming, talking, cycling, listening,* and so on. This sentence pattern may have one or more adverbials, but no direct object nor subject attribute. As you will see in Chapter 4, verbs like *running* are called *intransitive* verbs.

   ```
   S      P         (A)*
   John   is running (fast).
   ```

2. **The <u>being</u> pattern (copula verbs)**
   Sentences with the *being* pattern consist of a subject and predicator followed by a subject attribute. The subject attribute gives information about the subject only, not about the predicator. For the *being* pattern, you need a verb that does not have much meaning, but expresses the sense of the mathematical equal sign (=). The meaning of such a verb is merely to point out a link between the first participant and an attribute or a category. In the example below, *fast* expresses an attribute of John, and *the runner* indicates to what category John belongs.

   ```
   S     P   S A          (A)
   John  is  fast         (in the game).
   John  is  the runner   (as usual).
   ```

   By far the most common verb for this pattern is the lexical verb *be*, called a *copula* verb when used in this type of construction, but Table 2 shows a few more verbs that may be used with this pattern.

   * Here, the parentheses indicate that the constituent is optional. In other words, this constituent may be left off.

Table 2 Copula verbs (possible verbs used in the being pattern)

appear	grow	seem	look
be	make	smell	sound
become	prove	taste	
feel	remain	turn	

Remember, though, that words may have different senses in different contexts. So, for example, in a sentence like *He appeared suddenly*, the verb *appear* expresses an action, and this sentence has the *running* pattern. But in *He appeared sad* the verb *appear* has a sense somewhat similar to *be* and this sentence has the *being* pattern. Also, the verb *be* when followed by an adverbial expressing a place, as in *He is in the room*, is not used in the *being* pattern but the *running* pattern.

3 The doing/seeing pattern (monotransitive verbs)

Sentences with the *doing/seeing* pattern consist of a subject and predicator followed by a direct object. For this pattern, you need a verb that expresses an action or a (mental) experience such as perception involving two participants, one who does the acting or experiencing and one who is acted upon or perceived. There are many verbs like *doing*, for example, *holding, counting, building, kicking*, and many verbs like *seeing* that express (mental) experience like *feeling, hearing, believing, thinking* and so on. As you will see in Chapter 4, verbs used in this pattern are called *monotransitive* verbs.

```
S      P       DO          (A)
John   kicked  the ball    (when it was thrown by Peter).
John   saw     the ball.
```

4 The giving/buying pattern (ditransitive verbs)

Sentences with the *giving/buying* pattern consist of a subject, predicator, indirect or benefactive object, and direct object. Therefore, for this pattern to occur, there must be an event involving at least three participants, a person who gives something to someone or does something for someone (the subject), then the thing that is given or done (the direct object), and the receiver (the indirect or benefactive object). Very few verbs can be used in such patterns. The most common ones are *give, pass, send, tell, make, buy, offer,* and *ask*.

S	P	IO	DO	(A)
John	gave	Peter	the ball	(for his birthday).
John	bought	Peter	the ball	(for his birthday).

The difference between an *indirect object* and a *benefactive object* is that an indirect object has the thing given in hand after the transfer, whereas the benefactive object does not.*

John gave Peter the ball.	This sentence implies that Peter now has the ball in his possession.
John bought Peter the ball.	This sentence does not necessarily imply that Peter now has the ball in his possession; the ball may still be with John.

One easy way to keep these two apart is by changing the sentence word order and then seeing which preposition must be used. The preposition *to* indicates an indirect object, and the preposition *for*, a benefactive one.

IO		IO
I / give / you / the ball.	→	I / give / the ball / to you.

BO		BO
I / bought / you / the ball.	→	I / bought / the ball / for you.

As you will see in Chapter 4, verbs used in the *giving/buying* pattern are called *ditransitive verbs*.

* In many books, the distinction between indirect and benefactive object is not made. Both are then called *indirect object*.

5   **The <u>making/considering</u> pattern (complex-transitive verbs)**
Sentences with the *making/considering* pattern, which can occur with only a very limited number of verbs, consist of a subject and predicator followed by a direct object. This direct object, in turn, is followed by an object attribute describing only the direct object.

S	P	DO	OA	(A)
They	made	John	the umpire	
John	considered	the ball	out	(as it went past the line).

When used in this pattern, a verb like *make* has a sense of 'doing something' and thus causing the 'direct object' to belong to a new category. For example, a sentence like *We made him king* expresses something like 'we did something to him and this caused him to be king'. Other verbs like *make* are *call, crown, name,* or *elect*.

A verb like *consider*, when used with this pattern, expresses that in the subject's mind the 'direct object' belongs to a certain category. For example, a sentence like *We consider him king* expresses that in the subject's mind 'he is king'. Other verbs like *consider* are *assume, prove, declare, certify, regard,* or *deem*. The following are some more examples of this pattern.

The judge **declared** him guilty.	The judge thought something: he was guilty.
The We **crowned** her queen.	We did something and she became queen.
We **elected** him president.	We did something and he became president.
They **named** themselves Tracy.	They did something and they became Tracy.

As you will see in Chapter 4, verbs used in this pattern are called *complex-transitive verbs*.

1.6   Same verb, different patterns

Although there are typical verbs for typical sentence patterns, many verbs may be used in several patterns. Especially the verb *make* has several distinct senses.

S	P	SA	

He makes a good coach.   *make* used in *being* pattern

S	P	DO

He made a goal.   *make* used in *doing/seeing* pattern

S	P	BO	DO

We made them a cake.   *make* used in *giving/buying* pattern

S	P	DO	OA

We made her president.   *make* used in *making/considering* pattern

EXERCISE 4 In the following sentences, name the function of the sentence constituents, which have been separated with slashes. Then indicate which pattern the sentence as a whole has. The first one has been done for you.

	A	S	P	IO	DO

1 Last week / Michael / showed / us / how to prepare a 'fruit leather'.
   (*giving* pattern)

2 He / told / us / to buy over ripe and bruised fruit on sale.

3 We / bought / him / peaches, apricots, and strawberries.

4 He / showed / us / how to cut up the fruit.

5 He / put / the fruit / through a food mill.

6 Then / he / put / the fruit / in a large pot.

7 He / told / me / to add one tablespoon of honey per pound of fruit.

8 He / heated / the mixture.

9   He / stirred / it / until it boiled.

10 He / cooked / the mixture / for three minutes.

11 He / prepared / paper plates / to dry the fruit.

12 He / used / plastic wrap / to cover the plates.

13 After stretching the plastic around the plate, / we / taped / it / to the back.

14 The plastic / had to be / tight and flat.

15 We / spread / a thin layer of fruit / on each plate.

16 We / placed / the plates, covered with cheesecloth, / in a shadow box / to dry in the sun.

17 We / brought / the plates / inside / at night.

18 In about two days / the fruit / was / dry.

19 After three days,/ he / brought / us / the dried fruit leather.

20 We / considered / this snack / a real treat.

1.7 English word order

In order to be able to analyze sentences, you should be aware of a few more facts about English sentence constituents and their patterns. First of all, English word order is quite rigid. The subject almost always comes first, then the predicator, etc. One way to find out whether a sentence part is a subject or not is to make the sentence into a question. The subject will appear after the first verb:

> **He** told me to add one tablespoon of honey per pound of fruit.
> Did **he** tell me ...?

We spread a thin layer of fruit on each plate.
Did **we** spread ...?

The only constituent that may occur in many different places is an adverbial. Especially one-word adverbials like *not, always,* and *often* may occur almost anywhere in the sentence. In order to see if a sentence part is an adverbial or not, see if it is possible to move it to a different place in the sentence.

Last week Michael showed us how to prepare a 'fruit leather'.
Michael showed us how to prepare a 'fruit leather' **last week**.

He used plastic wrap **to cover the plates**.
To cover the plates, he used plastic wrap.

EXERCISE 5   In order to discover more about possible combinations of constituents, go back over the sentences in Exercise 4 and, assuming they represent typical English sentences, answer the following questions:

1. How many subjects can be found in a sentence?
2. How many direct objects can be found in a sentence?
3. If there is one object in a sentence, is it a direct, indirect, or benefactive object?
4. Is it possible to have a subject attribute and a direct object in one sentence?
5. Is it possible to have more than one adverbial in a sentence?
6. Which of the following are possible combinations, and which ones not?

   S — P — A   S — P — IO — IO — DO
   S — P — DO — A   S — P — OA
   S — P — DO — SA   S — P — SA — DO
   S — P — DO — OA   S — P

1.8 Summary

In this chapter, you saw that sentences may have different *communicative functions* and that each of these communicative functions is expressed with a typical *sentence pattern*, called the *declarative, interrogative, imperative* or *exclamatory* pattern. The declarative sentence pattern is the most common and will be studied the most in this book.

A typical declarative sentence gives information about a situation or event and may name one or more participants, a process, an attribute of one of the participants, and various aspects of the setting. The *sentence constituents* naming these are *subject*, and *predicate*. The predicate names the process, and possibly other participants, attributes or setting. The predicate consists of a *predicator*, which names the *process*, and its *complement*. The complement can be a *direct object* or *subject attribute*. If there is a direct object, there may also be either an *indirect* or *benefactive object* or an *object attribute* in the complement. Any sentence may have one or more *adverbials*, which give information about the setting. Table 3 shows the possible sentence patterns and gives an overview of these terms. English word order is quite rigid: usually, a subject is followed by a predicator and a complement. The only constituent that is moved around rather freely is the adverbial.

Table 3 Sentence constituents: A complete overview

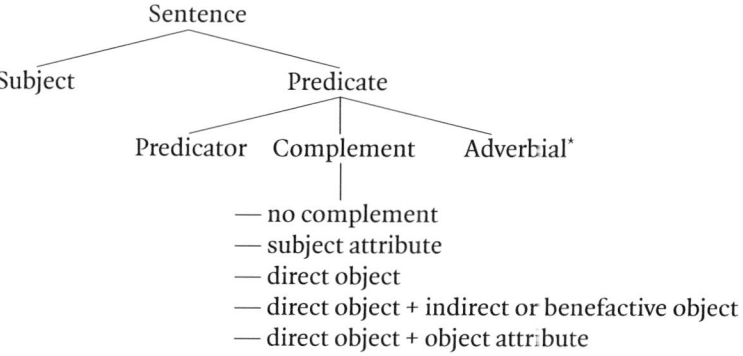

* In a few cases, an adverbial is not an optional, but a necessary part of the sentence as in *he put the book on the table*. The verb *put* needs both a direct object and an adverbial expressing a place to complete its meaning. In such a case the adverbial is also part of the complement. However, to keep the overview as simple as possible, this has not been shown in the table.

2 Sentences
Simple, compound, and complex

2.1 Introduction

In Chapter 1 we talked about different types of sentences, but what is a sentence? The term sentence is derived from Latin *sententia*, which literally means 'feeling' or 'opinion'. In the field of grammar, this meaning has specifically come to denote 'an utterance that expresses a feeling or opinion', but a more technical definition would be 'a grammatically self-contained speech unit consisting of a word, or a syntactically related group of words that express(es) an assertion, a question, a command, a wish, or an exclamation, which in writing usually begins with a capital letter and ends with a period, question mark, or exclamation mark'.

Actually, among linguists, there is still not one consensus on a definition of a sentence. For example, is "Hey, you!" a sentence or not? The answer would depend on whether you take the function or the form of the utterance as a starting point. "Hey you!" does express a complete thought; by saying it, the speaker means something like 'I want to get your attention', but in form it is rather incomplete as it does not have a subject or predicate. In this course, we will not worry too much about the right definition, but since we have decided to look mainly at the rather formal, standard written variety, we will be looking mostly at grammatically complete units, with their own subjects and predicates. However, as you may have noticed in the exercises in Chapter 1, some sentences may have more than one subject and/or predicate. Indeed, as humans we often want to convey complex thoughts. It is these more complicated types of sentences that we will look at in this chapter.

2.2 Sentences versus clauses

A *sentence* is a group of words that in writing starts with a capital letter and ends with a full stop, question mark or exclamation mark. A grammatically complete sentence expresses at least one complete whole event or situation with a subject and predicate. Some sentences consist of only one *clause*. A *clause* also expresses a whole event or situation with a subject and a predicate. In these contexts a sentence and clause coincide. In the following two examples, each is a simple sentence consisting of one clause.

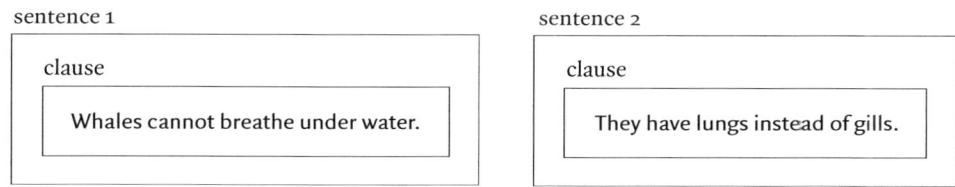

However, a sentence may also consist of two or more clauses. Note how the two simple sentences above are combined in different ways to form longer sentences using a connector (*for* and *because*, respectively). Both examples below illustrate one sentence, but they are both also examples of a sentence that consists of two clauses.

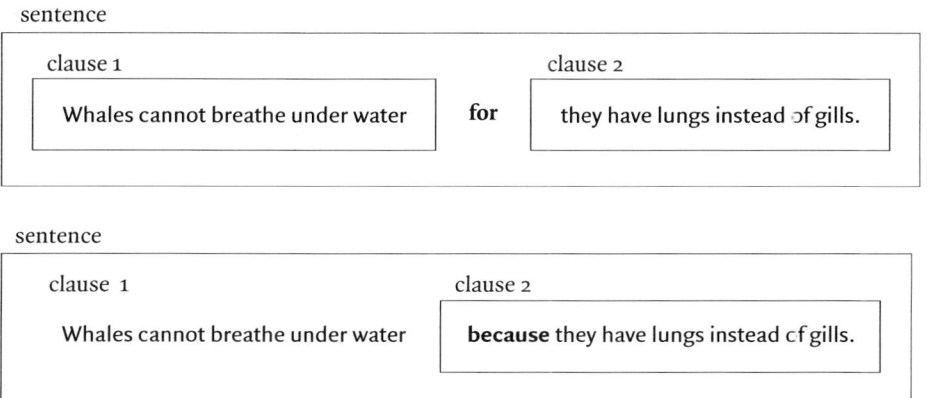

Even though the two sentences above do not differ much in terms of meaning, they are grammatically different because they consist of different types of clauses. Generally speaking, there are two types of clauses: those that form a meaningful unit by themselves, called *independent* or *main* clauses, and those that cannot stand on their own because they function as a constituent (subject, object, etc.) of another clause. These are called *dependent* or *subordinate* clauses. The distinction between main clauses and dependent clauses will be made clear in the following section on sentence types.

2.3 Sentence types

Sentences may have different degrees of complexity. They may consist of one or more main clauses or they may consist of one or more main clauses with one or more dependent clauses. They are called simple, compound, complex or compound-complex sentences, depending on the types of clauses they contain. Each type is explained in detail below.

1 Simple sentences

A *simple* sentence consists of one main clause only. However, this does not mean that the sentence has to be very short. The following is an example of a long sentence that is simple because it does not contain any dependent clauses. Even the last adverbial is not a full dependent clause because it does not start with the required type of connector, called a subordinator, and it does not have a full verb (which will be discussed in Chapter 3). Instead, the sentence contains one subject and one main verb, making it a simple sentence.

S   P   A   A
The waitresses / are basking / in the sun / like a herd of skinned seals.

2 Compound sentences

A compound sentence consists of two or more main clauses. The sentence *Whales cannot breathe under water for they have lungs instead of gills* is an example of a compound sentence because both clauses are independent and may stand on their own. The connecting word *for*, which expresses reason, connects these two clauses and expresses what these two situations have to do with each other.

One feature of a compound sentence is that the clauses have a fixed order, so they cannot be moved without changing their meaning. Note how turning the clause around results in what linguists term a semantically anomalous sentence; a sentence of which the meaning does not make sense.

> Whales cannot breathe under water, **for** they have lungs instead of gills.
> ? They have lungs instead of gills, **for** whales cannot breathe under water.

There are just a few other conjunctions like *for*, called *coordinate conjunctions*, that may be used to form a compound sentence. There are also a few variations on these coordinate conjunctions, consisting of a coordinate conjunction combined with another word or phrase, in turn called *correlative conjunctions*. We will use the term *coordinator* to refer to both types. Table 4 shows a complete list of coordinators.*

Table 4 Coordinators

Coordinate conjunctions		Correlative conjunctions
and	for	both … and
but	so	not only … but also
or	yet	either … or
nor		neither … nor

Another way to connect two main clauses and form a compound sentence is to put a *semi-colon* (;) between the main clauses.

---

* Since these are the only coordinators, it may be useful to memorize them; all other connecting words like *because, if, who*, and so on are subordinators and introduce dependent clauses. It is thus important to note that although *because* and *for* have roughly the same meaning, grammatically they result in different sentence types.

> Whales have lungs instead of gills; they cannot breathe under water.

To make the logical connection clear between two main clauses separated with a semi-colon, the semi-colon is often followed by a word like *therefore*, *besides*, or *similarly* called a *conjunctive adverb*.* Just like compound sentences with coordinate conjunctions, it is not possible to change the order of the two clauses.**

> Whales have lungs instead of gills; **therefore**, they cannot breathe under water.
> *****Therefore**, they cannot breathe under water; whales have lungs instead of gills.

Coordinate conjunctions and conjunctive adverbs have rather similar meanings; for example, both *and* and *moreover* express addition and both *so* and *therefore* express result, but they are different grammatically. Unlike a coordinate conjunction, a conjunctive adverb can be moved within the second clause:

> Whales have lungs instead of gills; they **therefore** cannot breathe under water.
> Whales have lungs instead of gills; they can **therefore** not breathe under water.
> Whales have lungs instead of gills, **so** they cannot breathe under water.
> *Whales have lungs instead of gills, they can **so** not breathe under water.***

3   Complex sentences

A *complex* sentence is a sentence that contains at least one full dependent clause with its own subject and predicate. A *dependent* clause is a clause that starts with a subordinator, a word like *because*, *although*, *if*, *who*, *where*, *when*, *that* and so on.****

The difference between a compound and complex sentence is that in a *compound* sentence, both parts are really just simple, independent sentences. In a *complex sentence*,

---

* For a complete list of conjunctive adverbs, see Table 20 in Chapter 5.

** An asterisk in front of a sentence indicates that it is grammatically incorrect.

*** 'So' with a sense of 'thus' cannot be moved in the sentence. However, with the right intonation this sentence would make sense for an American teenager.

**** For a complete list of subordinators, see Table 20 in Chapter 5.

the dependent clause cannot stand on its own and functions as a constituent (subject, object, adverbial, or attribute) of the main clause. There are three different types of dependent clauses.

The first kind of dependent clause functions as an adverbial. In the sentence below, the first clause can stand on its own, but the second one cannot as it starts with the connecting word *because*. The whole *because* clause answers the question *why whales cannot breathe under water* and is therefore not a sentence in itself but a constituent of the main clause: an adverbial.

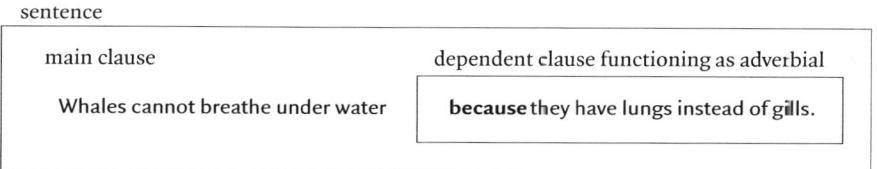

If you are unsure whether a clause functions as an adverbial, you can try moving it, as adverbials may occupy different positions in a sentence. The following sentence is a perfectly acceptable one: *Because they have lungs instead of gills, whales cannot breathe under water.*

The second type of dependent clause is not a sentence constituent, but part of a sentence constituent. It modifies, i.e. tells us something about, one particular noun. For example, the next sentence consists of one main clause and a dependent clause. The dependent clause says something about the noun *whales* and must occur directly after it. The complete subject of this sentence is *Whales, which cannot breathe under water*. If you omit the dependent clause, you are still left with a complete sentence because the main word of the subject is still in place: *Whales have lungs instead of gills*. However, the dependent clause cannot stand on its own because of the subordinator *which*.

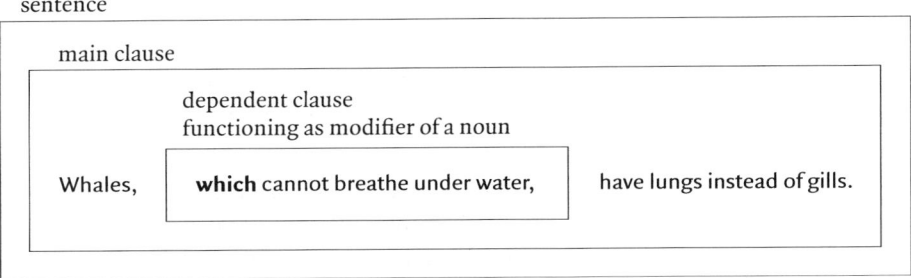

This type of clause is called a *relative clause*,* which will be dealt with more elaborately in Chapter 6. One way to test if a given clause is a relative clause is to leave it out. If what remains is still a complete sentence with a full subject and predicate, then it is likely that the dependent clause is a relative one.

	S	P	S A
	John, **who always kicks the ball hard**, /	is /	the player **who scores the most.**
	John, ~~who always kicks the ball hard~~, /	is /	the player ~~who scores the most~~.

The third type of dependent clause functions as subject, object, or subject attribute of a sentence, and since these are necessary parts of a sentence, they cannot be omitted or else you would be left with an incomplete sentence. One way to tell if the dependent clause functions as subject or object is to replace the whole clause with the word *it*.

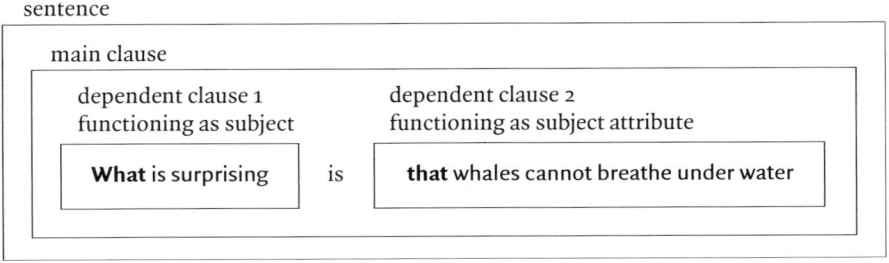

* Some grammar books may refer to these types of constructions as *adjective clauses*.

38   Sentences: Simple, compound, and complex

	S	P	SA
	That John kicks the ball hard	is	common knowledge.
	It	is	common knowledge.

	S	P	DO
	We all	know	**that John kicks the ball hard**.
	We all	know	**it**.

If a clause functions as subject attribute (with a copula verb like *be*), it does not always work to replace the whole clause with *it*. However, you can try turning the subject and subject attribute around. If they can take on another's place, it is likely that you have a clause functioning as subject attribute on your hands.

	S	P	SA
	The fact	is	**that John kicks the ball hard**
	That John kicks the ball hard	is	a fact.

In this section, the three different types of dependent clauses have been briefly introduced. In Chapter 5 the different types of subordinators are explained in much more detail and, in Chapter 7, each type of dependent clause will be dealt with in greater depth. For now, the important thing to understand is that clauses may function as constituents of other clauses or sentences.

EXERCISE 6   For each of the following sets of simple sentences, create two different types, (a) a compound sentence with two main clauses and (b) a complex sentence with a main clause and a dependent clause. The connector you may use has been given.

1   The human liver weighs three to four pounds. It is the heaviest organ in the human body.

   a   (*so*) _____

   b   (*which*) _____

2.3   Sentence types

2 In 1858, the first mechanical washing machine was invented by Hamilton E. Smith. It was a hand-cranked affair.

  a (but) _____

  b (which) _____

3 The aroma of coffee is not produced by the caffeine it contains. Caffeine imparts neither color nor flavor.

  a (for) _____

  b (because) _____

EXERCISE 7 In the following complex sentences underline each dependent clause. Then set off sentence constituents with slashes and identify each constituent as S, P, SA, DO, IO/BO, OA, A.

1 Thomas A. Edison did not make the first electric light bulb as it is popularly believed.

2 Cherrapunji, India, which has an average annual rainfall of 427 inches, is the wettest place on earth.

3 A state of intoxication is a condition in which there is recognizable disturbance of intellect, movement and coordination.

4 The largest fish anyone has ever caught was a white shark that weighed 2,176 pounds.

5 Only five percent of the people of the United States say that they dream in color.

4   Compound-complex sentences

It is also possible to have a compound sentence with complex parts, or a complex sentence with compound parts. We will call both types *compound-complex sentences*. The following example of a compound-complex sentence has two complete main clauses connected by the coordinate conjunction *and*. Each of these has a dependent clause with its own subject.

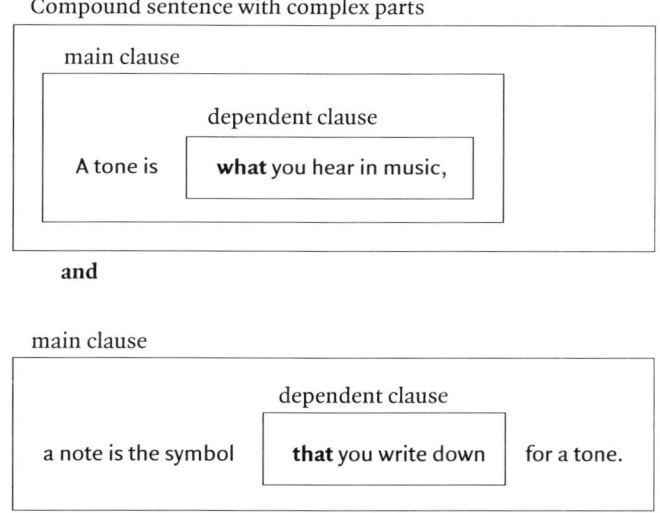

In the following example of a compound-complex sentence, there is only one main clause. The main word in the subject in this main clause is modified by two relative clauses which are connected to each other by *and*. Within the second relative clause there is another dependent clause, functioning as adverbial.

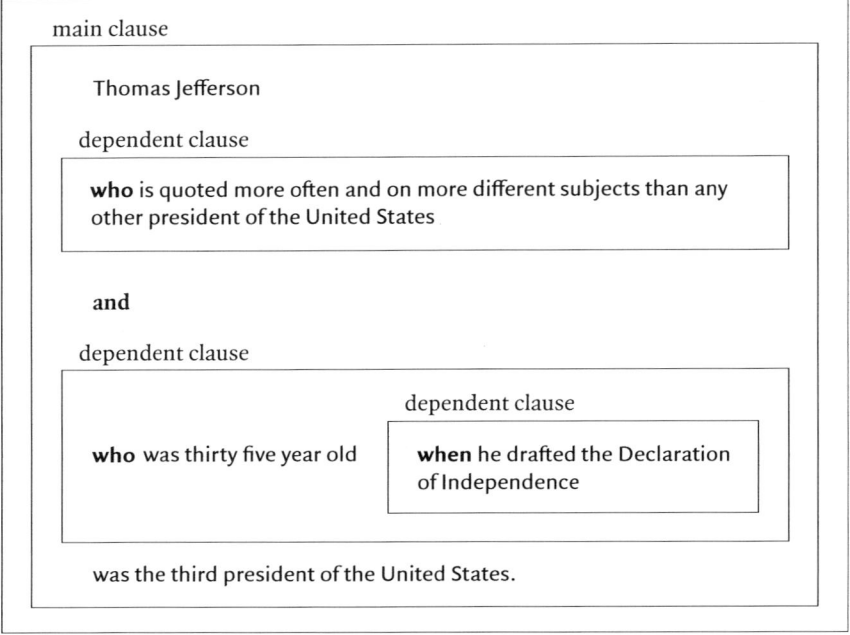

EXERCISE 8   In the following stream of words (adapted from Mark Twain's *Life on the Mississippi*), set off sentences with a period. How many sentences does this passage contain?

now when I had mastered the language of this water and had come to know every trifling feature that bordered the great river as familiarly as I knew the letters of the alphabet I had made a valuable acquisition but I had lost something too I had lost something which could never be restored to me while I lived all the grace the beauty the poetry had gone out of the majestic river

EXERCISE 9   In each sentence from Exercise 8, circle all subordinators and underline main clauses. Then identify the sentence type: simple, compound, complex or compound-complex.

2.4 Phrases

Phrases will be discussed in detail in Chapter 6, as there are many different kinds with different functions. For now it is enough to know that the main difference between a clause and a phrase is that a phrase does not express a complete event or situation and does not have its own subject and predicate.

For example, the first sentence in Exercise 8 (*now when I had mastered the language of this water and had come to know every trifling feature that bordered the great river as familiarly as I knew the letters of the alphabet I had made a valuable acquisition but I had lost something too*) consists of five clauses. Each of these clauses in turn consists of *phrases*, which are either single words or grammatically ordered groups of related words that together function as a constituent such as subject or predicator or part of a constituent. In the following clauses, the phrases are set off with slashes.

now / (when)* I / had mastered / the language of this water /
(and) had come to know / every trifling feature / **
that / bordered / the great river
as familiarly as / I / knew / the letters of the alphabet
I / had made / a valuable acquisition
(but) I / had lost / something / too.

* Most connecting words are set off in parentheses because they do not have a function within the clauses. They connect clauses. Therefore, they are not considered phrases.

** The part *now when I ... trifling feature* is considered one clause because the second part after *and* is not a full clause but just a predicate.

EXERCISE 10   In the following sentences, underline coordinators and subordinators and set off dependent clauses with square brackets and sentence constituents (subject, predicator, etc.) with slashes. Then name the function of the sentence constituents.

> I had lost something which could never be restored to me while I lived. All the grace, the beauty, the poetry had gone out of the majestic river.

2.5 Summary

A sentence can be *simple, compound, complex,* or *compound-complex,* depending on the types of clauses it contains. These clauses may be *main* (also called *independent*) *clauses* or *dependent* (also called *subordinate*) clauses. Main clauses can stand on their own, or two or more main clauses may be connected with a *coordinator* (a *coordinate* or a *correlative conjunction*) or separated with a *semi-colon,* to form a compound sentence.

Dependent clauses are introduced by *subordinators* and function as a clause constituent (subject, object, adverbial, and so on) or as part of a constituent as a relative clause; in other words, a dependent clause by itself does not form a complete sentence.

Each clause, in turn, has single words or groups of words that together form grammatical and meaningful units, called *phrases*. The difference between clauses and phrases is that phrases do not have a subject and predicate.

3 Verbs I

3.1 Introduction

In the previous chapters, we looked at different types of sentences and clauses as a whole. Now we will focus on smaller parts of sentences and clauses: phrases.

In Chapter 1, you saw that a sentence may have several constituents: subject, (S), predicator (P), complement (DO, IO, BO, SA, OA) and adverbial(s) (A).

S	P	IO	DO	A
Mary /	has written /	him /	a letter /	every day.

Each of the sentence constituents has a function in the sentence. The subject and objects name the main participants in an event or situation; the subject attribute or object attribute says something about the subject or object. Adverbials give information about the setting, when, where, how, and so on. The predicator names the process (action or state of being) in which the subject is involved.

When we call a group of words a subject or predicator, we name its *function*, that is we say what it does in the sentence and how it relates to the other parts of the sentence. But when we say subject or predicator, we do not go into what word or words together make up that subject or predicator. The technical term for 'words that together make up a sentence constituent' is *realized*. Each sentence constituent comprises one or more words, which together can form either a certain type of phrase or a certain type of clause.

In this chapter, we will look in more detail at the realization of the predicator. Since it always consists of verbs, it is called a *verb phrase* (VP). In this chapter and the next one, we will focus on the parts that may constitute a verb phrase. In this chapter and the next chapters, we learn that the function of sentence constituents is always presented first, followed by its form or realization. As the predictor is always realized by means of a verb phrase, we indicate this as follows:

P : VP
Mary / has written / him / a letter / every day.

3.2 Simple versus complex verb phrases

The verb phrase can be *simple* and consist of one word (*writes*) or *complex* and consist of two to five words (*will have been written*).

EXERCISE 11 In the following extract (from *Miles City, Montana* by Alice Munro) underline all verb phrases and indicate whether they are simple or complex.

> My father came across the field carrying the body of the boy who had been drowned. There were several men together, returning from the search, but he was the one carrying the body. The men were muddy and exhausted,* and walked with their heads down, as if they were ashamed. Even the dogs were dispirited, dripping from the cold river. When they all set out,** hours before, the dogs were nervy and yelping, the men tense and determined, and there was a constrained, unspeakable excitement about the whole scene. It was understood that they might find something horrible.

> * *Exhaust* is a verb, but here *exhausted* is used more like an adjective that describes the men. In this extract there are several of these 'verb-like' adjectives. Do not underline them. We will come back to these types of instances later in the book.

> ** The adverb *out* should be underlined too, as it is part of the verb *set out*. We will say more about these kinds of verbs in Chapter 4.

3.3 Lexical versus auxiliary verbs

There are two kinds of verbs: lexical and auxiliary verbs. The *lexical verb*, also called *main verb*, names the process taking place. It has the most 'meaning'. It may occur in several forms: *write(s), wrote, written, writing,* and *(to) write.* For a simple sentence or a clause to be meaningful, it must have a lexical verb, and if the verb phrase has more than one verb, the lexical verb always comes last.

Auxiliary verbs, also called *helping verbs*, stand in front of the lexical verb and help indicate when the process takes place, will take place, or took place or how the speaker feels of the whole process. Common helping verbs are *be, have, be able to, do, will, would, can, could, may, might* and so on.

EXERCISE 12   Go back to the extract in Exercise 11 and identify each underlined verb as *lexical* or *auxiliary*.

3.4 Finite versus non-finite verb forms

Verbs may have different functions in the sentence. Compare the following sentences; they all contain the form *walking*, but the form is used differently in all sentences. Only in the last sentence is *walking* part of the predicator.

Walking is good for you.	**walking** is used as a subject
I enjoy **walking**.	**walking** is used as direct object
The **walking** doll irritates me.	**walking** here says something about doll
I am **walking** to work every day to stay in shape.	**walking** is used as part of the predicator

Because both auxiliary verbs and lexical verbs may appear in so many different forms, and because not all verb forms are part of the predicator, it is necessary to be able to distinguish the different forms.

1   **Finite verb forms**

Within the predicator, the form of the verb depends on where it occurs in the verb phrase. In a complete English clause, the first verb is either in the present tense or the past tense and is called the *tensed verb* or the *finite verb*. It tells you whether the process denoted by the verb took place in the past or present. The word *finite* is derived from Latin *finitus* and means 'having definite or definable limits'. In grammar, *finite* refers to the verb form that is limited in tense, person, and number. In many languages, finite forms have different forms for each different subject such as *I, you, he, she, it,* (which are singular in number) and *we, you,* and *they* (which are plural in number). For every verb, English distinguishes in tense (e.g. *write* versus *wrote*) but marks only the third person singular in the present tense (e.g. *write* versus *writes*). However, as Table 5 shows, the verb *be* is an exception, as it has many irregular forms.

Table 5   Finite verb forms

	number	person	present tense	past tense
write	singular	first	*I write*	*I wrote*
		second	*you write*	*you wrote*
		third	*he/she/it writes*	*he/she/it wrote*
	plural	first	*we write*	*we wrote*
		second	*you write*	*you wrote*
		third	*they write*	*they wrote*

Table 5 (continued)

	number	person	present tense	past tense
be	singular	first	I am	I was
		second	you are	you were
		third	he/she/it is	he/she/it was
	plural	first	we are	we were
		second	you are	you were
		third	they are	they were

To test whether a verb is finite or not, you can change it from present to past, or in the present tense you can change the subject. If it is third person singular, change it to plural or vice versa. If the verb form changes, it is finite.

EXERCISE 13   In the next passage (from *A farm at Raraba* by Ernst Haveman), all verbs are underlined. Indicate whether they are finite or not.

> Next morning shortly after sunrise, just as the light <u>was</u> <u>beginning</u> <u>to come</u> <u>streaming</u> through the trees, while I <u>lay</u> <u>leaning</u> on my elbow <u>taking</u> my bread and tea, and <u>looking</u> across the canyon, <u>tracing</u> the dip of the granite headlands, and <u>trying</u> <u>to plan</u> a way to the river at a point likely <u>to be</u> fordable, suddenly I <u>caught</u> the big bright eyes of a deer <u>gazing</u> at me through the garden hedge. She <u>continued</u> <u>to gaze</u>, while I <u>gazed</u> back with equal steadiness, motionless as a rock. In a few minutes she <u>ventured</u> forward a step, <u>exposing</u> the fine arching neck and forelegs, then <u>snorted</u> and <u>withdrew</u>.

2 Non-finite verb forms

The forms that are not finite are called *non-finite* verbs. There are four non-finite forms: present participle, past participle, plain infinitive and *to* infinitive. The *present participle*, also called *-ing* form, always ends in *-ing*; the *past participle*, also called *-ed* form, has an *-ed* ending or an irregular form. The *plain infinitive* is the plain form of the verb, and a *to infinitive* is the same as the plain form, but preceded by *to*. Table 6 gives examples of these non-finite forms.

Table 6 Non-finite verb forms

plain infinitive	to infinitive	present participle	past participle
go	*to go*	*going*	*gone*
sell	*to sell*	*selling*	*sold*
type	*to type*	*typing*	*typed*
verify	*to verify*	*verifying*	*verified*

In dictionaries and grammar books, not all the finite and non-finite forms are typically presented, because if we just know the form of the plain infinitive, we can figure out what the present tense and present participle forms are. The verb forms that cannot always be figured out from the plain infinitive are the past finite and past participle form, because in English there are quite a few verbs that have irregular forms. So for these irregular verbs, dictionaries and grammar books usually present three forms, called *basic verb forms*, because once we know these, we can figure out what the other forms are. Take a look at Table 7.

Table 7 Basic verb forms of regular and irregular verbs

	base (plain infinitive)	past finite	past participle
regular	print	printed	printed
	talk	talked	talked
	call	called	called
	play	played	played
irregular	dig	dug	dug
	see	saw	seen
	go	went	gone
	be	was	been

The first form is the form that is listed first in any dictionary. It is called the *base form* or the *plain infinitive* form. To form a *to* infinitive, we just add *to* in front of the base (*to print*). To form the *present finite* form, we leave the base as it is, or add an *-s* (*I print, you print, he/she/it prints, we print, they print*). To form a present participle, we add *-ing* (*printing*). However, there may be some spelling changes in the third person singular or present participle forms, e.g. *sit/sitting, kiss/kisses, go/goes, write/writing*.

The second form is the past finite form, and the third form is the past participle form. Note that these forms are the same in case of a regular verb (*talked, talked*) as both add *-ed*. In the case of some irregular verbs, like *dig*, the past tense and past participle are also the same (*dug, dug*). Most irregular forms, though, have two different forms for the past and past participle (*wrote, written*).

EXERCISE 14   In the passage in Exercise 13 identify all the non-finite forms (plain infinitive, *to* infinitive, present participle, or past participle). Which two non-finite forms do not occur in this passage?

EXERCISE 15   Go back over the next passage (same as in Exercise 11) and identify the form of each verb (present finite, past finite, plain infinitive, *to* infinitive, present participle, or past participle), but only those that are part of a verb phrase.

> My father came across the field carrying the body of the boy who had been drowned. There were several men together, returning from the search, but he was the one carrying the body. The men were muddy and exhausted and walked with their heads down, as if they were ashamed. Even the dogs were dispirited, dripping from the cold river. When they all set out, hours before, the dogs were nervy and yelping, the men tense and determined, and there was a constrained, unspeakable excitement about the whole scene. It was understood that they might find something horrible.

As you can see in Exercise 15, non-finite verb forms may occur in all kinds of places within the sentence and have all sorts of different functions. However, if a verb is finite, it is always part of a predicator. In the next example, the finite verbs are printed in bold.

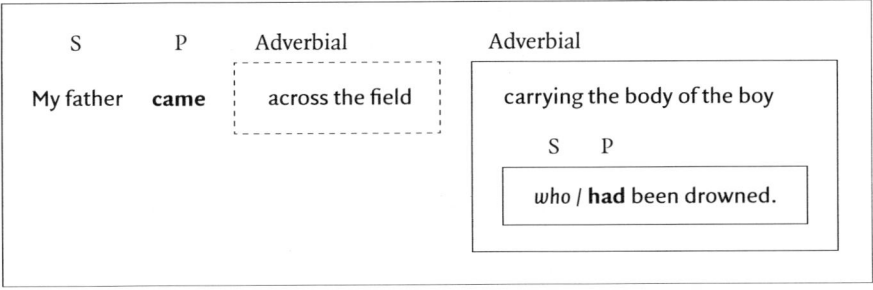

3.5 Auxiliary verbs

As you saw above, the lexical verb by itself names a process such as 'write', 'go', 'buy', and so on, but the verb phrase as a whole gives us a lot more information. By using a different tense or by adding a helping verb, we can express differences in how an event or situation is viewed: *aspect* refers to whether an event is ongoing or finished, *modality* refers to whether an event is viewed to be necessary, possible etc., and *voice* refers to whether the agent (active) is the subject of the verb or not (passive). Compare the following sets of sentences with just a simple verb phrase, consisting of only one verb, which is a lexical one in a finite form.

The men **are** muddy and exhausted.	present simple
The men **were** muddy and exhausted.	past simple

The difference between these sentences is that the lexical verb *be* has a different finite form. The verb in the first sentence has a present finite form, which places the situation in the present, and the other sentence a past finite form, which places the situation at a moment before the moment of speaking.

Besides placing a situation at a given moment in time, a speaker can express that he or she saw an action as ongoing, as still relevant, or as not really having taken place. A speaker can also focus on a second or third participant by making it the subject of a sentence. The next few sections explain which auxiliary verbs are used to express these different meanings.

1 Progressive *be* + present participle

Compare the sentence with a present simple below to those with a progressive one. With the first sentence, the speaker expresses that the men generally walk with their heads down. Using the second sentence, the speaker expresses that the men are in the actual process of walking with their heads down at the moment of speaking. The difference between *are walking* and *were walking* (in 2 and 3) is that the present progressive refers to an event as taking place now, whereas the *past progressive* refers to the event as having taken place at a particular moment in the past.

The men **walk** with their heads down.	present simple
The men **are walking** with their heads down.	present progressive
The men **were walking** with their heads down.	past progressive

To form a progressive, an auxiliary of progressive aspect, a form of *be* is used. The auxiliary can be in the present or past tense or a non-finite form. It must be followed by a present participle form (*-ing*) of a verb.

2 Perfect *have* + past participle

Compare the first sentence below, with a past tense, with the second and third one, each with *have* and a past participle. The first expresses that the event took place at a specific moment in the past and focuses on the event itself. In the second one, there is a present form of *have*, which implies that there is some connection with the present. The past participle form has a very general meaning of a process that is completed.

The *have* and past participle together form the *present perfect* and express that even though the event took place in the past, the focus is also somewhat on the present, namely the result of the setting out: the men are not here anymore. In the last sentence, too, the *past perfect* gives more focus on the result of the men setting out: they were not there when we arrived.

The men **set out** hours ago.	past simple
The men **have** already **set out**.	present perfect
The men **had set out** hours before we arrived.	past perfect

To form a perfect, an auxiliary of perfect aspect, a form of *have* (present or past) is used. It must be followed by a past participle (*-ed*) form of a verb.

3 Modals + (*to*) infinitives

Compare the following two sentences. The difference between *found* and *may find* is that with *found* the speaker indicates that indeed something horrible was found. In the second one with *may find*, the speaker indicates that the 'finding something horrible' has not taken place (yet) but is a possible event. In other words, the speaker is not sure something horrible will be found.

They **found** something horrible.	past simple
They **may find** something horrible.	present tense

An auxiliary verb like *may* is called a *modal auxiliary*. Together with the other verbs in the verb phrase, it expresses that an event is not seen as really having taken place, but as a possible, potential, or hypothetical event.

Besides *may* there are several modal auxiliary verbs that express different degrees of possibility, capability, or obligation. The ones most like *may* are *will, would, can, could, might, shall, should,* and *must*, each with a somewhat different meaning and range of uses. Even though these verbs can be seen as sets with present and past finite forms (*will/would, can/could, shall/should, may/might*), each of these, no matter whether it has a present or past form, can express a 'now' or 'future' meaning.

They **may** find something horrible.	refers to possible future event
They **might** find something horrible.	refers to possible future event

To create a 'past' meaning, a modal auxiliary must be followed by a perfect *have*.

They **may have** found something horrible.	refers to possible past event
They **might have** found something horrible.	refers to possible past event

This small set of verbs, called *central modals*, have in common that they are always finite (and come first in the verb phrase), but do not get an *-s* ending when the subject is *he, she,* or *it* and must be followed by a plain infinitive form of a verb.

Another small group of other auxiliary verbs, called *marginal modals*, are similar to these central ones in that they have only limited grammatical uses: *dare, need, ought to,* and *used to* and can express meanings similar to some of the central modals. *Dare* and *need* are followed by plain infinitives and *ought* and *used* are used with *to* infinitives.

They **dare** not think about what happened to the boy.	*dare* has a meaning somewhat similar to *can*
The boy **used to** play around the lake.	*used to* has a meaning somewhat similar to *would*

Finally, there is a whole group of auxiliary verbs like *to be able to, to be allowed to, to want to, to have to,* and so on, called *semi-modals*. They express meanings similar to the *will, would* group, so behave similarly to central modals. Because the uses of the central modals have become so limited (for example, they cannot express past permission or obligation), these semi-modals are used instead.

They **may/might** leave tomorrow.	expresses present permission
They **may leave** now.	expresses a possible future event
They **were allowed** to leave yesterday.	expresses past permission

What all the central, marginal, and semi-modals have in common is that they help the speaker express that they see an event or situation as a possible or hypothetical one rather than an actual one.

All these modal auxiliaries express modality in that they express the speaker's view towards the event. We will call these auxiliaries of mood for short.

4   **Passive *be* + past participle**
Compare the following three sentences. In the first one, the speaker focuses on the people and what they did. *They*, denoting the 'performers' of the action, is the subject of the sentence. In the second one, the focus is on what was found and *something horrible*, the 'undergoer' of the action, is now the subject. The performer can be mentioned in a *by*-phrase (as in 3.). A 'normal' sentence in which the subject performs the action is called a sentence in the *active voice*, or *active sentence* for short. A sentence in which the subject is not the 'performer' of the action is called a sentence in the *passive voice*, or a *passive sentence*.

They **found** something horrible.	active voice
Something horrible **was found**.	passive voice
Something horrible **was found** by the men.	passive voice

To form a passive sentence, an auxiliary of passive voice, the auxiliary verb *be* is used. It must be followed by a past participle.

Sometimes the helping verb of the passive voice is *get*, which is less formal and somewhat different from the helping verb *be* in that it shows more involvement of the 'undergoer' subject.

> He **was hurt** in the fight.   passive voice
> He **got hurt** in the fight.   passive voice

There are several different types of passive constructions, which will be discussed in more detail in Chapter 4.

5 **Do for questions, negation and emphasis**

Finally, as the examples below show, the auxiliary verb *do* is needed in English if we want to form a question, negate an action, or emphasize an action and there is no helping verb (or *be* form) in the predicate.*

> They **walked** with their heads down, as if they were ashamed.   affirmative
> **Did** they **walk** with their heads down, as if they were ashamed?   interrogative
> They **did** not **walk** with their heads down, as if they were ashamed.   negative
> They **did walk** with their heads down, as if they were ashamed.   emphatic

EXERCISE 16   In the following short sentences identify (a) the type of verb (lexical verb, modal auxiliary, auxiliary of perfect aspect, progressive aspect, passive voice, or *do*) and (b) the form of the verb.

1   Mary writes a letter every day.

2   Mary wrote a letter yesterday.

3   She will write a great deal more in the next few years.

4   Mary has been writing many letters.

---

* The auxiliary DO is often referred to as 'dummy' DO in these cases.

5   Mary <u>had</u> <u>been</u> <u>writing</u> many letters.

6   Mary <u>is</u> <u>writing</u> now.

7   Mary <u>was</u> <u>writing</u> yesterday.

8   She <u>could</u> <u>be</u> <u>writing</u> a letter to her grandmother.

9   She <u>need</u> not <u>write</u> to her sister.

10 She <u>is able to</u> <u>write</u> a letter in about one minute.

11 An average letter <u>is</u> <u>written</u> in about 30 minutes.

12 One letter <u>was</u> <u>written</u> in 10 minutes.

13 The next letter to her boyfriend <u>will</u> <u>be</u> <u>written</u> in 5 minutes.

14 Half of her letters <u>have</u> <u>been</u> <u>written</u> by hand.

15 Many of her letters <u>had</u> <u>been</u> <u>written</u> in pencil.

16 By next year all her letters <u>will</u> <u>have</u> <u>been</u> <u>written</u> on a word processor.

6   Ordering of auxiliary verbs

Just as there is a particular order in a phrase like *the body of the boy* rather than **body the boy of the*, there is a particular order that verbs adhere to in a complex verb phrase. If you look back at Exercise 16, you can see that the lexical verb *write* always comes last in the verb phrase. Consider the sentence *This book may have been being written by my teachers.** Note that the auxiliaries are ordered as follows:

---

* This sentence is only theoretically possible; the combination *been being* is so awkward that it is avoided in normal language use.

This book may [1. aux of mood] have [2. aux of perfect aspect] been [3. aux of progressive aspect] being [4. aux of passive voice] written [5. lexical verb] by my teachers.

1. a modal auxiliary comes before any other auxiliary
2. perfect *have* comes after a modal auxiliary but before the other ones
3. progressive *be* comes after a modal and/or perfect *have* but before a passive *be*.
4. passive *be* comes after any other auxiliary
5. lexical verb; the lexical verb is always the final one in a complex Verb Phrase.

Whichever verb comes first has present or past finite form. In other words, the first verb tells you whether the process the verb phrase describes took place in the past or present. When the lexical verb happens to be the only one in the verb phrase, it has a present or past finite form by definition. In other words, the first verb in the verb phrase carries tense. No matter which verb follows a modal, it always has a (*to*) infinitive form; a verb after perfect *have* always has the past participle form; a verb after progressive *be* has the present participle form; and a verb after passive *be* has the past participle form.

EXERCISE 17   In the following sentences, fill in the blank with the correct form of a verb. Even though you will probably intuitively know which form to use, explain your choice by referring to the order and form rules.

1. Mary _____ a book yesterday.
2. She _____ reading now.
3. She _____ read a great deal more in the next few years.
4. Mary has _____ reading a lot recently.
5. Mary _____ have read more if she had had more time.

3.6 One form, several senses: *Be, have* and *do*

Finally, it is important to remember that one language form often has different senses or functions. Verbs, too (especially *be, have,* and *do*), can be used with different senses. Compare the sets of example sentences below:

He **is** my friend.	*is* = lexical verb
He **is** writing a letter.	*is* = auxiliary verb of progressive aspect
The letter **was** written.	*was* = auxiliary verb of passive voice
He **is** to write many more letters.	*is* = auxiliary verb of mood
He **has** many friends.	*has* = lexical verb
He **has** written many letters.	*has* = auxiliary verb of perfect aspect
He **has** to leave now.	*has* = auxiliary verb of mood
He **does** a lot of work.	*does* = lexical verb
Does he write many letters?	*does* = auxiliary verb needed to form a question (dummy do)

EXERCISE 18 In the following passage (first paragraph in *A Hanging* by George Orwell) identify the function of each underlined *be* verb. Be prepared to explain your choice.

It <u>was</u> in Burma, a sodden morning of the rains. A sickly light, like yellow tinfoil, <u>was</u> slanting over the high walls into the jail yard. We <u>were</u> waiting outside the condemned cells, a row of sheds fronted with double bars, like small animal cages. Each cell measured about ten feet by ten and <u>was</u> quite bare within except for a plank bed and a pot of drinking water. In some of them brown silent men <u>were</u> squatting at the inner bars, with their blankets draped round them. These <u>were</u> the condemned men, due <u>to be</u> hanged within the next week or two.

3.7 Summary

To summarize, in a complete sentence or clause, the predicator is realized by the verb phrase. The *verb phrase* consists of one or more verbs. If there is one verb, it is called a *simple verb phrase*; if there are more verbs, *a complex verb phrase*. There are two types of verbs: there is only one that adds the lexical meaning; the others add grammatical meaning such as tense, aspect, or mood. As Table 8 shows, the one adding lexical meaning is called the *lexical verb*, and the ones adding more abstract, grammatical meanings are called *auxiliary verbs*.

Table 8 Auxiliary versus lexical verbs

	auxiliary verbs	lexical verb	
The letter	**may have been**	**written**	by John.

A verb may be *finite* or *non-finite*. There are two finite forms: *present* and *past*. There are four non-finite forms: *plain infinitive* (or *base form*), *to infinitive*, *present participle* (also called *-ing* form), and *past participle* (also called *-ed* form). See Table 9.

Table 9 Verb forms: A complete overview

finite	present		am, is, are	go, goes	talk
	past		was, were	went	talked
non-finite	participle	present participle	being	going	talking
		past participle	been	gone	talked
	infinitive	plain infinitive	be	go	talk
		to infinitive	to be	to go	to talk

In a complete sentence, when there is more than one verb (a complex verb phrase), one or more auxiliaries come in front of the lexical verb. There are five types of auxiliary verbs: *mood, perfect aspect, progressive aspect, passive voice* and *do* of negation, question, or emphasis. These auxiliaries are summarized in Table 10.

Table 10 Auxiliary verbs: A complete overview

auxiliary of		typical verb	other verbs sometimes used as auxiliary
mood	central modals	*will, would, can, could, shall, should, may, might, must*	
	marginal modals	*dare, need, ought to, used to*	
	semi-modals	*to be able to, to be allowed to, to want to, to have to*	*to be forced to, to be believed to, to seem to*
perfect aspect		*have*	
progressive aspect		*be*	*come, go, keep on, start, begin, continue, go on*
passive voice		*be, get*	
question, negation, emphasis		*do*	

In a complete sentence, there is always a lexical verb. Auxiliaries always come in front of the lexical verb. Table 11 shows the possible order, with some examples. Parentheses in the heading means that the item is optional.

Table 11 Ordering of auxiliaries and lexical verb in the verb phrase

(modal)	(perfect *have*)	(progressive *be*)	(passive *be*)	Lexical verb
will				*write*
could	*have*			*written*
should	*have*	*been*		*writing*
must	*have*	*been*	*being**	*written*
	has/had			*written*
	has/had	*been*		*writing*
	has/had		*been*	*written*
		is/was		*writing*
		is/was	*being*	*written*
			is/was	*written*
				writes/wrote

* Even though it is theoretically possible to have a verb phrase that is progressive as well as passive, the combination *been being* is so awkward that it is avoided in normal language use.

3.7 Summary

4 Verbs II

4.1 Introduction

As you saw in Chapter 3, the verb phrase may consist of one or more verbs. As far as meaning is concerned, there are two main types of verbs: auxiliary verbs and lexical verbs. In the last chapter, we looked more closely at the different subtypes of meanings that auxiliaries may express.

In this chapter we will first take a closer look at the subtypes of lexical verbs: intransitive, copula, and transitive verbs. We will also take a closer look at passive constructions. And, finally, we will turn to the morphological forms of verbs. You can think of morphology as the building blocks of language. Some verbs consist of one word, but others are combinations of two or more words.

4.2 Subtypes of lexical verbs

Just like auxiliaries, we can sub-classify lexical verbs. Lexical verbs express the central part of an action or state. In these events or states, there are participants. For example, an event like 'run' typically involves one main participant, the 'agent' of the running, as in *He runs*. In such a sentence, the focus is on the action part. However, *run* may also be used in a sentence like *He ran a mile*. In this sentence, the focus is not only on the action but also on the distance that he ran.

The same is the case with an action like 'read'. 'Read' by definition involves two entities, the person doing the reading and the object that is read, but still we can have sentences focusing on the action only as in *He is reading*. The sentence pattern used (with or without a direct object) lets us know whether the focus is on the action only or not.

Like *run* and *read*, many verbs can be used with slightly different senses in different patterns. They can be classified into three general kinds — intransitive, copula, and transitive lexical verbs — according to the type of complement they take in the sentence (see Chapter 2 for more details on complements)

1. **Intransitive verbs (the running pattern)**
   Intransitive verbs are verbs that do not take an object or subject attribute in the sentence. The focus is on the process or the action only. Also note that the verb *be*, when followed by an adverbial expressing place or time, is used as an intransitive verb.

   > He is **running**.
   > He is **reading**.
   > He is **turning around**.
   > He **is** in London at the moment.

2. **Copula verbs (the being pattern)**
   Copula verbs are verbs that take a subject attribute, which says something about the subject, in the sentence. Examples of copula verbs are *be, appear, become,* or *seem*. See Table 2 in Chapter 1 for a list of copula verbs.

   > He **is** friendly.
   > The soup **tastes** salty.
   > He **turned into** a monster.

3. **Transitive verbs (the doing/seeing pattern)**
   Transitive verbs are verbs that take a direct object in the sentence. The focus is not only on the action itself but also what or who else was involved in that action. Since transitive verbs are the only ones that may be used in a passive construction, all passively used verbs are transitive by definition.

active sentences	passive sentences
He **ran** a mile.	A mile was **run**.
He has **read** a book.	A book has been **read**.
He is **tasting** the soup.	The soup is being **tasted**.
He **turned** the page	The page was **turned**
He **understood** the lesson.	The lesson was **understood**.

EXERCISE 19   In the following passage (adapted from *A Hanging* by George Orwell), sentence constituents have been set off with slashes. First name each sentence constituent (S, P, DO, A, etc.). Then identify the type of lexical verb (*intransitive, copula,* or *transitive*) in the verb phrase, which has been underlined.

(1) One prisoner / had been <u>brought</u>* / out of his cell. (2) He / <u>was</u> / a Hindu, a puny wisp of a man, with a shaven head and vague liquid eyes. (3) He / <u>had</u> / a thick, sprouting moustache, absurdly too big for his body, rather like the moustache of a comic man on the films. (4) Six tall Indian warders / were <u>guarding</u> / him (and) / <u>getting</u> / him / ready for the gallows. (5) Two of them / <u>stood by</u> / with rifles and fixed bayonets; (6) the others / <u>handcuffed</u> / him, (7) / <u>passed</u> / a chain / through his handcuffs (8) (and) <u>fixed</u> / it / to their belts, / (9) (and) / <u>lashed</u> / his arms / tight to his sides. (10) They / <u>crowded</u> / very close about him, / with their hands always on him in a careful, caressing grip, as though all the while feeling him to make sure he was there. (11) It / <u>was</u> / like men handling a fish which is still alive and may jump back into the water. (12) (But) he / <u>stood</u>** / quite unresisting, yielding his arms limply to the ropes, / as though he hardly noticed what was happening.

* Note that this is a passive construction.

** Even though *stood* is usually an intransitive verb, it could also be argued that here it is used as a copula verb as *unresisting* may be interpreted as describing the subject.

4.3 Subtypes of transitive verbs

Of the different kinds of lexical verbs, transitive verbs are probably the most common, and they have several subtypes again, depending on whether there is an indirect object, benefactive object, or object attribute in addition to the direct object.

1 Monotransitive verbs (the doing/seeing pattern)

Monotransitive verbs are verbs that take only one object, a direct object, in the sentence.

> He is **running** a mile.
> He is **reading** a book.
> He **gave** a book.
> He **bought** a book.

2 Ditransitive verbs (the giving/buying pattern)

Ditransitive verbs are verbs that take two objects in the sentence: a direct object telling 'what' or 'whom' and an indirect object or benefactive object telling 'to' or 'for whom' the direct object is sent, given, made, bought, and so on.

> He **gave** me a book.
> He **gave** a book to me.
> He **bought** me a book.
> He **bought** a book for me.
> He **baked** me a cake.
> He **baked** a cake for me.

3 Complex-transitive verbs (the making/considering pattern)

Complex-transitive verbs are verbs that take a direct object and an object attribute in the sentence. The direct object tells 'what' or 'whom' and the object attribute describes a quality or characteristic pertaining only to the direct object.

> We **found** him friendly.
> We **considered** him our boss.
> We **wiped** the table clean.
> We **called** her Nosy.

EXERCISE 20   In the following sentences, name each sentence constituent (set off with slashes) and identify the type of lexical verb (*intransitive, copula, monotransitive, ditransitive,* or *complex-transitive*). Note: In this exercise there are a few passive sentences. The verb in a passive sentence is always *transitive*. To determine which kind of transitive, change the passive sentence into its active counterpart.

1. Here / I / will <u>describe</u> / an unconventional method that I have been using to help people learn to read French.

2. I / <u>begin</u> / by offering students a reading passage that is an almost literal word-for-word translation from French into English.

3. It / <u>has</u> / English words / in French word order.

4. A text of this sort / quickly / <u>conveys</u> / a sense of the overall patterns of French sentences.

5. In subsequent passages, / the most common French words / are <u>introduced</u> / into the reading materials, where they take the place of their English equivalents.

6. Step by step / an ever larger portion of French words / <u>appears</u> / in the reading passages / and the text / <u>turns</u> / progressively / into French.

7. Starting with a text that a monolingual English speaker can understand with no more than a minimum of explanation /, the student / is <u>led</u>, / by gradual steps /, to a text that is written in French.

8   In other words, / I / <u>offer</u> / students / a reading passage that is an almost literal word-for-word translation from French into English.

9   English words in French word order / <u>make</u> / the text / easy to understand.

10 I / <u>consider</u> / such a text / a helpful one in quickly conveying a sense of the overall patterns of French sentences.

11 In subsequent passages, / common French words / are <u>introduced</u> into the reading materials, where they take the place of their English equivalents.

12 Starting with a text that a monolingual English speaker can understand with no more than a minimum of explanation / <u>is</u> / useful / because the student is led, by gradual steps, to a text that is written in French.

4.4 Direct object forms

Not only are there three subtypes of transitive verbs, all these three types may have different kinds of direct objects. The direct object may be a phrase consisting of one or more words, a clause in itself with a finite verb, called a *finite clause* (FC) or a clause with a non-finite verb, called a *non-finite clause* (NFC). These will be discussed in more detail in Chapter 7, but examples of the different kinds of direct objects are given here so that you will be able to recognize them.

Remember that a direct object can often be replaced with the word *it* (unless it is a person) and answers to the question 'what' or 'whom'. For example, in *He is reading a book*, the direct object is *a book* because it can be replaced with *it* (*He is reading it*) and it answers the question 'what' (*What is he reading?* a book).

In the following three sentences, the direct object is a phrase, consisting of one or more words. In the third sentence, the main word *student* is modified by a clause, but the whole direct object is still considered a phrase because *the student* is the main part. We will come back to this later.

> I know **him**.
> I know **the student**.
> I know **the student who lives next door**

In the next two sentences, the direct object is no longer a phrase but a clause with a finite verb (underlined). In the second one, *him* is an indirect object.

> I know **that he <u>moved</u> here last year**.
> I have asked **him** on several occasions **whether he <u>could</u> turn his stereo down**.

The following are all examples of direct objects that are realized as non-finite clauses (underlined). The clauses are non-finite because they lack a finite verb. Some of these non-finite clauses have their own subjects (*him*), others don't. The non-finite form of the verb may be a present participle (or *-ing* form), plain infinitive, or *to* infinitive.

> I do not enjoy **<u>listening</u> to hard metal**.
> I certainly expect **him <u>to clean up</u> his act soon**.
> I forced **him <u>to arrive</u> on time**.
> I had **him <u>paint</u> the house**.
> I made **him <u>paint</u> the house**.
> I let **him <u>go</u> home early today**.

If you continue to study linguistics, you will find that there is a huge amount of literature on the non-finite noun clauses that we have just discussed. One of the main points of interest is how they should be analyzed. For example, in a sentence like *I told him to arrive on time* we may argue that there are two objects, an indirect one, *him* and a direct one *to arrive on time* because the verb *tell* is usually a ditransitive verb and has two objects. We could rephrase this sentence as *I told him something*.

With a sentence like *I forced him to arrive on time*, it is less clear whether *him* should be regarded as a separate indirect object or as part of the non-finite direct object clause because you cannot say *I forced him something*. However, we can find some arguments for both views because the sentence does mean something like *I forced him and he left*.

There is no one 'correct' answer as to which view is correct. In this course, though, we take the following position: If we are dealing with a verb like *tell* or *order*, which in other situations can clearly take an indirect object and a direct object (and so are ditransitive verbs), then we will analyze the sentence as follows:

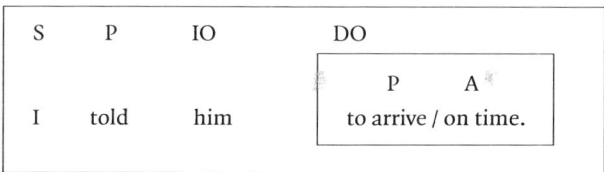

In all other cases, we will consider the pronoun or noun phrase to be part of the non-finite clause, as in the following example:

S	P	DO		
		S	P	A
I	forced	him /	to arrive /	on time.

These types of non-finite clauses will be discussed in more detail in Chapter 7.

EXERCISE 21   For each of the following verbs, create sentences with different types of direct objects: (a) a phrase consisting of one word (b) a phrase consisting of two or more words, (c) a finite clause and (d) a non-finite clause.

1   see

2   order

3   ask

4.4   Direct object forms

4.5 Passive constructions

On the whole, active sentences are more common than passive ones, especially in fictional writing. The passive voice is used only when we specifically want to focus on the 'recipient' or 'experiencer' of an action, rather than on the agent. In other words, the focus shifts. For example, instead of *Someone smashed the window*, we can say *The window was smashed* or *The window got smashed*.

However, we will discuss the passive in much more detail here because different types of passive constructions are possible. In Chapter 3, it was explained that the verb *be* (and sometimes *get*) can be used as a *passive auxiliary* to express that the speaker does not pick out the 'actor' or 'agent' as the main participant, but rather a 'patient', someone or something that is the receiver of an action. In other words, the first participant (the subject of the sentence) is not the one performing the action expressed by the lexical verb. Compare the next two sentences.

The boy held the balloon.	active sentence
The balloon was held high (by the boy).	passive sentence

In the active sentence the grammatical subject is *the boy*, who is seen as the main participant and who is doing the *holding*. In this sentence, *the balloon* is seen as the second participant and is therefore a direct object.

In the passive sentence, the grammatical subject is *the balloon*, which is now seen as the main participant, but which is not the 'actor' who does the holding. If you compare these sentences, you can see that they have similar meanings, but the main difference is that the second participant of the first sentence, *the balloon* is the first participant of the second sentence. Another difference is that the verb phrase has a *be* verb (*was*) followed by a past participle (*held*). The 'actor' is now mentioned in the adverbial *by*-phrase.*

Since a passive sentence is possible only when an action is involved with at least two participants (after all, if that is not the case you cannot have the perspective shift

---

* When the 'old subject' is not an 'actor' but an 'instrument', the preposition in the passive sentence is often another preposition like *of*, *with* or *through* as in *The floor was littered with paper*.

from actor to undergoer), only *transitive verbs* are used in a passive construction. In other words, if you see a passive verb phrase, you automatically know that the lexical verb is a transitive one. But since there are different types of transitive verbs and different types of direct objects, these are discussed in more detail below.

1   **Monotransitive verbs and passive constructions**
    As you have seen, there are three types of transitive verbs, those with one object (*mono-transitive verbs*), those with two objects (*ditransitive verbs*), and those with an object and object attribute (*complex-transitive verbs*). As you can see from the examples below, verbs such as *reading, buy,* and *give* may occur in different patterns.

    He / is reading / a book.
    He / bought / a book.
    He / gave / a book.

2   **Ditransitive verbs and passive constructions**
    Sentences with two objects have two passive alternates because either the second participant or the receiver may become subject of a passive sentence.

    S   P   IO   DO
    John / gave / Mary / a book.   Active sentence

    S   P   DO   A
    Mary / was given / a book / (by John).   Passive sentence 1

    S   P   IO   A
    A book / was given / to Mary / (by John).   Passive sentence 2

3   **Complex-transitive verbs and passive constructions**
    Sentences with a direct object and an object attribute have one passive alternative. But how should the passive counterpart be analyzed? Note that when the 'old' direct object becomes the 'new' subject, the 'old' object attribute now says something about

the subject, and therefore is no longer an object attribute, but a subject attribute. To remain consistent in naming the type of lexical verb, the lexical verb in the passive construction is still a complex-transitive one.

>   S   P   DO   OA
>   We / considered / him / a nuisance.   Active sentence

>   S   P   SA
>   He / was considered / a nuisance.   Passive sentence

4   **Non-finite clauses and passive constructions**
    Sentences with a non-finite clause functioning as direct object also have passive alternates. Usually, the subject of the non-finite clause becomes the subject of the passive sentence:

> I know **him** to be a noisy guy.
> **He** is known to be a noisy guy.
>
> I certainly expect **him** to clean up his act soon.
> **He** is certainly expected to clean up his act soon.

We just saw that an active sentence like *I know him to be a noisy guy* should be analyzed as follows:

>   S   P   DO
>   I / know / **him** to be a noisy guy.

This clear-cut solution is not without problems when you consider its passive counterpart. The subject of the non-finite clause may become the subject of the main clause as in *He was known to be a noisy guy*. If *him* in the active sentence is not an indirect object, why may it now be used separately as subject of the passive sentence? And what would we call *to be*, the leftover part after *known*? In the active sentence, *to be* is only part of a direct object. What is it now?

In this book, which takes a usage-based perspective, we have elected to have only a very limited number of syntactic categories (subject, predicator, direct object, and so on) and we have taken an approach to sentence analysis that is first and foremost determined by meaning rather than by form. Therefore, we will opt for the following analysis of such sentences, even though this is somewhat controversial and only one of several possible solutions.*

We will simply argue that the new passive verb phrase *was known to be* has a meaning quite similar to a verb phrase containing a modal auxiliary like *would* or *used to* and could therefore be regarded as one complex verb phrase.

```
S          P                 A

He    was known to be    on time.
      (= would/used to be)
```

Also when analyzing passive sentences with verbs like *believe* and *see* complemented by *to* infinitives, we will mainly consider the new meaning. Such sentences will be analyzed as follows:

```
S          P                 SA

He    is believed to be    honest.
      (= may be)
```

```
S          P                 A

He    was seen to walk    across the street.
      (= may have walked)
```

* The main reason for this choice is that it will enable an analysis of sentences at ever deeper levels, allowing for basically the same sentence patterns without having to resort to 'transformations'.

One question remains, though. What types of verbs are *know, believe,* and *see*? Even though they are now analyzed as part of a complex verb phrase to simplify the analysis of sentences, they are still monotransitive verbs because in their active counterparts they would occur in sentences with two participants like *someone knows something, someone believes something,* or *someone sees something* and the original lexical senses of knowing, believing, and seeing can still be felt to be there.

Finally, there is one other small group of passive constructions like *to be supposed to* or *to be allowed to* that is so commonly used in a passive construction like the one we just discussed that they are no longer seen as passive counterparts of active constructions; moreover, the original sense of the lexical verb like *suppose* has changed. Because these passive constructions are so conventionalized and clearly express a sense similar to that of a central modal auxiliary like *may* or *should,* they are considered *semi-modals.* Compare the following sentences.

I **suppose** (that) he is in his room.   *Suppose,* like *think,* is used
I **think** he is in his room.   as a monotransitive verb

He **is supposed to be** in his room.   The whole expression *is supposed to,* like *should,*
He **should** be in his room.   expresses obligation and is considered a semi-modal.

EXERCISE 22   In the following sentences, name each sentence constituent (set off with slashes) and identify the type of transitive verb (*monotransitive, ditransitive,* or *complex-transitive*). Then change the active sentence into a passive one. Be sure to keep tense, mood, and aspect constant. The first one has been done for you.

      S   P (monotransitive)   DO
1   Everyone / must have <u>admired</u> / him.

    He must have been admired (by everyone).

2   Students / must pay attention to / the teacher.

    The teacher ...

3   My brother / has given / me / some book cases. (2 passive constructions)

   Some book cases..

   I ...

4   They / made / me leave immediately.

   I ...

5   We / believe / him to be honest.

   He ...

6   We / are electing / her / chair.

   She ...

5   **Past participles as adjectives**
Normally, a passive construction is used to focus on what is considered the second participant in an active construction. In some cases, though, with verbs that express events involving a 'thing' doing something and a 'person' undergoing the event, the human is given more prominence and almost always made subject, and the passive form is much more common and actually preferred over the active one. Note that in such sentences, when the first participant is not really doing something, the preposition is not *by*, but *about* or *from*.

> The bad weather worried (upset, concerned, etc.) John.
> John was worried about the bad weather.
>
> The trip exhausted (tired) me.
> I was exhausted from/by the trip.

These passive-like constructions are so conventionalized that they have also lost their passive sense of a participant undergoing something. Therefore, the past participle is felt to be more of an adjective, describing the state of the subject and functioning as subject attribute, than a verb. Even many dictionaries list these words as adjectives.

```
       S  P         S A
       I / am / worried about him.

       S  P         S A
       I / am / interested in art.

       S  P         S A
       I / am / concerned about him.
```

EXERCISE 23   In the following passage (from *Miles City, Montana* by Alice Munro) identify the underlined past participle forms. Are they felt to be part of a passive construction in which the event itself is the focus of attention, or are they to be considered as adjectives describing the subject?

> My father came across the field carrying the body of the boy who had been <u>drowned</u>. There were several men together, returning from the search, but he was the one carrying the body. The men were muddy and <u>exhausted</u> and walked with their heads down, as if they were <u>ashamed</u>. Even the dogs were <u>dispirited</u>, dripping from the cold river. When they all set out, hours before, the dogs were nervy and yelping, the men tense and <u>determined</u>, and there was a constrained, unspeakable excitement about the whole scene. It was <u>understood</u> that they might find something horrible.

4.6   Identifying type of lexical verbs in complex sentences

In the preceding sections you have seen that lexical verbs may be one of three main types: intransitive, copula, and transitive. Transitive verbs, in turn, have three sub-types: monotransitive, ditransitive, and complex-transitive. Moreover, you have seen that transitive verbs may also occur in passive constructions. In very simple sentences, it is not difficult to see what type a verb is, but in sentences with dependent finite and non-finite clauses, the answer is not as obvious. To help you identify the type of verb, it helps to isolate the particular clause in which it functions and change it into a short simple (active) sentence so that it becomes clear how many participants are involved and who does what. Then you can decide what type of verb it is.

This idea **amused** him immensely. He **saw** himself **taken away** as a white slave-boy, **cozened** and **coddled** and **taught to play** the flute.

something **amused** him	monotransitive
he **saw** something	monotransitive
someone **took** him **away**	monotransitive
someone **cozened** him	monotransitive
someone **coddled** him	monotransitive
someone **taught** him something	ditransitive
he **played** the flute	monotransitive

EXERCISE 24   In the following passage (from *True Trash* by Margaret Atwood) identify each underlined verb as auxiliary (of mood, perfect aspect, progressive aspect, or passive voice) or lexical (intransitive, copula, monotransitive, ditransitive, or complex-transitive). If necessary, create a short sentence to help you identify the type of lexical verb.

Between two oval hills of pink granite there<u>'s</u> a small crescent of beach. The boys, <u>wearing</u> their bathing suits (as they never <u>do</u> on canoe trips but only around the camp where they <u>might</u> <u>be seen</u> by girls), <u>are</u> <u>doing</u> their laundry, <u>standing</u> up to their knees and <u>swabbing</u> their wet T-shirts and underpants with yellow bars of Sunlight soap. This only <u>happens</u> when they <u>run out of</u> clothes, or when the stench of dirty socks in the cabin <u>becomes</u> too overpowering. Darce, the counselor, <u>is</u> <u>supervising</u>, <u>stretched out</u> on a rock, <u>taking</u> the sun on his already tanned torso and <u>smoking</u> a fag. It'<u>s</u> <u>forbidden</u> <u>to smoke</u> in front of the campers but he <u>knows</u> this bunch <u>won't</u> <u>tell</u>. <u>To be</u> on the safe side he'<u>s</u> furtive about it, <u>holding</u> the cigarette down close to the rock and <u>sneaking</u> quick puffs.

4.7 Multi-word verbs

Terms like *intransitive, copula*, and *transitive verbs* refer to the 'meanings' of lexical verbs and are determined by the sentence pattern in which they occur. Terms like *finite* and *non-finite* refer to the grammatical forms of verbs. Another way to classify verbs, especially lexical ones, is by the number and type of words they consist of.

Most verbs consist of one word (*read, talk, write, run*, and so on). However, some verbs, combined with one or more words, take on a meaning of their own. For example, look at the different meanings of the verbs below:

> They **came** in the room.
> They **came in for** a surprise.
> He **took** a course.
> He **took up** the study of syntax.
>
> He **caught** the mouse.
> He **caught up with** him.
> He **caught sight of** him

In the first sentence, the verb *came* expresses a motion and *in* the direction into which he moved. In the second sentence, *in* has lost this literal direction sense and has become part of the standard expression 'to come in for', which means something like 'undergo' or 'experience'. The same applies for *took* versus *took up*, which means something like 'start'. In grammar, phrases like *come in for, take up, catch up with* and so on are considered to be one lexical verb. The verb part of a *multi-word verb* is usually a very frequently used verb like *come*, but the added adverb or preposition may change its meaning quite substantially.

Among these types of verbs, we can distinguish five different subtypes according to the word class of the added parts (see Table 12).

Table 12 Multi-word verbs

one-word verbs	verb	write, run
phrasal verbs	verb + adverb	write up, run off
prepositional verbs	verb + preposition	run into, agree to, agree with, agree on
phrasal prepositional verbs	verb + adverb + preposition	keep away from, come in for
idiomatic noun preposition verbs	verb + noun + preposition	catch sight of, set fire to, lose count of

Phrasal verbs and prepositional verbs may be hard to tell apart. Luckily, we can distinguish a phrasal verb from a prepositional verb by applying a simple test. If there is a direct object, replace it with a pronoun (*it, him, her, them*). The pronoun always comes after a preposition, but in front of an adverb.

He **looked into** the problem.
He **looked into** it.   prepositional verb

He **looked up** the word.
He **looked** it **up**.   phrasal verb

If there is no direct object, the multi-word verb is a phrasal one by definition.

The airplane **touched down** a few minutes ago.   phrasal verb

Often, it is not easy to tell if a preposition and/or adverb or noun phrase is part of the verb or not and so to determine whether we are dealing with a verb plus preposition or adverbs or, indeed, a prepositional or phrasal verb. To find out, you can apply several tests. First of all, you should see if the preposition or adverb gives the verb a specific sense that is distinct from the verb in isolation.

He **stood**.   a static action
He **stood up**.   a dynamic action

If you can substitute the verb and preposition or adverb with another expression covering the same meaning, it is likely that you have a prepositional or phrasal verb on your hands.

He **ran out of** clean clothes.   multi-word verb
i.e. He no longer had clean clothes.

Finally, if the preposition or adverb or noun can easily be substituted with another preposition, adverb or noun, it is not a multi-word verb.

He stood **up** to his knees in the mud.   *Stood* is not part of a multi-word verb because
He stood **down** to his knees in the mud.   *up* is part of the phrase *up to his knees* and can
                                               be substituted with another preposition.

EXERCISE 25   For the following expressions, first create a meaningful sentence. Then indicate the function of the verb (transitive or intransitive). Also identify the type of multi-word verb.

1	come about	6	come off
2	come across	7	come on
3	come by	8	come out
4	come down	9	come up with
5	come in for	10	come round to

4.8 Summary

In this chapter, you have seen that there are different types of lexical verbs, determined by the type of complement they take in a sentence. *Copula verbs* are verbs that take a subject attribute as complement, *intransitive verbs* are verbs that neither take an object nor a subject attribute as complement, and *transitive verbs* are verbs that take a direct object as complement.

Among transitive verbs there are three subtypes: *monotransitive verbs* have only a direct object, *ditransitive verbs* have a direct and an indirect or benefactive object. *Complex-transitive verbs* have a direct object and an object attribute. Table 13 gives an overview of the different types of lexical verbs with an example and an analysis of the sentence pattern.

Table 13 Types of lexical verbs

type of lexical verb		example	sentence pattern
intransitive		He is **running.**	S P
copula		He **is** a teacher.	S P SA
transitive	monotransitive	He **bought** a book.	S P DO
	ditransitive	He **gave** her the book.	S P IO/BO DO
	complex-transitive	She **found** the book interesting.	S P DO OA

Transitive verbs may be used in two different sentence patterns: an *active* or a *passive* sentence pattern. Depending on the type of transitive verb, different passive sentence patterns are possible. A ditransitive verb may have two alternate passive constructions. Not only the 'old' direct object, but also the 'old' indirect object may become the 'new' subject of a passive sentence. In the case of a *complex-transitive verb* like *consider*, the 'old' object becomes the 'new' subject, and the 'old' object attribute now becomes the 'new' subject attribute. See Table 14.

Table 14 Passive constructions

type of transitive verb	active sentence	passive sentence
monotransitive	He read the book.	S P The book / was read.
ditransitive	He gave her the book.	S P IO The book / was given / to her. S P DO She / was given / he book.
complex-transitive	He found the book interesting.	S P SA The book / was found / interesting.

Direct objects may have all kinds of forms: they may consist of a phrase consisting of one word, a phrase consisting of two or more words, a non-finite clause, or a finite clause. Especially non-finite clause direct objects can give rise to passive constructions that are difficult to analyze. Some of such passive forms like *to be supposed to* or *to be allowed to* have become so conventionalized that they have taken on meanings similar to those of modals such as *should* or *may* and are therefore considered to be *semi-modals*. Finally, there are also some conventionalized passive forms, which have lost their real passive sense, and the past participle is considered part of the subject attribute rather than the verb phrase. Table 15 reviews how sentences with these passive constructions should be analyzed.

Table 15 Analyzing conventionalized passive constructions

S	P	A
He /	was forced to leave /	this afternoon.

S	P	A
He /	is supposed to leave /	this afternoon

S	P	S A
He /	was /	worried about the trip.

Finally, there are lexical verbs that consist of more than one word, called *multi-word verbs*. These are verbs like *come in for* or *take off* consisting of a verb followed by a preposition, an adverb, or a preposition and adverb, or even a whole phrase as in *to catch sight of*, which together means something like *see*.

5 Word classes

5.1 Introduction

In Chapters 1 and 2, we looked at sentence constituents, and in Chapters 3 and 4, we looked more closely at the central part of a sentence or clause, the verb phrase, which always consists of verbs. When we use the term *verb*, we name the type of class a word belongs to, called *word class*.

In this chapter, we will discuss the different types of word classes. But before doing so, we will first examine briefly at what level of analysis word classes play a role, so that you will understand how this chapter relates to the previous ones and the following ones. Consider the following sentence:

> My late dad was a magnificent hunter.

We know that this sentence can be analyzed as follows:

> S   P   S A
> My late dad / was / a magnificent hunter.

The subject, predicator, and the subject attribute contain one or more words that 'belong together' and are called *phrases*. Phrases consisting of more than one word have one word that is semantically the most important. If these most important words were used by themselves (without the other words in the phrase), the sentence would still be meaningful: *Dad was hunter*. *Dad*, *was* and *hunter* are called the *heads* of their respective phrases. Both *dad* and *hunter* happen to be nouns, so both *my late dad* and *a magnificent hunter* are called *noun phrases*, abbreviated as NP. We already know that the predicator is called a *verb phrase*, abbreviated as VP.

The terms *subject, predicator* and *subject attribute* name the *functions*, which refer to the roles the constituents play in the sentence. The terms *noun phrase* and *verb phrase* name the *realizations*, which describe what form the constituents have.

Once we know both the function and realization, we can analyze the sentence in more detail. In this book, we will use the colon (:) to stand for 'is realized by'. The following example shows this more detailed analysis.

S : NP   P : VP   SA : NP
My late dad / was / a magnificent hunter.

In the next chapter, we will look more closely at the different types of phrases, the different parts they may contain, and how these parts may be combined, but to be able to analyze them, you first need to know the names of all the word classes and how these word classes may be combined. Therefore, we will discuss word classes first.

To determine the word class of a word, you cannot just look at its form or meaning, but you have to look at its function in the phrase, clause, or sentence in which it occurs. For example, when you see the word *walk*, you probably think of an 'action', which is usually a verb, but in different sentences the same word (with a similar meaning) can be used in different ways.

I **walk** to school every day.	verb
We went for a long **walk** yesterday.	noun
I had on my **walking** shoes.	adjective
The trip **exhausted** me.	verb
The trip was **exhausting**.	adjective
It was **exhausting**.	adjective

In all, there are about eleven different word classes in English. Note that word classes, just like any other category, include not only members that are really good examples of that word class but also members that only marginally belong to that word class.

Moreover, one particular word may belong to more than one class, depending on how it is used in the sentence.

One distinction that can be made among word classes is the 'open' versus 'closed' classes. Nouns, verbs, adjectives, and adverbs are very clearly 'open' classes because new members are added almost every day and old members are used with completely new senses. Just think of an expression like *to surf the internet*. Here, *surf* is used with a new sense, and *Internet* is a rather new word in the English lexicon. The total number of prepositions, coordinators, subordinators, numerals, pronouns, and articles is much smaller, and new ones are added only sporadically. Therefore they are considered 'closed' classes. Table 16 gives examples of both classes.

Table 16 'Open' versus 'closed' word classes

open classes		closed classes	
noun	*mother, bird, pleasure, walk*	preposition	*after, at, in, on, during, amongst, like, since*
verb	*walk, say, cry, consider, be*	coordinator	*and, but, or, nor*
adjective	*big, rich, happy, exhausted, walking*	subordinator	*after, since, because, although*
adverb	*happily, merely, very, up, however*	pronoun	*I, you, she, someone, which, this*
interjection	*alas!, oops!, wow!*	article	*the, a,*
		numeral	*two, fifth*

5.2 Nouns

Nouns and verbs represent the two most important word classes. They are the first ones to be learned by children and usually the most meaningful. They name the things around us and the processes they are involved in.

Nouns name things and persons. If people were asked to name 'things' or 'persons', they would probably quickly come up with a list like *woman, man, boy, book, desk, chair,* and so on. These persons and things are quite obviously in this world because we can clearly see their contours. Other things cannot be seen directly but inferred from facial expressions because they describe a human emotion or another mental state: *puzzlement*, *annoyance*, and *idea*. Other things such as *air* and *noise* we are not really able to see, but from what we know about the world we know they are there. Some things people would probably mention in the plural form because the items appear as a group: *books* and *houses*. Besides naming things (*house*, *bicycle*) or persons (*boy*, *girl*, *John*, *Mary*), nouns name events (a *walk*) or situations seen as things (a *gathering*).

Among nouns, several distinctions can be made along different, but overlapping dimensions: *proper* versus *common*, *concrete* versus *abstract*, and *count* versus *non-count*. And, as can be expected, the same word may be used as a different kind.

Proper nouns, usually capitalized in English, are names for a particular person or thing: *Peter*, *Dorothy*, *Great Britain*, *the Netherlands*, and so on. Most proper names are singular, but also plural nouns like *the United States* and *the Alps* are used as proper nouns. *Common nouns* refer to persons and things by their general name: *boy*, *girl*, *country*, *idea*, and so on.

Concrete nouns refer to things that are tangible like *mountain*, *bicycle*, and *table*. *Abstract nouns* refer to things that are not tangible like *idea*, *thought*, and *dream*. Nouns referring to processes like *transportation*, *move*, *adaptation*, *walk*, and so on are also considered abstract nouns. However, the distinction between concrete and abstract is not always clear-cut. For example, a *bicycle* refers to a concrete thing and *love* to an abstract thing, but especially nouns expressing actions (*a walk*, *a yelp*, *a smoke*) are not clearly one or the other. In other words, we have to do with a continuum and can say nouns can be more concrete or abstract.

Count nouns refer to things that are clearly 'bounded' and are seen as separate things like *house* and *bicycle*. *Non-count nouns*, also called *mass nouns*, refer to things that consist of a whole group of separate (small) items that are not seen as clearly separate things but as a whole such as *grass*, *furniture*, and *cattle*. Non-count nouns may also refer to things that do not have clear boundaries such as concrete things like *water*, *gold*, and *glass* or abstract things like *love* and *war*.

As creative beings, people often use the same 'form' in different ways, usually affecting its meaning. Consider the semantic differences between the following sentences.

John has lots of **love**.   non-count and abstract
Bill has lots of **loves**.   count and concrete

In France, a lot of **wine** is produced.   non-count and concrete
France produces a lot of **wines**.   count and concrete

To be sure that a word in a sentence is used as a noun, you can apply the following grammatical tests:

- See if you can put *the* in front of it. (This works for most nouns, except *proper nouns*.)
- See if you can change it from singular to plural or vice versa. (This works for *count nouns* but not for *non-count nouns*.)
- See if you can substitute it with a pronoun like *it* or *they*.

EXERCISE 26   In the following passage (from *A Farm at Raraba* by Ernst Havemann), underline all nouns and identify whether it is (a) proper or common, and (b) count or non-count.

> My late dad was a magnificent shot. One time when we were hunting in the Low Veld and had paused for a smoke, there was the yelp of a wild dog, and a troop of impala came bounding over the tall grass. Opposite us, three hundred yards off, was a stony ridge like a wall, six feet high. You would think those buck would avoid it, but no, they went straight at it. One after the other, without pausing or swerving, they leapt over it. They cleared it by three feet. I tell you, friend, it was a beautiful sight. You can't beat Nature for beauty, eh.

5.3 Verbs

As you saw in Chapter 4, *verbs* usually denote processes, actions, or states: *walk, run, be, become, think, believe,* and so on that may take place or occur over time. The referents of lexical verbs may range from very concrete to very abstract processes. For example, *walk* and *run* have concrete meanings because they stand for actions that can be clearly visualized. On the other hand, *have* or *become*, which refer to a state of possession or a change of state, *believe* and *think*, which refer to mental processes or states, and *be*, which refers to a vague state that takes place over time, have more abstract meanings referring to states that occur over time. And as you saw in Chapter 3, the auxiliary verbs of mood like *will, can, may,* and so on also have rather vague, abstract meanings.

In some cases it is difficult to determine whether a word is used as noun or verb as nouns may be used as verbs and vice versa. For example, a non-finite verb form like *to study* or *studying* can keep a lot of its 'verb quality' but is used as a subject, as in *To study is necessary*. In this case, *to study* is still regarded as a verb because it still has a lot of 'verbal' characteristics. It can be followed by a direct object as in *To study* <u>English syntax</u> *is necessary* or be modified by an adverb as in *To study* <u>hard</u> *is necessary*. *To study, to study hard,* and *to study English Syntax* are all non-finite clauses functioning as subject, which will be studied in more detail in Chapter 7.

In case of an *-ing* form, the 'verb' may lose all of its 'verb' properties and then it should be regarded as a noun. Compare the following sentences:

Painting the room is difficult.	*Painting* still has verbal qualities because it is followed by a direct object, *the room; painting the room* as a whole is a non-finite clause, functioning as subject. In this dependent clause *painting* is the verb phrase.
The painting of the room was the most difficult chore.	*Painting* now has more noun qualities because it is preceded and followed by noun modifiers, *the* and *of the room*. *The painting of the room* is a noun phrase, functioning as subject.
The painting in the room is by a famous artist.	*Painting* has lost all of its verb qualities and is a full noun; it could even be made plural. *The painting in the room* is a noun phrase, functioning as subject.

5.4 Adjectives

Adjectives are words that *modify* (= say something about) a noun; they either name an inherent attribute of a thing, like *a glass door* or an attribute granted to it like *a beautiful door* or tell what kind of thing it is as in *a shed door*. Prototypical adjectives are words that can occur in the *comparative forms* like *big, bigger, biggest*, but many other adjectives are nouns or verbs used as adjectives, as in *city life* or *walking shoes*, and do not have comparative forms. To determine whether a word is used as an adjective, you should see if it modifies a noun.

- See if it is in front of a noun as in *a busy street*. *Street* is a noun and *busy*, which is in front of it, tells what kind of street it is.
- See if it functions as the main part of a subject attribute or an object attribute as in *This street is very busy* and *I find this street very busy*.
- In a few fixed expressions, the adjective may also occur after a noun as in *all the students present* or *China proper*.

5.5 Adverbs

Whereas adjectives have only one function (they can modify only nouns), different kinds of *adverbs* can have different functions. Typical adverbs are words like *here, home, there,* and *yesterday* expressing 'where' or 'when' an event or situation is taking place. Also question words themselves like *where, when* and *how* are adverbs, called *interrogative adverbs*. By themselves these words may function as adverbial in a sentence or clause.

He ran **yesterday**.	The adverb *yesterday* functions as adverbial and tells when the event took place.
He writes **well**.	The adverb *well* functions as adverbial and tells how he *writes*.
How does he write?	The interrogative adverb *how* functions as adverbial.

Other adverbs modify one particular word in a phrase. For example, adverbs like *very* express 'degree' and modify adjectives or adverbs. Some adverbs modify a whole phrase.

He runs **very** quickly.	The adverb *very* expresses the degree to which he runs *quickly*. It modifies the adverb *quickly*.
He is **very** fast.	The adverb *very* expresses the degree to which he is *fast*. *Fast* is here an adjective and *very* modifies it.
He went **completely** out of his mind.	The adverb *completely* modifies the phrase *out of his mind*.

Some adverbs, like *clearly* or *obviously* modify a whole statement. Other adverbs like *however* and *therefore*, called *conjunctive* or *sentence adverbs* (see Chapter 2), have meanings similar to coordinate conjunctions and express the logical relationship between main clauses or sentences.

Obviously he is very fast.	The adverb *obviously* expresses the degree of certainty with which the statement in the sentence should be taken. *Obviously* modifies the whole sentence.
He is very fast; **however**, he does not have much stamina.	The conjunctive adverb *however* shows the 'thought link' between two sentences. It functions as an adverbial within the sentence.

Finally, there are two types of adverbs that may have a double function. They can introduce a dependent question (*interrogative adverb*) or a modifying clause (*relative adverb*). Below are two example sentences, but these two types will be discussed further in the section on connectors.

Where does he live?	The adverb *where* is an interrogative adverb.
I don't know **where** he lives.	The adverb *where* is an interrogative adverb with the double function of subordinator.
Do you remember the place **where** we met last week?	The adverb *where* is a relative adverb with the double function of subordinator.

Note that the form of the word is not always an indication of its class. In English, the adverb often (but not always) has a -ly suffix (*beautiful* versus *beautifully*). However, not all adverbs have an -ly suffix (*fast*, *well*) and the -ly ending is not only used for adverbs but also for some adjectives (*friendly*).

EXERCISE 27   In the following passage (from *The Catch* by Nadine Gordimer), underline and identify all words used as adjectives and adverbs.

> His* thin strong bony legs passed by at eye level every morning as they lay, stranded on the hard smooth sand. Washed up thankfully out of the swirl and buffet of the city, they were happy to lie there, but because they were accustomed to telling the time by their nerves' response to the different tensions of the city, children crying in flats, lorries going heavily and bicycles jangling for early morning, skid of tyres, sound of frying and the human insect noise of thousands talking and walking and eating at midday — the tensionless shore keyed only to the tide gave them a sense of timelessness that, however much they rejoiced mentally, troubled their habit-impressed bodies with a lack of pressure. So the sound of his feet, thudding nearer over the sand, passing their heads with the deep sound of a man breathing in the heat above the rolled-up, faded trousers, passing away up the beach and shrinking into the figure of an Indian fisherman, began to be something to be waited for. His coming and going divided the morning into three; the short early time before he passed, the time when he was actually passing and the largish chunk of warm midday that followed when he had gone.
>
> * Ignore words like *his, the* and *every*. These will be discussed in the next sections.

5.6 Pronouns

The term *pronoun*, which literally means 'instead of a noun' is not really correct. Sometimes a pronoun does stand for a noun, but often it doesn't. What is odd about pronouns is that they may have two different functions. On the one hand, they may stand on their own and function *independently*, like a noun, as the subject or object of a clause. On the other hand, they may function *dependently*, very much like adjectives, in that they occur before a noun. In some books they are even called adjectives. In this course, we will just use the term *pronoun* to stand for both kinds and indicate whether they are used *dependently* or *independently*.

Michael bought **these** books, and Claire bought **those**.	The first pronoun is used dependently; the second one, independently.
Each book costs over $ 100. **Each** costs over $ 100.	The first pronoun is used dependently; the second one, independently.
His book costs more than **hers**.	The first pronoun is used dependently; the second one, independently.

When pronouns are used dependently, before a noun, they are somewhat similar to adjectives, but rather than describing a quality or characteristic of a thing as *old* in *old books*, they do not say anything about the thing itself. Instead these pronouns help locate and identify the things in the world the speaker and hearer share.

For example, in phrases like *my telephone* and *that telephone* words like *my* and *that* do not describe the telephone itself, but help the speaker locate the thing in space, usually from the speaker's perspective. Such words function as *determiners* in a noun phrase as they help us determine 'which' or 'whose' telephone it is. Determiners will be discussed in more depth in Chapter 6.

There are nine kinds of pronouns: personal, possessive, relative, interrogative, demonstrative, reflexive, reciprocal, and indefinite. Finally, there is the pronoun *so*. Each will be discussed below.

1. **Personal pronouns**

   Personal pronouns are always independent and refer to people or things: *I/me, you, he/him, she/her, it, we/us,* and *they/them*.

   > I saw **them** yesterday.

2. **Possessive pronouns**

   Possessive pronouns are related to personal pronouns and express 'ownership'. There are dependent and independent ones. The dependent ones are *my, your, his, its,** *her, our, their*. They function as a determiner and tell 'whom' or 'what' something or somebody belongs to. The independent ones are *mine, yours, his, hers, its, ours, theirs*.

   > Consider **my** book **yours**.
   > These are **mine**.

3. **Relative pronouns**

   Relative pronouns are the pronouns *who, whom, whose, which,* and *that*, which have a double function. They are pronouns in that they refer to a person or thing and at the same time they introduce a dependent clause. In the clause that they introduce, they function as a constituent (for example, a subject or object). Except for *whose*, they are all independent, but *whose* is a dependent one, very much like a possessive pronoun.

   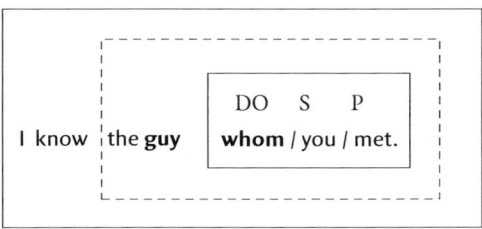

   * Note that the possessive pronoun related to *it* (*its*) is spelled as one word (just like *his* and *hers*). The spelling with an apostrophe (*it's*) is used to stand for *it is*.

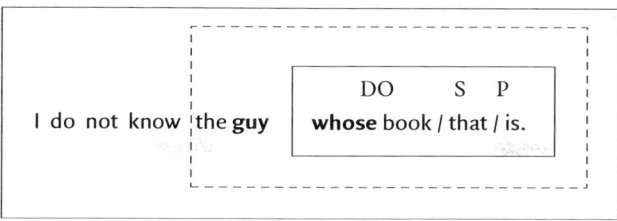

4 Interrogative pronouns

Interrogative pronouns are words like *whose, who, whom, which* and *what*, which introduce questions. They may be used dependently or independently.

Whose book is that?	*whose is used dependently*
Whose is that?	*whose is used independently*

These same interrogative pronouns may be used as *subordinators* to introduce dependent clauses functioning as subject, object, or attribute. Actually, many of such clauses can be seen as dependent questions. Note that the word order in dependent questions is very much the same as that of a declarative sentence, and different from the word order in an interrogative sentence.

Whom did you see?	*Whom introduces an independent question and the finite verb precedes the subject.*
I asked **whom** you saw.	*Whom introduces a dependent question and the subject precedes the finite verb.*

5 Demonstrative pronouns

The demonstrative pronouns are this, that, these, and those, which have a 'pointing' sense. This and that refer to 'singular' things, these and those to 'plural' ones. They can also be used independently and dependently.

Did you see **this/that**?	*This and that are used independently*
Did you read **this/that** book?	*This and that are used dependently*

Did you see **these/those**?	*These* and *those* are used independently
Did you read **these/those** books?	*These* and *those* are used dependently

6 Reflexive pronouns

Reflexive pronouns are words like *myself, himself,* and so on and consist of a personal or possessive pronoun followed by *self* or *selves*. They are always used independently. They may be used as object to refer back to another noun or pronoun in the sentence, or they may be used to emphasize part of a subject or object.

They saw **themselves** in the mirror.	The reflexive pronoun functions as direct object.
They **themselves** saw the UFO.	The reflexive pronoun is used as part of the subject.

7 Reciprocal pronouns

The *reciprocal pronouns* are *each other* and *one another*. They are always used independently.

> We saw **each other** quite often.

8 Indefinite pronouns

Indefinite pronouns are words like *someone* and *somebody* that begin with *some, every, no,* or *any* and end in *person, body* or *thing*. They are used independently. Indefinite pronouns are very much like personal pronouns, but they have a vaguer sense. Other indefinite pronouns are words like *no, every, all, any, both, enough, much, several* and so on, which refer to a quantity and are like vague numerals. The last group may be used both dependently and independently.

> **Someone** thought that **all** of the books would be too **much**.

Some books make a distinction between indefinite pronouns and quantifiers like *no, several* and so on. Because it is difficult to distinguish between indefinite pronouns and quantifiers on the one hand and quantifiers and numerals on the other hand, we have decided to call all quantifying expressions indefinite pronouns. The term numeral is reserved for expressions containing a number.

There are also some expressions that consist of a noun or pronoun, sometimes followed by a preposition, that have meanings and functions very similar to these indefinite pronouns. To keep things simple, we will call these phrases indefinite pronouns, too.

A great many	books
A few	books
Many a	book
A lot of	books
A great deal of	books

⎫ indefinite pronouns

9 **So**

Finally there is one unnamed type of pronoun, *so*, which is always used independently, and which usually refers to a whole event.

> I asked you to leave. Please do **so** immediately.

5.7 Numerals and articles

Numerals are words like *one*, *second*, and so on, referring to numbers. Like pronouns, they can be used independently and dependently.

Michael bought **two** books, and Claire bought **three**.	The first numeral is used dependently; the second one, independently.

A *numeral* is a 'count word'. There are *cardinal numerals* (*one, two, three*) which name the number and *ordinal numerals* (*first, second, third*), which show the order.

He is number **one**.	independent cardinal numeral
He is the **first**.	independent ordinal numeral
He has **one** book.	dependent cardinal numeral
He has read the **first** page.	dependent ordinal numeral

English has two *articles*: *the* and *a(n)*. Historically they come from the demonstrative pronoun *this* and the cardinal number *one*, but now they have a much vaguer meaning. Articles are always used dependently as determiners, that is in front of a noun.

He has **a** new car. **The** car is old.

EXERCISE 28   In the following passage (same as Exercise 26) identify the word class of all underlined words and indicate whether they are used dependently or independently.

His thin strong bony legs passed by at eye level every morning as they lay, stranded on the hard smooth sand. Washed up thankfully out of the swirl and buffet of the city, they were happy to lie there, but because they were accustomed to telling the time by their nerves' response to the different tensions of the city, children crying in flats, lorries going heavily and bicycles jangling for early morning, skid of tyres, sound of frying and the human insect noise of thousands talking and walking and eating at midday — the tensionless shore keyed only to the tide gave them a sense of timelessness that, however much they rejoiced mentally, troubled their habit-impressed bodies with a lack of pressure. So the sound of his feet, thudding nearer over the sand, passing their heads with the deep sound of a man breathing in the heat above the rolled-up, faded trousers, passing away up the beach and shrinking into the figure of an Indian fisherman, began to be something to be waited for. His coming and going divided the morning into three; the short early time before he passed, the time when he was actually passing and the largish chunk of warm midday that followed when he had gone.

5.8 Connectors

There are many different types of connectors. The term *connectors* is used in a very broad sense as a superordinate term for all words that 'link.' Coordinators link parts that have 'equal' syntactic value. Subordinators link a dependent clause or phrase to a clause or phrase of a higher level. Subordinators, in turn, may be subclassified again according to the type of dependent phrase or clause they introduce and according to whether they have a function within the clause or phrase they introduce. Each will be discussed separately below.

1 Coordinators

Coordinators link two 'equal' parts, which may be two or more single words, phrases, dependent clauses, or main clauses. As you saw in Chapter 2, there is a small number of *coordinators*, the *coordinate conjunctions* (*and, but, or, nor, for, so, yet*) and *correlative conjunctions: not only ... but also, neither ... nor, either ... or,* and *both ... and*. Note that the term *conjunction* is reserved for connectors that have no function within the clause they introduce.

The following examples show how these coordinators may be used to form compound subjects, objects, and compound sentences.

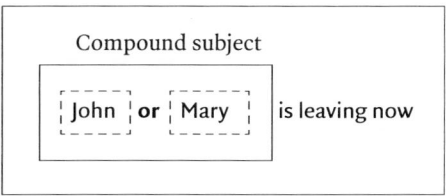

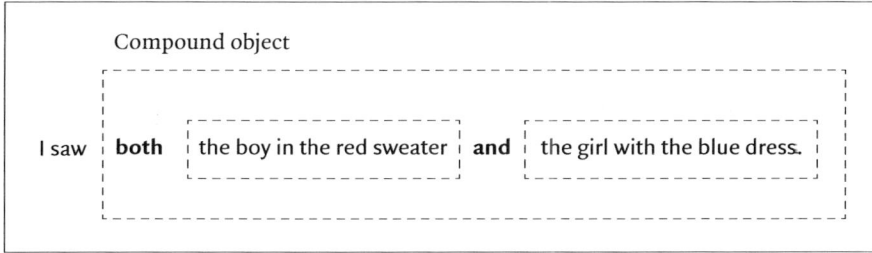

Compound sentence

> He is studying for his exam now,
>
> **for**
>
> he will not have enough time next week.

Coordinators may also be used to show the logical connection between two separate sentences.

sentence 1

> He is studying for his exam.

sentence 2

> **So** he has no time to come visit next week.

Note that the structures within the boxes are very similar to each other. For example, a noun is connected to a noun, or a noun modified with a prepositional phrase to a noun with a prepositional phrase. This phenomenon is called *parallel structures*, which is often a sign of effective writing (see Chapter 9).

Remember that in Chapter 2 it was explained that compound sentences may also be formed by placing a semicolon between two main clauses. Often, the second clause contains a *conjunctive adverb*. Several conjunctive adverbs have a meaning very similar to coordinate conjunctions, but they are different as far as grammatical properties are concerned (they may be moved within the clause), and therefore they are punctuated differently. When main clauses are linked with a coordinate conjunction, they are separated with a comma. When main clauses are logically linked with a conjunctive adverb, these main clauses should not be separated with a comma (which would result in a comma splice, see Chapter 9) but with either a period (.), a semicolon (;) or sometimes a colon (:).

Compound sentence separated with semicolon

> He is studying for his exam now
>
> ;
>
> A
> therefore, he will not have enough time next week.

EXERCISE 29   In the following passage (same as Exercise 26) underline all words used as coordinators. Set off the parts that they connect with square brackets. Has this author kept the structures connected with a coordinator parallel?

> His thin strong bony legs passed by at eye level every morning as they lay, stranded on the hard smooth sand. Washed up thankfully out of the swirl and buffet of the city, they were happy to lie there, but because they were accustomed to telling the time by their nerves' response to the different tensions of the city — children crying in flats, lorries going heavily and bicycles jangling for early morning, skid of tyres, sound of frying and the human insect noise of thousands talking and walking and eating at midday — the tensionless shore keyed only to the tide gave them a sense of timelessness that, however much they rejoiced mentally, troubled their habit-impressed bodies with a lack of pressure. So the sound of his feet, thudding nearer over the sand, passing their heads with the deep sound of a man breathing in the heat above the rolled-up, faded trousers, passing away up the beach and shrinking into the figure of an Indian fisherman, began to be something

5.8   Connectors

to be waited for. His coming and going divided the morning into three; the short early time before he passed, the time when he was actually passing and the largish chunk of warm midday that followed when he had gone.

2 Subordinators

Subordinator is a superordinate term for all words that introduce a dependent clause. They can introduce three types of dependent clauses: (1) clauses functioning as subject, object, subject attribute, or object attribute, (2) clauses modifying a noun, and (3) clauses functioning as adverbial.

Among the subordinators, we can distinguish between those that do not have a function in the clause they introduce (so they are only subordinator and called conjunctions, like coordinators) and those that *do* have a function within the clause they introduce (so they are subordinator and pronoun or adverb at the same time).

A clause functioning as subject, object, or attribute is introduced by subordinators like *that, when, where, who, whom, whose, what, whether, how, which,* and *if*. In the following example, *when, where,* and *if* introduce direct object clauses and the coordinator *or* connects these three.

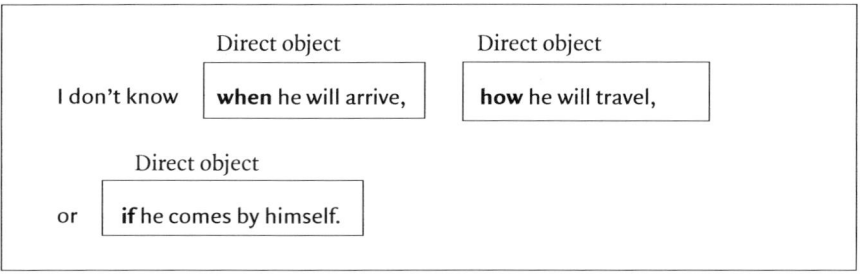

Among the noun clause subordinators, there are two types: those that have a function within the clause they introduce and those that don't. Compare the more detailed analysis of each direct object. *When* and *how* both are constituents in the clauses they introduce, so they are interrogative adverbs with a subordinating function. *If* is not a clause constituent, so it is purely a subordinating conjunction. We will reserve the term *conjunction* for connectors that do not have a function within the clause they introduce, so *if* and *whether* are called *subordinating conjunctions*.

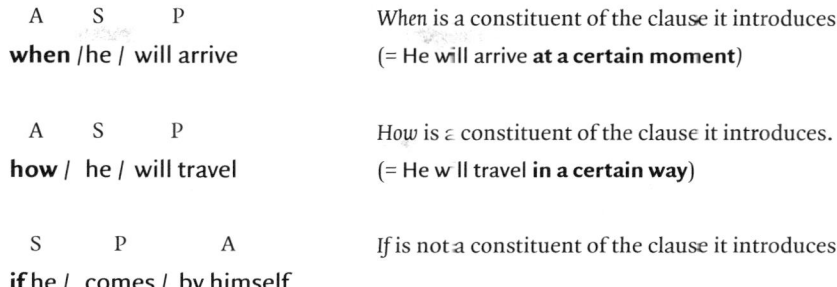

	A	S	P
	when /	he /	will arrive

When is a constituent of the clause it introduces.
(= He will arrive **at a certain moment**)

	A	S	P
	how /	he /	will travel

How is a constituent of the clause it introduces.
(= He will travel **in a certain way**)

	S	P	A
	if he /	comes /	by himself

If is not a constituent of the clause it introduces.

Clauses functioning as modifiers of nouns are called *relative* (or *adjective*) *clauses*. They are introduced by the subordinators *that, which, who, whom, whose* (called *relative pronouns*), and *where* and *when* (called *relative adverbs*). Note that a relative clause comes after the noun it modifies, and the pronoun or adverb refers to this noun.

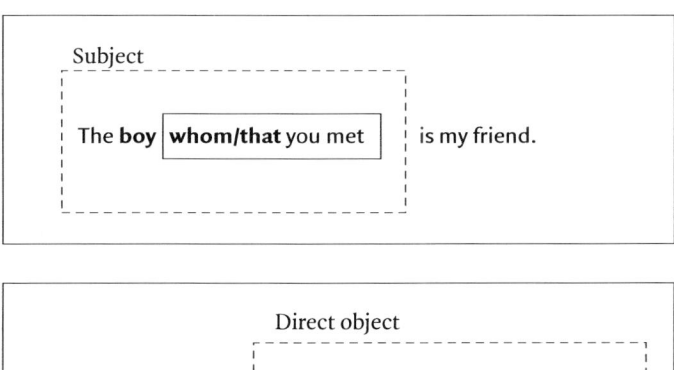

5.8 Connectors

Relative pronouns and adverbs always have a double function. They are subordinators and they are a constituent of the clause they introduce. Look at the more detailed analysis of the relative clauses.

        DO   S   P   Whom is a constituent of the clause it introduces.
whom / you / met   (= *you met* **him**)

        A   S   P   DO   When is a constituent of the clause it introduces.
when / we / played / hooky   (= *we played hooky* **then**)

Clauses functioning as adverbial are introduced by words like *when, where, after, before, since, although, because, before, even though, if, in order that, now that, once, rather than, since, so that, that, though, unless, until, when, whenever, where, whereas, wherever, while,* and so on. None of the subordinators introducing an adverb clause have a double function. All they do is link the dependent clause to another clause and show the meaning relation, but they do not function as a constituent of the clause they introduce. So just like *if* and *whether*, which introduce clauses functioning as subject, object, or attribute, they are called *subordinating conjunctions*.

In the summary, in Table 18, a complete list is given of all the connectors, but remember that the same word may have different functions. The same is true for subordinators. For example, in the following sentence the subordinator *who* introduces a clause functioning as direct object and in the next one *who* introduces a relative clause.

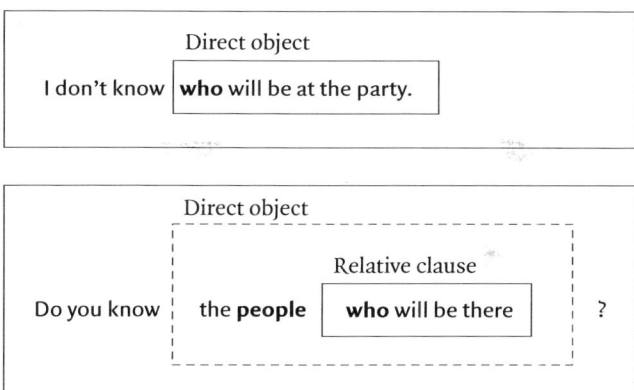

In the next sentence *if* functions as subordinator introducing a clause functioning as direct object, but in the one after that, *if* functions as subordinator introducing an adverbial.

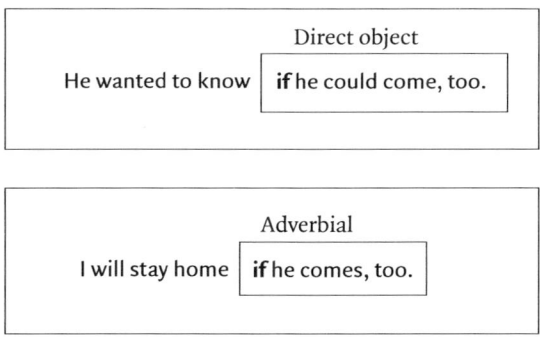

EXERCISE 30   In the following passage (same as Exercise 26) underline all words used as subordinator. Set off the parts that they introduce with square brackets. Note that some dependent clauses occur within other dependent clauses. Identify the subordinator as subordinating conjunction (SC), relative pronoun (RP) or relative adverb (RA), or as interrogative pronoun (IP) or interrogative adverb (IA).

His thin strong bony legs passed by at eye level every morning as they lay, stranded on the hard smooth sand. Washed up thankfully out of the swirl and buffet of the city, they were happy to lie there, but because they were accustomed to telling the time by their nerves' response to the different tensions of the city, children crying in flats, lorries going heavily and bicycles jangling for early morning, skid of tyres, sound of frying and the human insect noise of thousands talking and walking and eating at midday — the tensionless shore keyed only to the tide gave them a sense of timelessness that, however much* they rejoiced mentally, troubled their habit-impressed bodies with a lack of pressure. So the sound of his feet, thudding nearer over the sand, passing their heads with the deep sound of a man breathing in the heat above the rolled-up, faded trousers, passing away up the beach and shrinking into the figure of an Indian fisherman, began to be something to be waited for. His coming and going divided the morning into three; the short early time before he passed, the time when he was actually passing and the largish chunk of warm midday that followed when he had gone.

3 **Prepositions**

Prepositions are not traditionally called subordinators, but they have been put here because they are very similar to them. What they have in common is that they do not really have a function within the phrase or clause they introduce. They purely link and show a meaning relationship. The difference between a subordinating conjunction and a preposition is that subordinating conjunctions introduce dependent clauses and prepositions introduce dependent noun phrases.

* *However much* is used as a multi-word subordinator.

Prepositions are usually short words like *in, on, at, about, with, of, to, by, beside, before,* and *after.* (See the summary for a complete list.) When put in front of a noun phrase, which denotes a person or a thing, the noun phrase changes into a prepositional phrase, denoting a manner, place, time, and so on.

> The boy **in** the room running **in** a circle was crazy **about** the fact that his dog had barked **at** his cat.

In the previous sentence, *in the room* expresses 'where', *in a circle* expresses 'how', *about the fact* expresses 'why' and *at his cat* expresses 'in which direction'.

Whereas most prepositions are short words, there are also some multi-word prepositions like *by way of* or *in addition to, in spite of, in contrast to, apart from*. Multi-word prepositions are really made up of a noun phrase followed by a prepositional phrase, but they are combinations that are so commonly used together that they can be considered as one preposition.

> **In contrast to** his roommate, he likes to keep his room clean.

One problem is again that some words have more than one function. For example, in the following sentence *after*, which is followed by a noun phrase, functions as a *preposition*, but in the next one, when followed by a clause, *after* functions as a subordinator of a clause.

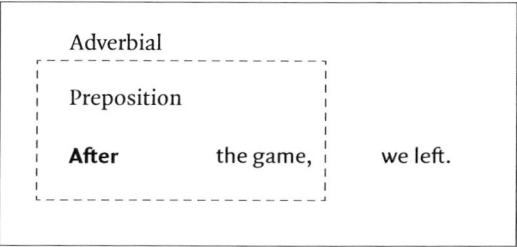

109   5.8   Connectors

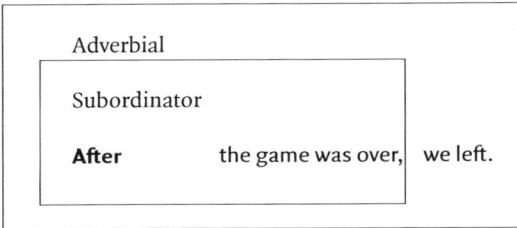

EXERCISE 31 In the following passage (same as Exercise 26) underline all words used as prepositions. Set off the parts that they introduce with square brackets. Note that some prepositional phrases contain other prepositional phrases.

His thin strong bony legs passed by at eye level every morning as they lay, stranded on the hard smooth sand. Washed up thankfully out of the swirl and buffet of the city, they were happy to* lie there, but because they were accustomed to** telling the time by their nerves' response to the different tensions of the city, children crying in flats, lorries going heavily and bicycles jangling for early morning, skid of tyres, sound of frying and the human insect noise of thousands talking and walking and eating at midday — the tensionless shore keyed only to the tide gave them a sense of timelessness that, however much they rejoiced mentally, troubled their habit-impressed bodies with a lack of pressure. So the sound of his feet, thudding nearer over the sand, passing their heads with the deep sound of a man breathing in the heat above the rolled-up, faded trousers, passing away up the beach and

* *To* as part of a *to* infinitive is not considered a preposition. It is considered part of the verb, like *–ing* would be part of a verb like *walking*.
** This is not a *to* of a *to* infinitive but a preposition before *telling*, which is used as a noun.

shrinking into the figure of an Indian fisherman, began to be something to be waited for.* His coming and going divided the morning into three; the short early time before** he passed, the time when he was actually passing and the largish chunk of warm midday that followed when he had gone.

5.9 Interjections

Interjections are words that literally are interjected into a sentence, *oh, well, blast, damn,* and so on. They do not have a function like subject or object, but express the speaker's attitude towards something.

> **Oh**, I didn't know you wanted to leave.

EXERCISE 32 In the following passage from *A Farm at Raraba* by Ernest Havemann identify the word class of each word. Remember to look at *how* it is used in the sentence. For an overview of word classes see the summary.

> My late dad was a magnificent shot. One time when we were hunting in the Low Veld and had paused for a smoke, there was the yelp of a wild dog, and a troop of impala came*** bounding over the tall grass. Opposite us, three hundred yards off, was a stony ridge like a wall, six feet high.**** You would think those buck would

---

* In normal word order it would be *to wait for* something.

** Here *before* is a subordinator because it introduces a clause.

*** The verb *come* is usually used as a lexical verb. In this sentence it can be argued that it functions as an auxiliary verb as it can easily be replaced with the auxiliary of progressive aspect *be*.

**** Remember that in some standard expressions, adjectives occur after a noun.

avoid it, but no, they went straight at it. One after the other, without* pausing or swerving, they leapt over it. They cleared it by three feet. I tell you, friend, it was a beautiful sight. You can't beat Nature for beauty, eh.

5.10 Summary

The term *word class* is a relative one. One particular word may be used in different ways, and its word class is determined by how it is used in a sentence. The following three tables give examples for each word class as discussed in this chapter. Table 20 provides rather complete lists of prepositions, subordinators, coordinators and conjunctive adverbs.

Table 17 Open word classes

noun	proper	*Peter, January, Great Britain, the Alps*
	common	*boy, girl, country*
	concrete	*bicycle, mountain*
	abstract	*idea, thought, transportation*
	count	*boy, bicycle, idea*
	non-count	*grass, furniture*
verb	lexical	*walk, run, think, become*
	auxiliary	*be, have, will, would, can, could, shall, should, is supposed to, is going to*
adjective		*beautiful, good*
adverb		*now, here, very, obviously, therefore*
interjection		*oh, well, my goodness*

* Remember that only noun phrases may occur after a preposition.

Table 18 Pronouns, articles, and numerals

pronoun		
	personal	I, me, you, he, him, she, her, we, us, they, them, one
	reflexive	myself, yourself, himself, herself, itself, ourselves, yourselves, themselves
	reciprocal	each other, one another
	possessive	my, mine, your, yours, his, her, hers, it, its, our, ours, their, theirs, one's
	relative	who, whom, whose, which, that
	demonstrative	this, that, these, those
	interrogative	who, which, what
	indefinite	somebody, anything, nobody, each, several, much
article		the, a(n)
numeral		
	cardinal	one, two, one-fifth
	ordinal	first, second

5.10 Summary

Table 19 Connectors

coordinate conjunctions		*and, but, or, nor, for, so, yet;*	
correlative conjunctions		*not only ... but also, either ... or, both ... and*	
subordinators			
	for clauses functioning as subject, object or attribute	interrogative pronouns	*who, what, which whose*
		interrogative adverb	*where, when, how*
		subordinating conjunction	*if, whether*
	for clauses functioning as adverbial	*before, while, as, although, etc.*	
	for clauses modifying nouns	relative pronouns	*who, whom, whose, which, that,*
		relative adverbs	*where, when, how, as, whence*
preposition		*in, on, at, before, etc.*	

Table 20 Lists of prepositions, subordinators, coordinators, and conjunctive adverbs

prepositions		subordinators	coordinators	conjunctive adverbs
about	inside	after	and	accordingly
above	in spite of	although	but	also
across	into	as	or	anyway
after	like	as if	nor	besides
against	near	as though	for	certainly
along	of	because	so	consequently
among	off	before	yet	finally
apart from	on	even though	not only …but also	furthermore
around	onto	however much	both …and	hence
as	out	if	either…or	however
at	out of	in order that	neither…nor	incidentally
because of	outside	now that		indeed
behind	over	once		instead
below	past	rather than		likewise
beneath	regarding	since		meanwhile
beside	since	so that		moreover
between	through	that		nevertheless
beyond	throughout	though		next
by	to	unless		nonetheless
concerning	toward	until		now

5.10 Summary

Table 20 (*continued*)

prepositions		subordinators	coordinators	conjunctive adverbs
despite	under	when		otherwise
down	underneath	whenever		similarly
during	until	where		still
except	up	whereas		then
for	upon	wherever		thereafter
from	with	while		therefore
in	with regard	that		thus
in addition to	to	who		undoubtedly
in case of	within	whom		
in contrast to	without	whose		
		which		
		if		
		how		
		where		
		when		
		what(ever)		
		whether		
		which(ever)		
		who(m) (ever)		

6 Phrases

6.1 Introduction

In Chapter 2, we briefly discussed the difference between a clause and a phrase. Whereas a clause has its own subject and predicate, a phrase does not. In Chapter 5, we discussed the eleven different word classes. In this chapter, we will examine how members of these word classes may be put together to form a phrase.

What do phrases do? They can be used as subject, object, predicator, and so on of a sentence or a clause. But phrases can also be parts of other phrases. For example, *the garden* is a phrase, which could be combined with *the chair* with a preposition, as in *the chair in the garden*, which in turn can be combined with *the cushion*, as in *the cushion in the chair in the garden*, and so on. Within a phrase, we can even add a clause like *that you made* as in *the cushion that you made for the chair in the garden*.

A phrase can consist of one word or more words. If it consists of more words, it usually has one main word that is the most important one as far as meaning is concerned. For example, in the phrase *the cushion in the chair in the garden* the thing talked about is the *cushion*. This main word is called the *head* of the phrase. Since the main word in this phrase is realized by a noun, the whole phrase is called a *noun phrase*.

When we name a *head*, we talk about the *function* of a word in a phrase. Once we have identified a function, we can again specify how it is *realized*. Many students have trouble with this distinction, so an analogy to make this distinction more clear may be useful. Suppose you have some vessels such as a cup, a bowl, and a vase. Each of these could be made of glass, porcelain, earthenware, or even a kind of metal. The words *cup*, *bowl*, and *vase* refer to what you can do with them (their *functions*) and the words *glass, earthenware, porcelain,* and *metal* refer to what they are made of (their *realizations*). If I say 'cup' I only refer to its function and if I say 'glass' I only refer to what it is made of. Since these functions and realizations do not have a one-on-one relation, it can be useful to name both.

In language, too, a particular type of constituent with a particular kind of function can have different realizations, and one particular type of structure can have different functions. That is why in this course we prefer to name both. However, there are many grammar books, especially introductory ones, that do not make this distinction, or if they do, not consistently.

Phrases can also be analyzed into smaller parts (also called constituents, each with a function and realization). As you can see from the examples in Table 21, the head of a phrase is realized by a noun, pronoun, verb, adjective, adverb, or preposition. In total, there are five kinds of phrases, each of which will be discussed separately.

Table 21 Types of phrases

	abbreviation	example
noun phrase	NP	the **boy** **they**
verb phrase	VP	has been **walking**
adjective phrase	AdjP	very **tired**
adverb phrase	AdvP	**faster** than usual
prepositional phrase	PP	**before** school

EXERCISE 33   Name the type of phrases, underlined in the following passage (from *The Catch* by Nadine Gordimer).*

> <u>After a few days</u>, he began to say <u>good morning</u>, and <u>looking up</u> they found his face, a long head with a <u>shining</u> dark dome surrounded with curly hair given a strong liveliness by the sharp coarse strokes of gray hairs, the beautiful curved nose handed out <u>so impartially</u> to Indians, dark eyes <u>slightly bloodshot from the sun</u>, a wide muscular mouth smiling on strong uneven teeth that projected <u>slightly like the good useful teeth of an animal</u>. But it was by his legs they would have known him; the dark, dull-skinned feet with the few black hairs on the big toe, the long hard shaft of the shin tightly covered with smooth shiny skin, the pull of the tendons at his ankle like the <u>taut</u> ropes that <u>control</u> the sail of a ship.

6.2   Noun phrases

The possible constituents of noun phrases are determiner, premodifier, head, and postmodifier. The central element of a noun phrase is called its *head*. The head may have words before it called *determiners* (abbreviated as *det*) and *premodifiers* (abbreviated as *premod*) and words after it called *postmodifiers* (abbreviated as *postmod*). Premodifiers of nouns are always realized as *adjective phrases*. Note that even when there is only one word to modify a noun, it is still called a *phrase* because potentially it could have more than one word.

> * Some of the underlined phrases are sentence constituents (subject, object, and so on) and some are parts of other phrases. We will look at the different functions of phrases at the end of this chapter.

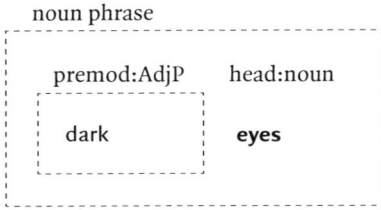

A noun may be premodified by one or more separate adjective phrases, as each modifies the noun independently. For example, in the phrase *sad, dark eyes*, both *sad* and *dark* tell us something about *eyes*.

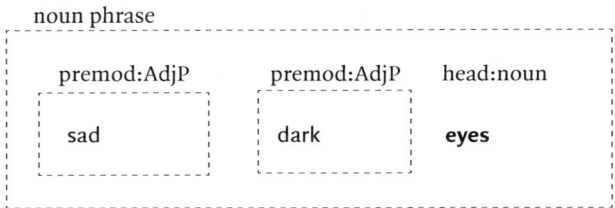

Even when nouns are used to modify another noun, they are to be considered adjectives, as can be seen in the following example.

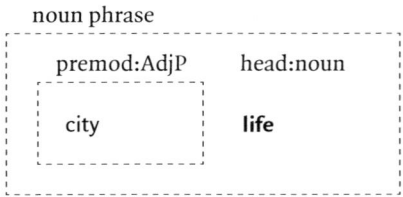

Postmodifiers of nouns are either phrases or clauses, which we will deal with in more detail in Section 6.3.

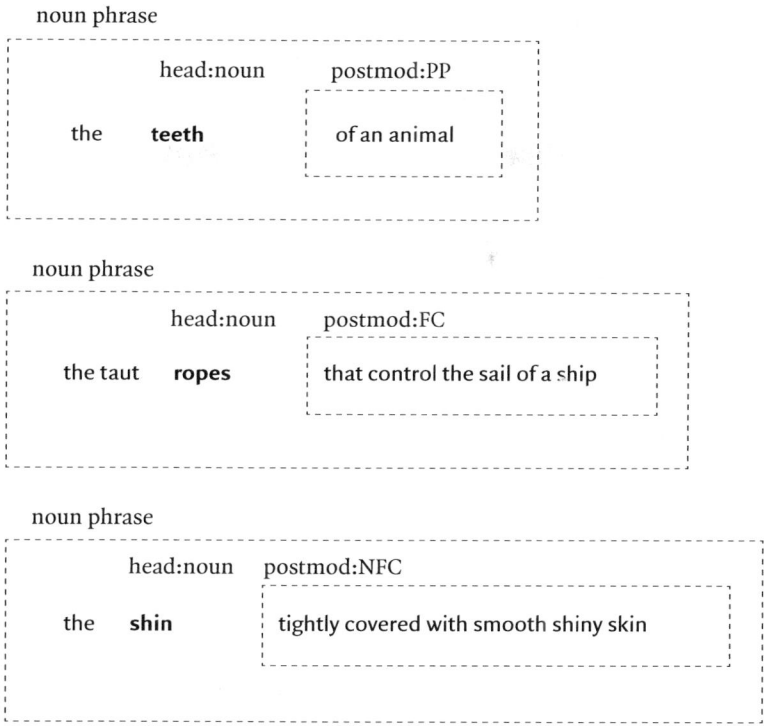

In some standard expressions, as in *China proper*, the postmodifier may be an adjective phrase.

1   **Determiners**

One additional constituent of the noun phrase functions as determiner. As you saw in Chapter 5, *determiners* are words somewhat like adjectives in that they come before a noun, but they are different in that they do not say anything about the quality or status of the 'thing', but tells 'where' (in relation to the speaker) the thing/person can be found. Determiners may be the articles *a(n)* or *the* or any of the dependent pronouns and numerals, including some expressions like *a few, a number of, a lot of* and so on, which we also call indefinite pronouns.

Articles, dependent pronouns and dependent numerals are often used in combination. Many books subclassify the determiners into pre-determiners, central determiners, and post-determiners, but in this course we will avoid this sub-classification and call them all determiners.

When we analyze a phrase, we name the constituents at phrase level (head, determiner, modifier) and its realization.

noun phrase			
det:indef. pron.*	det:article	head:noun	postmod:FC
All	the	books	we read

noun phrase			
det:dem. pron	premod:AdjP	head:noun	postmod:NFC
These	boring	**books**	discussed in class

2   Specifying versus classifying genitives

When a noun is used before another noun to denote a kind of possession, it often ends with a *genitive -s* as in *John's book* or *the children's book*. There are two main kinds of genitives, which have different functions and meanings and should therefore be analyzed differently.

Some genitives express 'where' (in relation to the speaker) a thing/person can be found, or more precisely to whom something or someone belongs. In this case the genitive could be substituted with a possessive pronoun like *her*, *his*, *its*, or *theirs*;

---

* It is difficult to argue which of the determiners is the more important, so we will name them separately.

therefore, it functions as a determiner and it is called a *specifying genitive*.

Another type of genitive, which occurs much less, expresses 'what kind' of thing something is, and it is called a *classifying genitive*. This type functions more like a premodifier and should be regarded as an adjective phrase.

When we analyze a noun phrase with a genitive, we have to be aware of another difference between a specifying and a classifying genitive. In a noun phrase with a specifying genitive, the article and the possessive noun together function as one determiner as the article is the determiner of the genitive noun, not the head noun. In a noun phrase with a classifying genitive, the article functions as determiner of the head noun.

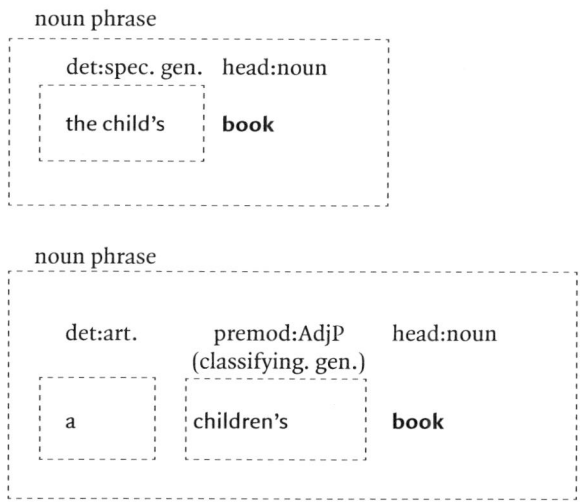

In some cases, the same genitive phrase can be used with two different senses depending on the context. Compare the following two sentences. In speaking, they would be pronounced differently. For a specifying genitive, the phrase *the children's books* would be pronounced with more stress on *books*; for the classifying genitive, there would be equal stress for *children's* and *books*.

The **children's** books were torn.	their books: specifying genitive
The **children's** books were fun to read.	those kinds of books: classifying genitive

EXERCISE 34   In the following passage (same as Exercise 33) several nouns, functioning as heads of noun phrases, have been underlined. Indicate with square brackets the beginning and end of the noun phrase and analyze the phrase further as has been done in the examples above. The first complex one has been done for you.

After a few <u>days</u>, he began to say good morning, and looking up they found his face, a long head with [a (det:art) shining (premod:AdjP) dark (premod:AdjP) <u>dome</u> (head:noun) surrounded with curly hair given a strong liveliness by the sharp coarse strokes of gray (postmod:NFC)], the beautiful curved <u>nose</u> handed out so impartially to Indians, dark <u>eyes</u> slightly bloodshot from the sun, a wide muscular mouth smiling on strong uneven <u>teeth</u> that projected slightly like the good useful teeth of an animal. But it was by his <u>legs</u> they would have known him; the dark, dull-skinned <u>feet</u> with the few black hairs on the big toe, the long hard <u>shaft</u> of the shin tightly covered with smooth shiny <u>skin</u>, the <u>pull</u> of the tendons at his ankle like the taut ropes that control the sail of a ship.

They idly watched him go, envious of his fisherman's <u>life</u> not because they could ever really have lived it themselves, but because it had about it the frame of their holiday <u>freedom.</u>

6.3 Postmodifiers of nouns

Noun phrases are the most complex types of phrases. Not only do they have two possible constituents before the head noun (determiners and premodifiers), they also have a great many types of postmodifiers. As the following examples show, postmodifiers may be realized as phrases, finite clauses, or non-finite clauses.

	function:	realization
the boy **ahead**	Postmod:	AdvP
the boy **in the room**	Postmod:	PP
the boy **who walked into the room**	Postmod:	FC
the guy **living next door**	Postmod:	NFC

We will discuss adverb phrases and prepositional phrases later in this chapter. Here we will take a closer look at the types of clauses that modify nouns, as they are very common in English. The use of relative pronouns may be rather confusing and there are different types with different punctuation rules.

Another point is that in quite a few cases the relative pronoun and *be* verb may be ellipted (left out) from a finite relative clause resulting in a postmodifier realized as a phrase or a non-finite clause. Therefore, we will discuss below restrictive versus non-restrictive postmodifiers, the use of the relative pronoun in finite relative clauses, and ellipsis in relative clauses.

1 Restrictive versus non-restrictive postmodifiers

Postmodifiers may be added to a noun phrase to help identify the head noun, or they may be given as extra information. Consider the following pair of sentences:

> My **friend** who has recently moved to London called last night.
> **Peter,** who has recently moved to London, called last night.

Assuming that the speaker has more than one friend, the NP *my friend* in the first sentence has rather vague reference, and the postmodifier *who has recently moved to London* in this sentence helps to identify which friend is meant. In other words, this clause specifies or restricts the reference of the noun phrase. Therefore, it is called a *restrictive* or *specifying modifier*. The following figure illustrates how the clause 'restricts' or 'specifies'.

my friend who has recently moved

possible friends

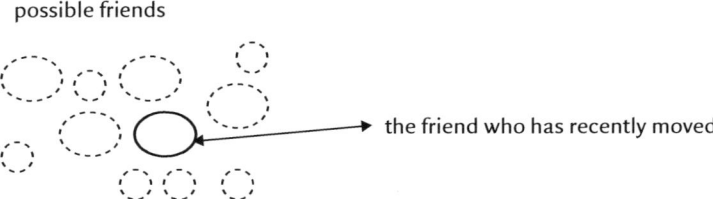

the friend who has recently moved

In the second one, assuming that the speaker and hearer both know the same Peter, the function of the postmodifier is not to help identify which Peter is meant, but to give extra information. This information may be very relevant for the context, because people usually do not give information unless it is relevant, but it is not needed to understand who or what the head of the noun phrase refers to because this person or thing does not need to be identified. This type of modifier is called a *non-restrictive modifier*. If the head noun is a proper name (like *Fred, Germany, Budapest*) or a unique/general thing (*the earth, tennis, soccer*) the clause is usually non-restrictive. The following illustrates how a non-restrictive clause does not identify which one, but gives extra information.

Peter, who has recently moved, ..

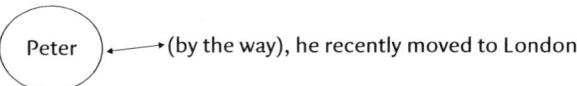

(by the way), he recently moved to London

In speaking these two types of modifiers are easily distinguished because they are pronounced differently in terms of prosody: restrictive ones have rising intonation (which gives more emphasis to that part of the sentence) and non-restrictive ones have falling intonation (which gives less emphasis to that part of the sentence). In writing, the distinction is marked with commas. A non-restrictive modifier, which has the falling intonation, is set off with commas. The restrictive one is not.

As the following two sentences show, commas or not can make a big difference in meaning.

The students who attended class regularly will do well on their exams.
The students, who attended class regularly, will do well on the exam.

In the first one, the students who will do well are only those who attended regularly and in the second one, all the students attended class regularly and all will do well.

The meaning of each of these sentences is illustrated below:

The students who attended class regularly will do well on their exams.

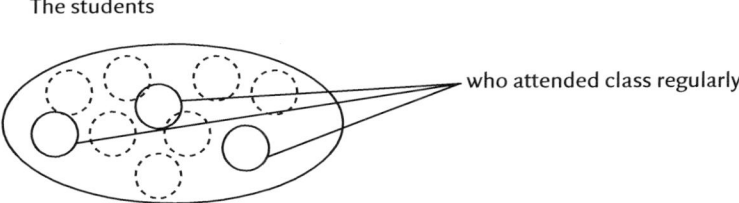

The students, who attended class regularly, will do well on the exam.

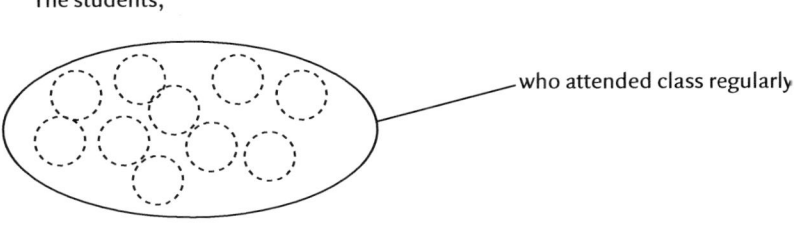

EXERCISE 35   In the following sentences noun phrases are underlined and any postmodifying clause or phrase has been put between parentheses. Identify the PostMod (a) as finite clause, non-finite clause, or phrase and (b) as restrictive or non-restrictive. The first one has been done for you.

1. Lincoln, (who was one of the truly great men of all time), led the US during the Civil War.

   Head: *Lincoln*

   Postmod: Finite non-restrictive clause

2. Lincoln once said that his wife had got a notion (that he would be assassinated).

3. His attempt (to reassure her) was to carry a cane on his nightly walks to the War Department.

4. Any person (plotting to kill him) was going to find a way (to do it anyway), he believed.

5. Lincoln, (a very public figure), simply was not willing to live in fear despite this ever present threat.

6. The fact (that Lincoln was on assassinated), now seems to take on an ironic meaning.

7. The stories (concerning President Lincoln's courage and humor) have made him a legend.

2 Relative pronouns and adverbs

In Chapter 5, relative pronouns and adverbs were discussed. We will now look at their functions within the relative clause. There are five relative pronouns: *who, whom, whose, which,* and *that. Who, whom,* and *whose* are normally used to refer to persons (or animals or things seen as persons) and *which* refers to things. The pronoun *that* may be used for both, but only in restrictive clauses. In other words, *that* is used only when there are no commas! There are also four commonly used relative adverbs *when, where, how,* and *as.* A rather archaic relative adverb is *whence.*

As mentioned earlier, these relative pronouns and adverbs have a double function. They are subordinators introducing a dependent clause and at the same time they function as a clause constituent: they may function as subject, object, or adverbial within the clause itself.

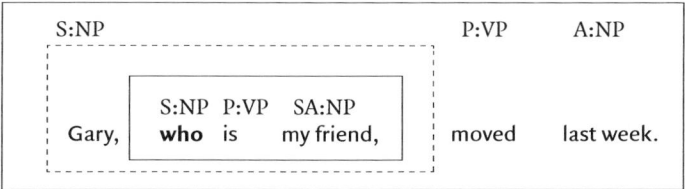

In addition, as you can see in the following example, the pronoun *that* may be left out, but only if it does not function as subject.

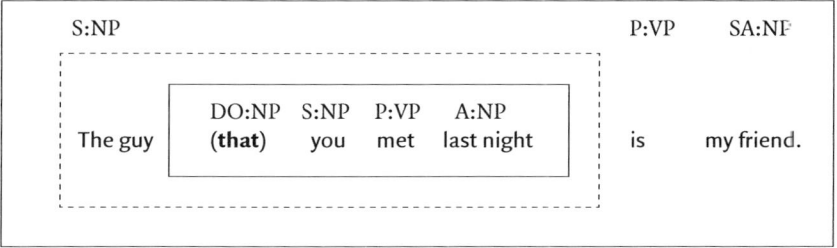

The relative pronoun *whose* is different in that it is not an independent pronoun but a dependent one, like the possessive pronoun *his*. Therefore, it is not a clause constituent, but a phrase constituent: the determiner of a noun phrase. For example, the

6.3 Postmodifiers of nouns

relative clause in the following example is related to the sentence *You borrowed **his** bike*, where *his* functions as determiner in the phrase.

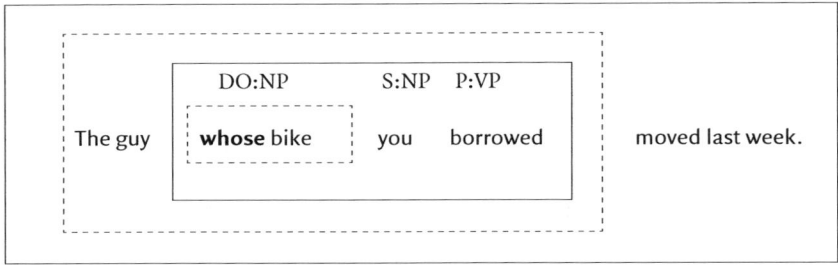

One problem that students may come across is the use of *which* with a possessive sense. Consider the following. For a person, a possessive is often formed with a possessive pronoun like *his* or a genitive, as in *his bike* or *Gary's bike*, and for the pronoun *who*, we can use the possessive form *whose*, e.g. *whose bike*. But for things, possession is usually expressed with a postmodifying *of* phrase. One would say *the tires of the bicycle* rather than *the bicycle's tires*. The same is the case for *which*. When *which* is used in a possessive construction it becomes *of which*, which occurs after the noun it modifies. However, even native speakers often have trouble with this construction and try to avoid it as much as possible. To solve the problem, sometimes *whose* is used for a thing, and in spoken English we might even hear a sentence like *The bike of which the tires are flat belongs to me*. But the following example shows the grammatically 'correct' construction.

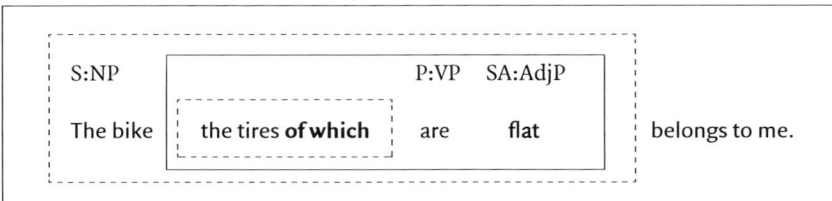

Finally there are relative adverbs: *where* and *whence* (place), *when* (time), *how* (manner), and *as* (manner). Like relative pronouns, they are sentence constituents, but function as adverbial. For example, in the sentence *The place **where** he lives is beautiful*, the relative clause is ***where** he lives*. Within the relative clause, the subordinator ***where*** has the same function as *there* in the sentence *He lives there*.

The place (where he lives) is beautiful. He lives there.

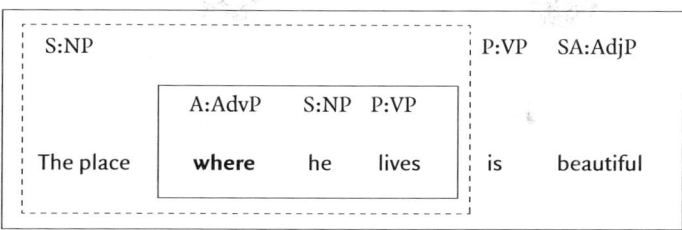

EXERCISE 36   In the following passage (from *The Wind and the Boy* by Bessie Head) underline all finite relative clauses. Remember that they must modify a noun. Double underline the (head) noun and circle the relative pronoun (or indicate where the pronoun *that* could occur) and identify the function the relative pronoun has within the clause that it introduces. The first one has been done for you.

Until they became ordinary, dull grown <u><u>men</u></u>, (who) drank beer and made babies, [subject] the little village boys were a special set all on their own. They were kings whom no one ruled. They wandered where they willed from dawn to dusk and only condescended to come home at dusk because they were afraid of the horrible things in the dark that might pounce on them. Unlike the little girls who adored household chores and drawing water, it was only now and then that the boys showed themselves as useful attachments to any household. When the first hard rains of summer fell, small dark shapes, which were quite naked except for their loin-cloths, sped out of the village into the bush. They knew that the first downpour had drowned all the wild rabbits, moles and porcupines in their burrows in the earth. As they crouched down near the entrances to the burrows, they would see a small drowned nose of an animal peeping out; they knew it had struggled to emerge from its burrow, which had been flooded by the sudden rush of storm water and as they pulled out the animal they would say, pityingly:

> Birds have more sense than rabbits, moles and porcupines. They build their homes in trees.

3 Ellipsis in relative clauses

When communicating, people try to be as efficient as possible. One way to 'save time' is to ellipt (= leave out) parts that are clearly understood in the context, especially if the part already occurs in a preceding part of the sentence.

Compare the following sentences and note that a subject, a predicator, or subject and predicator may be ellipted.

> The dock workers are discontented and ~~the dock workers~~ have gone on strike.
> Peter is leaving tonight and Joan ~~is leaving~~ tomorrow.
> We lived in Kansas City from 1989 to 1991 and ~~we lived~~ in Monroe before that.

One particular combination that is often ellipted in English is a subject (if it is clearly understood in the context) followed by a form of the *be* verb, but only in dependent clauses. This type of ellipsis takes place very frequently in relative clauses and the resulting postmodifier is no longer a finite clause, but a phrase or a non-finite clause

> Where is Sandra, **who is** the girl who lives next door?   PostMod:FC
> Where is Sandra,   the girl who lives next door.   PostMod:NP

The following are all pairs of sentences, the first with a postmodifier realized by a finite clause, the second with a postmodifier realized as a particular kind of phrase or non-finite clause. The realizations of the different postmodifiers have been given below.

Where is Dr. Wilcox, **who is** the head of the English Department?		FC
Where is Dr. Wilcox, the head of the English Department?		NP

Dr. Wilcox, **who is** unable to attend the meeting, will be here later.		FC
Dr. Wilcox, unable to attend the meeting, will be here later.		AdjP

I do not know the people **who are** in this room.		FC
I do not know the people in this room.		PP

The student **who has been** sitting next to me all term is from Taiwan.		FC
The student sitting next to me all term is from Taiwan.		NFC

The vet treated the puppy **that was** hit by a car.		FC
The vet treated the puppy hit by a car.		NFC

The first person **who was** to stand on the moon was Neil Armstrong.		FC
The first person to stand on the moon was Neil Armstrong.		NFC

There are some postmodifying non-finite clauses with an *-ing* form in which there is no ellipted *be* verb. Also some *to* infinitive constructions have a meaning similar to a modal auxiliary. Compare the following pairs of sentences.

I can't find the book **that belongs** to Chris.		FC
I can't find the book **belonging** to Chris.		NFC

I need a bag **that I can carry** on the plane.		FC
I need a bag **to carry** on the plane.		NFC

6.3 Postmodifiers of nouns

EXERCISE 37   In the following passage, underline all phrases and finite and non-finite clauses that function as postmodifiers of nouns. Circle the noun that is modified. Identify how it is realized (what type of phrase or clause) and whether it is restrictive or non-restrictive. The first two have been done for you.

In the (summer) of 1859, a French (acrobat) called Blondin strung a rope across the gorge just below Niagara Falls. On June 30, he was ready to walk from the United States to Canada across that rope, which was more than 150 feet above Niagara's violent waters.

Blondin, sitting down on the rope halfway across, scared the crowd as he lowered a string to a boat below, pulled up a bottle and took a drink. Then he continued his terrifying walk. Eighteen minutes after he began his stroll, he was greeted by a crowd cheering tremendously as he stepped on the Canadian side. In less than seven minutes he completed his trip back to the United States.

People coming to the Falls that summer to see what the acrobat would do next were never disappointed by Blondin, who always thought of different tricks. He walked across with a sack over his head! He pushed a wheelbarrow across! He did a headstand on the rope! And once Blondin, ready for a snack, took a table, chair and stove with him to the middle of the rope and fixed an omelet!

One time, he convinced his manager, Harry Colcord, to ride across on his back; however, he did not try that stunt, a near disaster, again. A support wire snapped and jerked the main rope sideways. Finally, Blondin, managing to keep himself and his manager from falling, was able to land safely on the other side after forty-five agonizing minutes.

6.4 Verb phrases

In Chapters 3 and 4, we have discussed verb phrases extensively. Here we will give a brief review again. A verb phrase consists of a group of verbs, which must contain a lexical verb* (which is its *head*, as it is semantically the most important one) and which may be preceded by one or more auxiliary verbs. There is not really a good, standard term to name the function the group of auxiliaries that may precede the lexical verb may have. In many books, the group is simply called *aux*, which does not say much about its semantic contribution. We could argue that the group of auxiliaries are somewhat like determiners of nouns, because just like them, they do not give information about the process itself but on how the speaker views the process. By using auxiliaries, the speaker may indicate whether he sees the process as ongoing, finished, and so on. However, to avoid confusion with other methods and books, we shall call the function of this group *aux*.

```
verb phrase
┌─────────────────────────────────────────┐
│   ┌─────────────────────┐               │
│   │ aux:aux. verbs      │  head:lex. verb│
│   │                     │               │
│   │ may have been       │  talking      │
│   └─────────────────────┘               │
└─────────────────────────────────────────┘
```

EXERCISE 38 In the following passage (same as Exercise 33) underline each verb phrase and identify whether it is finite (F) and non-finite (NF).

> After a few days, he <u>began (F)</u> to say good morning, and <u>looking up</u> (NF) they found his face, a long head with a shining dark dome surrounded with curly hair given a strong liveliness by the sharp coarse strokes of gray hairs, the beautiful curved nose handed out so impartially to Indians, dark eyes slightly bloodshot from the

---

* Remember that a lexical verb may consist of more than one word. See Chapter 4.

sun, a wide muscular mouth smiling on strong uneven teeth that projected slightly like the good useful teeth of an animal. But it was by his legs they would have known him; the dark, dull-skinned feet with the few black hairs on the big toe, the long hard shaft of the shin tightly covered with smooth shiny skin, the pull of the tendons at his ankle like the taut ropes that control the sail of a ship.

6.5 Adjective phrase

An *adjective phrase* consists of an adjective that may be preceded and/or followed by other words. The premodifier is always one or more adverb phrase(s), but the postmodifier can be an adverb phrase, a prepositional phrase, or even a clause. It is also possible to have a modifier that is partly in front and partly behind the head, called a *discontinuous modifier*, abbreviated as *disc-mod*.

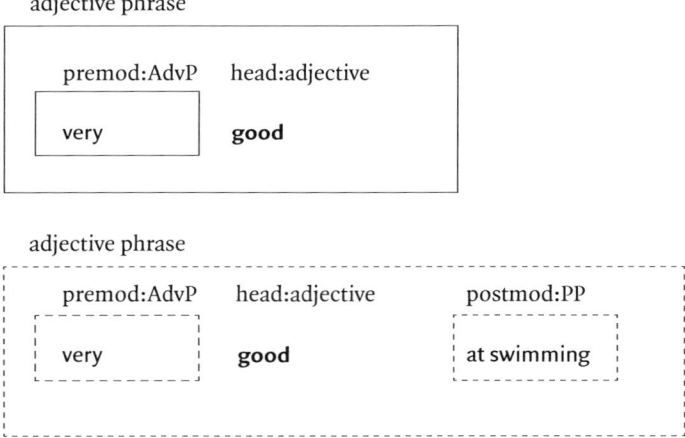

* *So...that* is here regarded as one subordinator to introduce an adverbial clause of result.

6.5   Adjective phrase

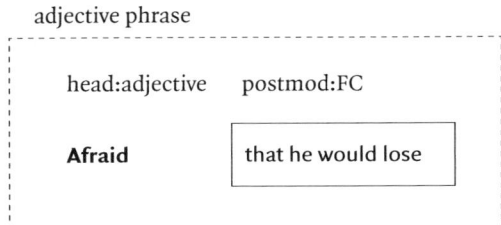

EXERCISE 39   In the following passage (same as Exercise 33) underline each adjective, and indicate with brackets the beginning and end of the phrase of which it is the head. The first has been done for you.

> After a few days, he began to say [good] morning, and looking up they found his face, a long head with a shining dark dome surrounded with curly hair given a strong liveliness by the sharp coarse strokes of gray hairs, the beautiful curved nose handed out so impartially to Indians, dark eyes slightly bloodshot from the sun, a wide muscular mouth smiling on strong uneven teeth that projected slightly like the good useful teeth of an animal. But it was by his legs they would have known him; the dark, dull-skinned feet with the few black hairs on the big toe, the long hard shaft of the shin tightly covered with smooth shiny skin, the pull of the tendons at his ankle like the taut ropes that control the sail of a ship.

6.6 Adverb phrase

An *adverb phrase* is very similar to an adjective phrase in that it consists of an adverb, which may be preceded and/or followed by other words. Here, too, the premodifier is always an adverb phrase, and the postmodifier can be an adverb phrase, a prepositional phrase, or a finite or non-finite clause. An adverb may also have a *discontinuous modifier*.

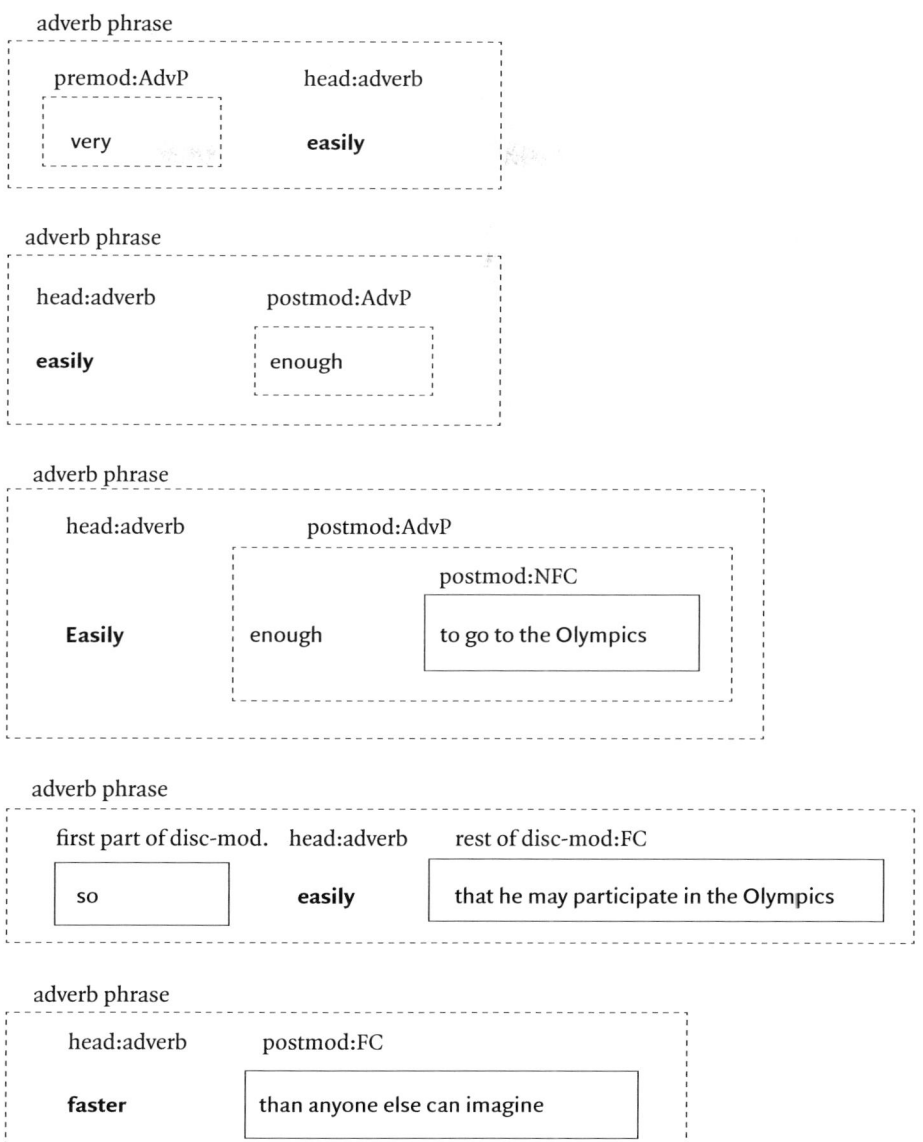

139   6.6   Adverb phrase

EXERCISE 40 In the following adapted passage (also from *The Catch* by Nadine Gordimer) underline each adverb, and with square brackets indicate the beginning and end of the phrase of which it is the head.

> They idly watched him go, not because they were so envious of his fisherman's life that they would really have liked to live it themselves, but because it had about it the frame of their holiday freedom. They looked at him enough to think that they should have respect for one who has put a little space between himself and the rest of the world. It's a good life, said the young man, the words not quite hitting the nail of this respect. "I can just see *you*...' said the girl, smiling. She saw him in his blue creased suit, carrying a bottle of gin wrapped in brown paper, a packet of banana and the evening paper.

6.7 Prepositional phrase

A *prepositional phrase* has two constituents, a *head*, always realized by a preposition and a *complement*, always realized by a noun phrase. In the case of a prepositional phrase, it is not really consistent to call the preposition a 'head', as it is semantically not really the most important word of the whole phrase. As you saw in Chapter 5, the function of the preposition is merely to connect and it could even be argued that it is a kind of subordinator that introduces not a clause but a noun phrase.

However, to keep things consistent for all five phrases, we will call the preposition the 'head' of a PP. As you saw in Chapter 5, a preposition is usually a short word like *in*, *on*, or *at*, but there are also prepositions that consist of several words, *in spite of*, *because of*, *in case of*, and there are prepositions like *concerning* that have developed from verb forms.

The complement of a preposition is always a 'noun-like' construction. It can be a noun phrase or a clause (finite or non-finite) that functions as a noun.

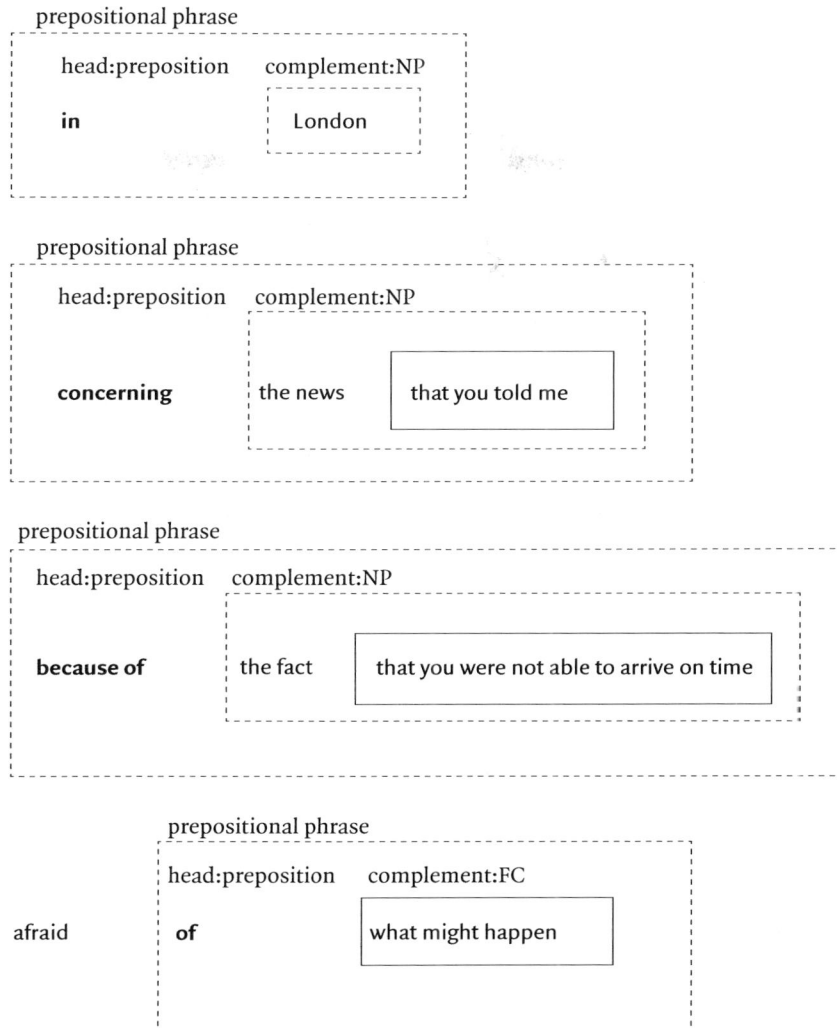

141   6.7 Prepositional phrase

	prepositional phrase	
	head:preposition	complement:NFC
looking forward	to	seeing you

EXERCISE 41　In the following passage (same as Exercise 33) underline each preposition and indicate with square brackets the beginning and end of the phrase of which it is the head. Note that some prepositional phrases are sub-components of other prepositional phrases. The first complex case has been done for you.

> After a few days, he began to say good morning, and looking up they found his face, a long head [with a shining dark dome surrounded [with curly hair given a strong liveliness [by the sharp coarse strokes [of gray hairs]]], the beautiful curved nose handed out so impartially to Indians, dark eyes slightly bloodshot from the sun, a wide muscular mouth smiling on strong uneven teeth that projected slightly like the good useful teeth of an animal. But it was by his legs they would have known him; the dark, dull-skinned feet with the few black hairs on the big toe, the long hard shaft of the shin tightly covered with smooth shiny skin, the pull of the tendons at his ankle like the taut ropes that control the sail of a ship.

6.8　Functions of phrases

In the preceding sections you have seen how each different type of phrase may be analyzed into phrase constituents, each with its own function and realization. Now we will look at how these phrases may be used within a sentence, clause, or other phrase, all at different levels.

Remember that sentences and clauses have S, P, DO, IO, BO, SA, OA, or A as constituents. The realization of a predicator is always a phrase (VP). The realization of the other constituents can be either phrases or clauses. When the sentence constituent is a clause, no matter whether it is finite or non-finite, it can be analyzed further into sentence/clause constituents such as S, P, DO, and so on.

If the constituent is a phrase, it can be analyzed further into phrase constituents with heads and modifiers. All the different types of phrases we have discussed (except the verb phrase) can have functions at the sentence/clause level or at the phrase level. For example, at the sentence/clause level, a noun phrase may function as subject, direct object, indirect object, benefactive object, subject attribute, or object attribute. At the phrase level, a noun phrase may function as a postmodifier in noun phrases, adjective phrases, and adverb phrases, or as complement in a prepositional phrase.

To make these functions at sentence/clause level versus phrase level clear, we will look at one sentence in more detail. In the following sentence, there are two noun phrases functioning at sentence level, which we will call Level 1, the first one as subject, and the second one as subject attribute.

Level 1

S:NP   SA:NP

He / was / a Hindu, a puny wisp of a man, with a shaven head and vague liquid eyes.

If we look at the subject attribute, we can see all kinds of noun phrases functioning at different phrase levels. At level 2, a noun phrase functions as postmodifier of a noun.

Level 2

This noun phrase postmodifier can be analyzed further and further. At the third level, the postmodifier itself contains another postmodifier, this time a prepositional phrase.

Level 3

The prepositional phrase can be analyzed further at level 4. A prepositional phrase always contains a complement, which is always realized by a noun phrase:

Level 4

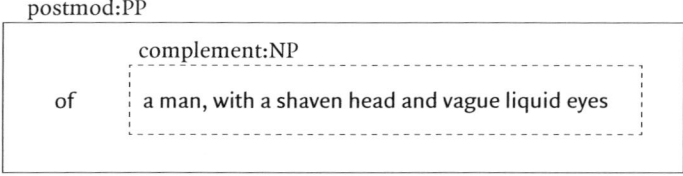

The noun phrase that functions as complement of a preposition is postmodified again with a prepositional phrase at level 5:

Level 5

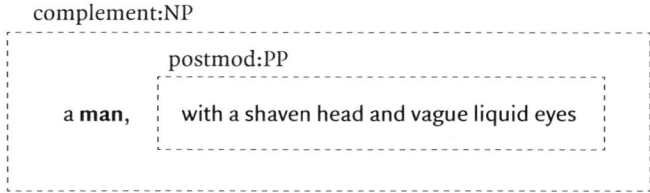

The postmodifying prepositional phrase in turn contains a noun phrase at level 6:

Level 6

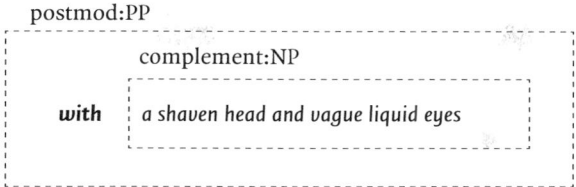

Now, we have identified all the functions of the noun phrases in the sentence *He was a Hindu, a puny wisp of a man, with a shaven head and vague liquid eyes*. Even though the sentence has five noun phrases, only two have a function at the first level: the sentence level. *He* is subject and *a Hindu* is the main part of the subject attribute. All the other noun phrases function at ever lower levels as postmodifier of a noun or as complement of a preposition. This is also signaled by means of the commas in non-restrictive postmodifiers.

We could show the same type of detailed analysis at the different levels for adjective phrases, adverb phrases, and prepositional phrases, but it would take too much room to do so. Therefore, a brief example is given here, one with the phrase functioning at the sentence/clause level, and one at the phrase level.

The boy / is / **quite tall**.	Adjective phrase as subject attribute
The **tall** boy	Adjective phrase as premodifier of a noun
The boy / walks / **quite fast**.	Adverb phrase as adverbial
Quite fast	Adverb phrase as premodifier of an adjective
The boy / lives / **in the city**.	Prepositional phrase as adverbial
Life **in the city**	Prepositional phrase as postmodifier of a noun

6.9 Summary

In this chapter, we looked at the constituents of the five different types of phrases: noun phrases, verb phrases, adjective phrases, adverb phrases, and prepositional phrases. Below, the possible constituents and realizations of each phrase is briefly summarized in separate tables.

A noun phrase has the most possibilities. The head is either a noun or a pronoun. It may or may not (indicated by parentheses) have one or more determiners, premodifiers, and/or postmodifiers, each of which may have one of several realizations.

Table 22 Noun phrase

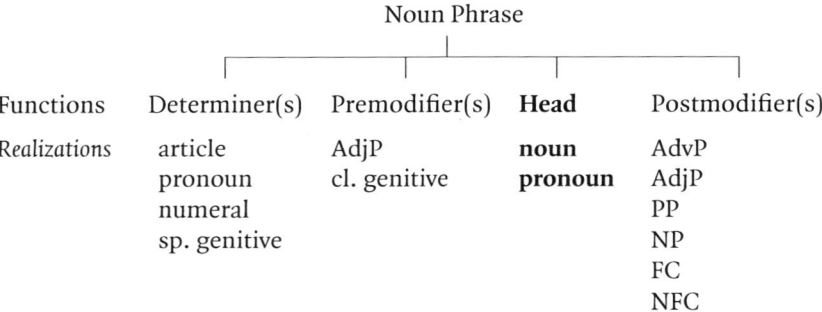

As you can see above, postmodifiers of nouns may be all kinds of different phrases or clauses. Postmodifiers may be restrictive or non-restrictive, depending on whether or not they are needed to identify the noun that they modify. A restrictive clause, which helps identify, is not set off with commas, and a non-restrictive one, which gives extra information, is not. A *that* clause is never set off with commas.

When the postmodifier is a finite clause, the subordinators are the relative pronouns *who, whom, whose, which*, and *that* depending on whether they refer to persons or things. When the clause modifies a noun denoting a place or time, the relative adverbs indicating place, time, and manner may be used, such as *where, when, how,* and *as* may be used. Non-finite relative clauses, which can often be considered ellipted clauses, may have a *to* infinitive, an *-ing*, or an *-ed* form.

An adjective phrase has an adjective as its head. It may or may not have one or more premodifiers and/or postmodifiers, and even a discontinuous modifier.

Table 23 Adjective phrase

functions	premodifier(s)	**Head**	postmodifier(s)
	discontinuous	....	modifier
realizations	AdvP	**adjective**	AdvP
			PP
			FC
			NFC

An adverb phrase has an adverb as its head. Like an adjective phrase, it may or may not have one or more premodifiers, postmodifiers, and a discontinuous modifier.

Table 24 Adverb phrase

functions	premodifier(s)	**Head**	postmodifier(s)
	discontinuous	....	modifier
realizations	AdvP	**adverb**	AdvP
			PP
			FC
			NFC

Note that in our analysis, modifiers are always realized as either phrases or clauses, even though especially premodifiers often consist of only one word. The reason is that modifiers could consist of more than one word, which in turn could be analyzed into heads and modifiers.

A prepositional phrase has a preposition as its head, and its complement is almost always realized by a noun phrase. In some cases, though, a finite or non-finite clause can function as a complement of a preposition.

Table 25 Prepositional phrase

functions	**Head**	complement
realizations	**preposition**	NP
		FC
		NFC

Finally, a verb phrase has a lexical verb as its head, and it may have one or more auxiliaries in front of it. The group of auxiliaries is called aux.

Table 26 Verb phrase

functions	(aux)	**Head**
realizations	of mood	**lexical verb**
	of perfect aspect	
	of progressive aspect	
	of passive voice	
	do	

In Section 6.7, we also briefly discussed the different functions these phrases may have. After the next chapter, we will discuss in great detail how a sentence may be analyzed at ever deeper levels: how phrases may be used as constituents of either clauses or phrases. For right now, it is enough for you to realize that these different levels are possible.

EXERCISE 42   In the following sentences (from *The Catch* by Nadine Gordimer), the constituents at sentence level have been set off with square brackets. For each constituent, identify its function (S, P, DO, etc.) and its realization (type of phrase or finite or non-finite clause).

[They] [did [not] know]* [his name,] and** [now,] [although they might have asked the first day and got away with it,] [it] [was] [suddenly] [impossible,] [because he didn't ask them theirs.] So [their you's and he's and I's] [took on] [the positiveness of names,] and [yet] [they] [seemed to deepen]*** [their sense of communication] [by the fact that they introduced none of the objectivity that names must always bring.] [He] [spoke [to them] [quite a lot] about]**** [Johannesburg, to which he assumed they must belong, as that was his generalization of city life,] and [he] [knew,] [sympathetically] [that they were city people.] And [although they didn't live there, but somewhere near on a smaller pattern,] [they] [answered] [as if they did.] [They] [also] [talked [a little] of] [his life, or rather of the processes of the sugar refinery from which his life depended.] [They] [found] [it] [fascinating].

* *Did* and *know* are one phrase

** Coordinate conjunctions are not constituents of sentences or clauses, so they can be skipped in the analysis.

*** Here *seem* is regarded as a semi-auxiliary.

**** *Spoke* and *about* belong to one phrase

6.9 Summary

7 Sentence constituents realized as clauses and non-canonical constructions

7.1 Introduction

We have now discussed almost all relevant facts that you need to analyze almost any English sentence at ever deeper levels. In Chapter 1 you learned that a sentence or clause may consist of two or more constituents: subject, predicator, subject attribute, direct object, indirect or benefactive object, object attribute, and adverbial. In several chapters, we have talked about the realizations of constituents. In this chapter we will try to show how all the detail you have seen so far fits together. We will also address some remaining issues, especially those concerning non-finite dependent clauses and non-canonical constructions, but before doing so, we will briefly review the pertinent distinctions between sentences, clauses, and phrases.

In Chapter 2, you learned that a *sentence* is an independent grammatical unit that expresses a complete thought. To be grammatically complete, it must contain a *main clause* with a subject and a predicate and the predicate must contain a *finite verb*. The following are not grammatically complete sentences for various reasons.*

because he was sick	no main clause
has been famous for many years	no subject
him having been late over three times	no finite verb

* In speaking, people often use incomplete sentences. In writing, especially academic or other formal writing, the use of grammatically incomplete sentences is usually avoided.

A *clause* is a group of words that expresses a whole event or situation, containing a subject and a predicate. It is a grammatical unit that may be independent or dependent. A *main* or *independent clause* can stand by itself and form a grammatically complete sentence. A *dependent clause* always starts with a *subordinator*, except when that is understood (see Chapter 5.) There are three types of dependent clauses: those functioning as subject, object, or attribute, those functioning as postmodifiers of a noun, and those functioning as adverbials.

Don was sick	main clause
I know **that Don was sick**	clause functioning as DO
Don, **who was sick**, stayed home	clause modifying the noun *Don*
Because Don was sick, he stayed at home.	clause functioning as A

As you learned in Chapter 6, a *phrase* is a grammatically ordered group of related words that does not have a subject and/or predicate and functions as a constituent of a sentence, of a clause, or of another phrase. A phrase has one main word, called the *head*, and words in front of or behind it. And as you can see from the examples below, phrases, especially noun phrases, may consist of more phrases and phrases may even contain dependent clauses, usually relative clauses.

you
behind you
the **door** behind you
the **door** behind you in the closet
the **door** behind you in the closet that he recently bought.

Sometimes it is difficult to distinguish a clause from a phrase. What is even more confusing is that different books may use different terms for the same thing. The trouble comes in especially when a group of words has a verb, but not a finite one. Compare the following:

	Robert was sick	clearly a clause, in this case even a main clause, because it does not have a subordinator and it contains a subject, predicate and a finite verb

Robert was sick — clearly a clause, in this case even a main clause, because it does not have a subordinator and it contains a subject, predicate and a finite verb

because Robert was sick — also clearly a clause, this time a dependent one, because it contains a subordinator, subject, predicate and finite verb

very sick — clearly a phrase because there is no subject nor verb

Robert being sick — in some books, this is called a phrase because it does not contain a finite verb; in others, it is called a *non-finite clause* because it contains a subject and a predicate

In this book we will use the term *non-finite clause* (NFC) for groups of related words like *Robert being sick*, mainly because they have a subject and predicate and should be further analyzed as clauses.

In this chapter we will look especially at how each sentence constituent may be realized. Table 27 below gives an overview of the possible functions of sentence or clause constituents and their possible realizations, marked with •.

Table 27 Functions and realizations at sentence or clause level

	NP	VP	AdjP	AdvP	PP	FC	NFC
S	•					•	•
P		•					
DO	•					•	•
IO/BO	•					(•)	
SA	•		•			•	•
OA	•		•			•	•
A	•			•	•	•	•

As you can see from Table 27, subjects and objects are always realized by a noun phrase or a clause. Subject attributes and object attributes may also be realized by a noun phrase or clause, or by an adjective phrase. Subjects, objects, and attributes will be dealt with together because they are quite similar.

Predicators are always realized by verb phrases and indirect object and benefactive objects are usually realized by a noun phrase. We will not deal with these constituents in this chapter because we have already dealt with noun phrases and verb phrases extensively.

Adverbials may have the most kinds of realizations. We will deal with these in a separate section.

7.2 Subjects, objects, and attributes

Subjects and objects are the main participants in an event or situation and are usually persons or things. Therefore, they are commonly realized by a noun phrase. Subject and object attributes, when they name a category to which a person or thing belongs to, may be realized by a noun phrase as well. In Chapter 6, noun phrases were discussed in great detail. Here we will take a closer look at the finite and non-finite clauses.

Sometimes a whole event or situation is seen as a 'thing' and be seen as a participant. An event or situation is expressed by means of a clause. The type of clause that may function like an NP, often called a *noun clause*, may be finite or non-finite.

1 Finite clauses

A subject, object, or attribute can be realized by a finite clause. There are different types of finite clauses: those related to a statement or a question.

If the noun clause is related to a statement, it can be quoted directly, marked with quotation marks, or it is introduced by the subordinator *that*. However, *that* is often understood (= left out), especially when it introduces a direct object clause as in *I heard* ~~that~~ *he was sick*. The examples show a statement and a finite clause related to the statement, functioning as direct object.

statement	Abraham Lincoln was one of the truly great men of all time.
direct quotation	The encyclopedia states, **"Abraham Lincoln was one of the truly great men of all time."**
indirect quotation	The encyclopedia claims **(that) Abraham Lincoln was one of the truly great men of all time.**

A clause may also be related to a question: a yes/no question or a question starting with an interrogative pronoun (called WH-*question* for short). If it is related to a yes/no question, the subordinator is *if* or *whether*. The examples show a yes/no question and finite clauses related to the yes/no question, functioning as direct objects.

yes/no question	Are you leaving early today?
direct quotation as direct object	Eric asked **"are you leaving early today?"**
indirect quotation as direct object	Eric asked **whether/if you were leaving early today.**

If the noun clause is related to a question starting with an interrogative pronoun, the interrogative pronoun *who(ever)*, *what(ever)*, or *which(ever)* or interrogative adverb *when(ever)*, *where(ever)*, or *how(ever)* gets the double function of a subordinator. Note that in the finite dependent clause, which functions as subject, the word-order changes, and the helping verb *do* is not needed.

wh-question	What did he do?
wh-question as subject	**What he did** was lead the US during the Civil War, which was the greatest crisis in US history.

As you learned in Chapter 5, the subordinators *that*, *if*, and *whether* do not have a function in the clause that they introduce, but interrogative pronouns and adverbs functioning as subordinators do when the next level is analyzed.

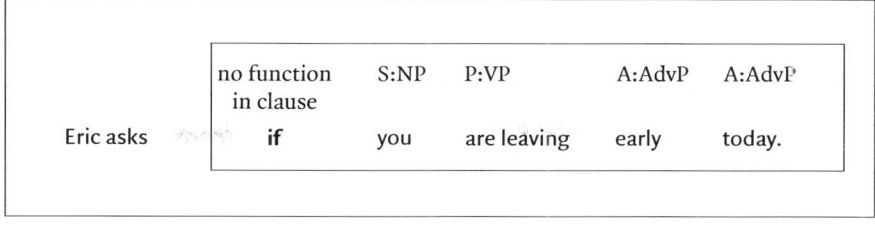

2 Non-finite clauses

Much more common than the finite clauses just discussed are the non-finite ones with *to* infinitives, *-ing* forms, and sometimes even plain infinitive forms. Note how a sentence like *Lincoln wanted to end slavery in the nation and keep the American Unit from splitting apart during the war* can be analyzed.

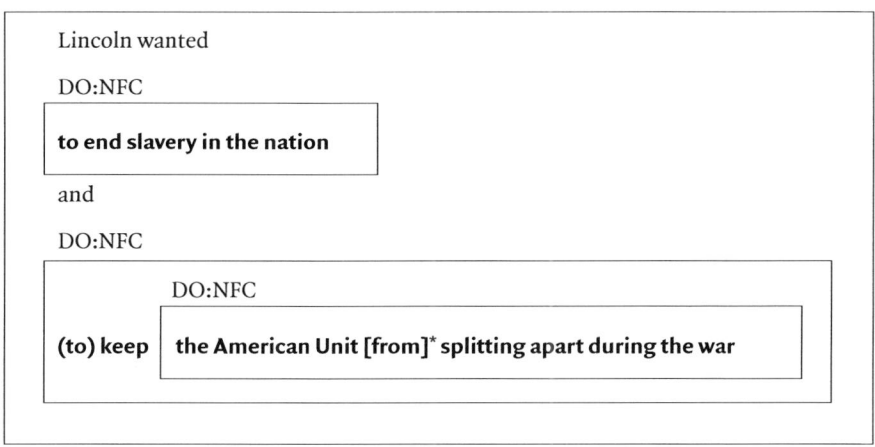

* *from* is part of the multi-word verb *to keep from*

In this sentence there are non-finite clauses at different levels. At Level 1, the sentence level, there are two non-finite clauses *to end slavery in the nation* and *to keep the American unit from splitting apart during the war*. Both function as direct objects of *want*. At Level 2, within the second non-finite clause, there is another non-finite clause, which functions as the direct object of the verb *keep from*.

EXERCISE 43   In the following passage (adapted from *Daily Life in the Industrial United States, 1870–1900* by Julie Husband and Jim O'Loughlin) analyze each sentence at sentence level by setting off sentence constituents with slashes and naming their function and realization. Do not analyze the constituents further.

> At a hearing of a Senate committee investigating working conditions in New York City in 1883, Conrad Carl, a tailor, testified that before the Civil War his had been "a very still business, very quiet." Then the sewing machine appeared. "We admit it stitched very nicely, nicer than the tailor could do. And the bosses said: 'We want you to use the sewing machine …'" Then he was asked how this innovation affected the tailors. Carl replied: "We work now in excitement — in a hurry. It is hunting; it is not work at all; it is a hunt."

There are three types of non-finite clauses that may function as subject, object, or attribute. Some have a *to* infinitive, some have an *–ing* form, and some have a plain infinitive as the first verb in the non-finite verb phrase.

For direct objects, the non-finite form used depends on the context and the particular meaning with which the lexical verb is used in the main clause. There are many lexical verbs, especially verbs expressing some mental state, attitude, or process like *love, hate, want, enjoy, regret, manage, advise, suggest, imagine, suggest*, and so on that take non-finite clauses as their objects. Although the use of these different non-finite forms is quite complex and subject to very subtle semantic differences, the following observations may be used as a general guide.

Verbs that express a cause, a mental state, or an order related to something that will happen at a future time are followed by a *to* infinitive clause functioning as direct object.

> I caused **him to fall**.
> He wants **to go home**.
> He refused **to answer**.
> I told him **to go home**.
> He began **to leave**.*

Also verbs that have in their meaning an element of '(dis)belief' or '(un)certainty' or 'I am (not) sure it is true' towards something can be followed by a non-finite *to* infinitive clause functioning as direct object.

> I believed **him to be in his room**.
> He claimed **to be going home**.

The use of a non-finite plain infinitive clause as direct object is more limited. Only verbs expressing a very direct cause (*have, let, make*, and sometimes *help*) or very direct perception (*see, notice, observe, hear,* and *feel*) may take direct objects realized by a non-finite plain infinitive clause.

> I had **him paint the room**.
> I made **him leave**.
> I let **him leave**.
> We helped **him paint his room**.

I did/said something; this caused something directly.

> We saw **him leave**.
> We heard **him leave**.
> I felt **the ant crawl on my toe**.

I saw/heard/felt something directly.

---

* Verbs like *begin, continue, stop*, which express a point in time in an event, are originally transitive verbs that take a direct object. When used with a non-finite verb as object, they can also be seen as auxiliary verbs of aspect, very much like *be* in *He is leaving*.

Finally, the *-ing* form is used as direct object after quite a few different types of verbs: those expressing a direct perception (also imagination), a feeling towards something, a positive or negative attitude towards something, a suggestion, or a 'playing around' in the mind.

> I saw **him walking down the street.**
> I imagined **sitting on the beach.**
> I enjoy **swimming in the summer.**
> I regret **leaving so early.**
> I avoid **working too hard.**
> I suggest **taking your time.**
> We advise **leaving early.**
> I considered **leaving early.**

As you may have noticed, some lexical verbs may take different non-finite clauses as their object, usually with a (slightly) different sense. Below some of these are illustrated, with their semantic differences explained.

> I saw **the ship sink**.
> I saw **the ship sinking**

With the plain infinitive, the focus is more on the event as a whole and the sentence implies that the ship really sank. With the *-ing* form, the focus is more on an ongoing part of the event; this sentence does not have to imply that the ship sank completely.

> I remember **taking out** the garbage.
> I remembered **to take out** the garbage.

With the *-ing* object, the event can be seen as happening in the mind again. With the *to* infinitive object, the event is construed as something that still had to be done.

> I advise **studying** hard.
> I advise you **to study** hard.

With the –*ing* object, only an idea is suggested. With the *to* infinitive object, the speaker is trying to impose their will on the listener

EXERCISE 44 In the following passage (from *The Wind and a Boy* by Bessie Head), several non-finite clauses have been underlined. Which ones are used as direct objects of a sentence or a clause?

> Until they became ordinary, dull grown men, who drank beer and made babies, the little village boys were a special set all on their own. They were kings whom no one ruled. They wandered where they willed from dawn to dusk and only condescended <u>to come home at dusk</u> because they were afraid <u>to encounter</u> the horrible things in the dark that might pounce on them. Unlike the little girls who adored <u>doing household chores</u> and <u>drawing water</u>, it was only now and then that the boys showed themselves as useful attachments to any household. When the first hard rains of summer had started* <u>to fall</u>, small dark shapes, quite naked except for their loin-cloths, sped out of the village into the bush. They knew that the first downpour had drowned all the wild rabbits, moles and porcupines in their burrows in the earth. As they crouched down near the entrances to the burrows, they would

---

* *Start* could be regarded as a lexical verb, in which case *to fall* is DO. It could also be regarded as a helping verb of aspect, in which *to fall* is part of the VP. Semantically, the latter case makes more sense.

159   7.2   Subjects, objects, and attributes

see a small drowned nose of an animal <u>peeping out</u>; they knew it had struggled <u>to emerge from its burrow</u>, flooded by the sudden rush of storm water and as they pulled out the animal they would say, pityingly:

'Birds have more sense than rabbits, moles and porcupines. They build their homes in trees.'

3   **Extraposed subject or object clauses**

As you have just seen, finite *that* clauses and non-finite *to* infinitive clauses may be the subject or object of a sentence or a (dependent) clause. However, in English, it sounds very awkward to have such a long subject, which is referred to as 'frontal overloading'. The following are examples of such awkward sentences.

> **That he enjoys studying English** is a fact.
> I think **to study hard** is necessary.

To avoid using such long subjects, speakers usually prefer another type of construction. They put the pronoun at the beginning of the sentence or the clause as a *temporary subject* and move the real subject after the subject attribute. The technical term for such a construction is *extraposition*. *Extraposed* constructions occur especially when the lexical verb expresses an opinion, or the subject attribute contains an adjective or noun expressing an evaluation, opinion, or attitude (*nice, a mistake, necessary, worthwhile, clear,* and so on). In Section 7.4, we will discuss how such sentences can be analyzed.

> **It** is a fact **that he enjoys studying English.**
> **I** think **it** is necessary **to study hard.**

7.3 Adverbials

An adverbial gives some background information about an event or state of affairs. It may tell when, where, why, how, to what degree, under what condition, or in spite of what condition an event or state of affairs may take place. Adverbials are commonly realized by adverb phrases, prepositional phrases, or sometimes even noun phrases.

   He / left / **yesterday**.   A: AdvP
   He / left / **by car**.   A: PP
   He / left / **Monday**.   A: NP

Very often, though, an adverbial is realized by a finite or non-finite clause. As you learned in Chapter 5, a finite clause functioning as an adverbial is introduced by a subordinate conjunction such as *because, although,* or *if*.

There is one type of finite clause we have not discussed yet, which functions as an adverbial but looks very much like a relative clause. As you know, a relative clause modifies one particular noun in a phrase. Sometimes, though, a *which* clause is used to modify not one particular noun but a whole clause.* In such cases, we no longer have to do with a noun modifier but a clause modifier, which per definition is an adverbial. This type of clause, which expresses some kind of 'afterthought' is usually set off with commas.

   I had to go to work at 6:00 in the morning three times a week, **which** I didn't like at all.

The sentence above should be analyzed as follows:

   S:NP   P:VP   A:PP   A:PP
   I   /   had to go /   to work   /   at 6:00 in the morning   /

---

* Many prescriptive grammars discourage the use of such constructions because they argue that *which* should refer to a particular noun rather than a whole clause.

A:NP	A:FC
three times a week, /	which I didn't like at all.

Adverbials are also frequently realized by non-finite clauses. It may be a *to* infinitive clause (usually to express a purpose or a hypothesis), such as *I went to the store to buy some bread*. An adverbial *-ing* clause may express a 'while' or 'because' meaning at the beginning, such as *Being hungry, I went to the store*. It can also express 'at the same time' or 'result' meaning at the end of the sentence, such as *I rushed out of the door, tripping over all my kids' toys*.

Non-finite adverb clauses may also modify adjectives as in *He is too tired TO RUN*, with *to run* modifying the adjective *tired*.

EXERCISE 45   Analyze the following sentences into sentence constituents and name their realizations. Then state in your own words what the logical relationship between the non-finite adverbial clause and the main clause is. The first one has been done for you.

	A:NFC	S:NP	P:VP

1   Running down the street, / he / fell down.

2   *Running down the street* expresses a 'while' or 'because' meaning.

3   They ran down the street, stumbling over everything that was in their way.

4   He went to the store to buy some groceries.

5   To think that she had so much homework, it surprises me that she went out last night.

EXERCISE 46　In the following passage (same as the Exercise 44), analyze each sentence at sentence level by inserting slashes to set off sentence constituents. Then give the function and realization of each sentence constituent. Do not analyze any further. The first one has been done for you.

1. Until they became ordinary, dull grown men, who drank beer and made babies, (A:FC) / the little village boys (S:NP) / were (P:VP) / a special set all on their own (SA:NP).

2. They were kings whom no one ruled.

3. They wandered where they willed from dawn to dusk and only condescended to come home at dusk because they were afraid to encounter the horrible things in the dark that might pounce on them.

4. Unlike the little girls who adored doing household chores and drawing water, it was only now and then that the boys showed themselves as useful attachments to any household.*

5. When the first hard rains of summer had started to fall, small dark shapes, quite naked except for their loin-cloths, sped out of the village into the bush.

6. They knew that the first downpour had drowned all the wild rabbits, moles and porcupines in their burrows in the earth.

7. As they crouched down near the entrances to the burrows, they would see a small drowned nose of an animal peeping out; they knew it had struggled to emerge from its burrow, flooded by the sudden rush of storm water and as they pulled out the animal they would say, pityingly: 'Birds have more sense than rabbits, moles and porcupines. They build their homes in trees.'

* What is unusual about this sentence pattern?

7.3　Adverbials

7.4 How to analyze non-canonical constructions*

In this section we will discuss some non-typical but frequently occurring constructions that may be difficult to analyze. As you learned in Chapter 1, and as you can see in Table 28, a typical (=canonical) English sentence or clause has one of several basic patterns, consisting of a number of constituents in a typical order. The complement may be a subject attribute or a direct object. If there is a direct object, there may also be one of the following: an indirect object, a benefactive object, or an object attribute. Except for in a few particular cases, adverbials are optional.

Table 28 Review of typical sentence patterns

subject	predicator	no complement	(adverbial(s))
		S A	
		D O	
		IO/BO + DO	
		DO + OA	

However, as you have already seen in previous chapters, *passive* and *extraposed* sentences are variations to this basic pattern. You have also seen that some clauses have parts that are *ellipted*. There are two other variations we have not discussed yet: *existential* and *cleft* constructions. We will briefly review the first three and introduce the other two below.

1 Passive constructions

Remember that a passive sentence can be recognized by its verb phrase, which contains *be* (or *get*) followed by a past participle. Even though a *passive sentence* contains a *transitive verb*, there is often not a direct object as the 'former' direct object is now the subject of the sentence (See Chapter 4).

---

* The term *constructions* refers to a sentence, finite clause, non-finite clause or part of clause that is left over after some other part has been ellipted

In the case of a *ditransitive verb*, like *give* or *buy*, there may still be a direct object as the receiver, the 'former' indirect object, can become the subject, too. The 'former' subject becomes a prepositional phrase, often with *by* and is considered an adverbial. In the case of a *complex transitive verb*, the 'old' object attribute becomes a subject attribute. Note how each type is analyzed below.

        S: NP   P:VP   A:PP
The lecture /   was given /   by a teaching assistant.

    S: NP   P:VP   DO:NP   A:PP
The girl /   was given /   a book /   by her teacher.

    S: NP   P:VP   SA:NP
The girl /   was considered /   a genius.

Some conventionalized passive constructions, depending on their meaning, are no longer seen as passive verbs but multi-word auxiliaries of mood. For example, in the following sentence, *to have been allowed* has a meaning similar to the modal *may* expressing permission. In Chapter 4, it has also been suggested that passive constructions such as *to be forced to* or *to be believed to* could be analyzed as one auxiliary verb.

   S:NP   P:VP   DO:NP
   He /   has been allowed to attend /   the concert.
   He /   has been told to buy /   the ticket.
   He /   is believed to have bought /   one.

Complete passive sentences are not all that common, but passive constructions do occur very commonly in postmodifiers of nouns. Remember that in dependent constructions a subject and *be* are often ellipted. In these ellipted clauses, the remaining parts can be analyzed as follows:

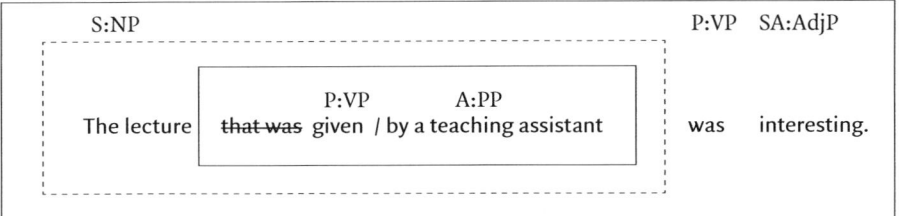

2 Extraposed constructions

Another variation on the standard pattern is an *extraposed construction*, which was presented earlier in this chapter. If the real subject is a *that* or a *to* infinitive clause and the predicate expresses an evaluation, opinion, or attitude, the sentence may start with *it* as a placeholder (also referred to as "dummy" *it*) and the real subject is moved after the predicate. Such sentences are analyzed as having two subjects, with *it* functioning as a temporary one. It is also possible to have a *temporary object*.

tempS:NP	P:VP	SA:AdjP	S:FC
It	is	necessary	**that you study hard**
It	was	nice of you	**that you called me**

tempS:NP	P:VP		S:FC
It	is hoped		**that all students work hard**
It	seems		**that they are honest**

S:NP	P:VP	tempDO:NP	OA:NP	S:NFC
I	consider	**it**	my duty	**to work hard**

3 Ellipsis

As you have seen in several chapters, repeated or clearly understood sentence constituents may be *ellipted*, often resulting in compound predicates or other compound structures, which are rather straightforward to analyze.

S:NP	P:VP	coord. conj.	P:VP	A:PP
The dock workers /	are discontented /	and /	have gone /	on strike.

S:NP	P:VP	A:AdvP	coord. conj	S:NP	A:AdvP
Peter /	is leaving /	tonight /	and /	Joan /	tomorrow.

In Chapter 5, it was also shown that many noun postmodifiers are related to relative clauses in which the relative pronoun and *be* are ellipted. When naming the constituent and realization of the postmodifier, we just name the left-over part. So in the sentence below, the direct object is realized by a noun phrase. The noun phrase is in turn realized by a head (noun), preceded by a determiner realized by an article, and postmodified by the prepositional phrase *in the room*.

level 1	S:NP	P:VP	DO:NP		
level 2			det: art	head: noun	postmod: PP
	I	/ do [n't] know /	[the]	[people] ~~who are~~	[in this room].

However, in some cases, it is difficult to decide on how ellipted constructions should be analyzed. Should they be analyzed with the ellipted parts understood, or should we just analyze what is left?

Consider the analyses of the clause *that he is absent* in the following example. At first glance, this clause looks very much like any other relative clause modifying the noun *fact*, but when you consider that it is related to the clause *which is that he is absent*, you realize that the postmodifying clause is a clause functioning as a subject attribute, not a relative one. Therefore *that* is not a relative pronoun but a subordinating conjunction and has no function in the clause that it introduces.

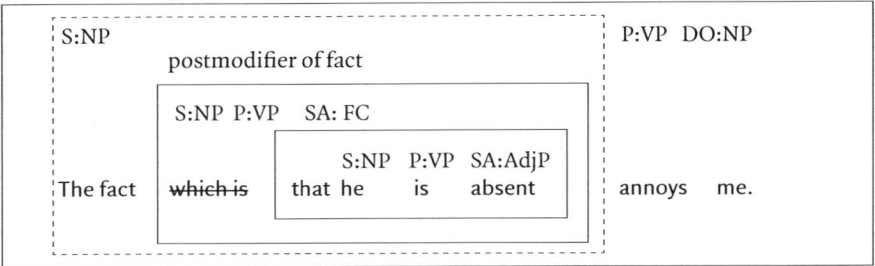

Another tricky example comes from one of the following exercises. Consider the following sentence:

> When the act of sneezing exists because it communicates, it becomes symbolic: a handshake is for friendship or frankness, a bow for deference or submission, an affected sob to evoke sympathy or pity.

The parts after the colon are obviously three items in a series:

> a handshake is for friendship or frankness,
> a bow for deference or submission,
> an affected sob to evoke sympathy or pity.

However, rather than using three full clauses joined by a coordinating conjunction, the author elected to use ellipted structures (leaving out a finite form of the *be* verb). So, when we analyze the last two structures, should we consider them noun phrases with postmodifiers or should we consider them clauses with subjects and subject attributes? A *bow for deference or submission* by itself would be a good example of a noun phrase with a prepositional phrase as postmodifier. However, we also need to look at context and in a case like this one. As we explained in the introduction of the book, our approach to sentence analysis is based on usage-based construction grammar. We should therefore base our analytical choices on what we know about actual language use, as well as good writing practice. A good writer will usually make use of parallel structures. Therefore, the preferred analysis for all three would be as follows:

S:NP	P:VP	SA:PP (first two) and SA:NFC (last one)
a handshake	is	for friendship or frankness,
a bow		for deference or submission,
an affected sob		to evoke sympathy or pity.

To conclude this section on analyzing elliptical constructions, you should analyze what you see and not worry too much about ellipsis. However, in some unusual cases like the ones just discussed, it is useful to consider what the full clause would have been without parts ellipted.

4 Existential sentences with *there*

A typical sentence describes an event or situation. An event usually involves some kind of change or movement and a situation usually describes what or how something is. When describing such an event or situation, the speaker typically focuses on the thing or person he or she wants to say something about. However, sometimes the setting (the place) in which an entity exists receives more prominence, especially if the thing or person is not clear. In such cases, English sentences can start with *there*, which is a very vague indication of place. In such sentences, called *existential sentences*, the person or thing talked about is still the subject, but it occurs after the predicator. In some books *there* is considered a 'dummy subject'; in other books, it is called an adverbial. We will call it an adverbial because it does indicate a vague 'place'.

A:AdvP	P:VP	S:NP	A:PP
There	are	some mice	in the cellar.

A:AdvP	P:VP	S:NP
There	will come	a time when he will regret this.

5 Cleft constructions

There is one construction in English that looks very similar to a relative clause, but is different, especially because it occurs not only after nouns but also after other parts of speech. This construction, called a *cleft construction*, is used to give some extra emphasis to a particular sentence constituent. Note how in the following proposition different parts can be 'lifted out' and given special emphasis.

>John Benjamins published this book in 2022 in Amsterdam.
>It is **John Benjamins** who published this book in Amsterdam.
>It is **this book** that John Benjamins published.
>It was **in 2022** that John Benjamins published this book.
>It was **in Amsterdam** that this book was published.
>It was **yesterday** that the book was published.

The basic construction is 'It is X *who/that/which/* …', where X can be a subject, object, or adverbial in the non-emphasized sentence. But how should we analyze these cleft sentences? The *who/that/which* clauses after the emphasized nouns are different from relative clauses because they are never non-restrictive and the pronoun *that* is used in places where we do not normally expect it. However, to keep things simple we will consider them postmodifiers and analyze them as follows.

S:NP	P:VP	SA:NP
It	is	**John Benjamins** who published this book in Amsterdam.
		SA:NP
It	is	**this book** that John Benjamins published.
		A:PP
It	is	**in 2022** that Benjamins published this book.
		A:PP
It	is	**in Amsterdam** that this book was published.
		A:AdvP
It	is	**yesterday** that the book was published.

The following example shows how such a sentence may be analyzed at lower levels.

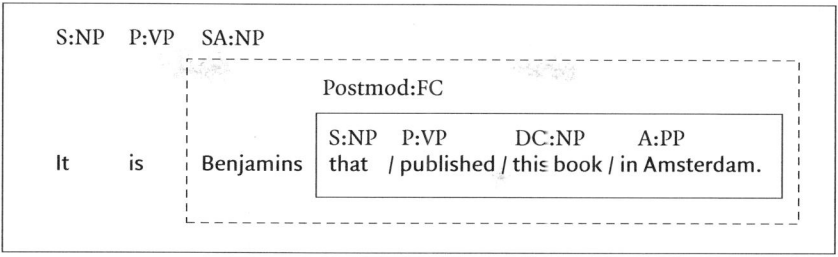

The *it* cleft sentence can give prominence to subjects, objects, or adverbials, but when we want to give prominence to a predicator or subject attribute, we can use a *what* subject clause in what is called a *pseudo-cleft construction*.

John is a fool.	**What John is** is a fool.
John writes books.	**What John does is** write books.
You need to study a lot.	**What you need to do** is study a lot.

Note how such sentences are analyzed.

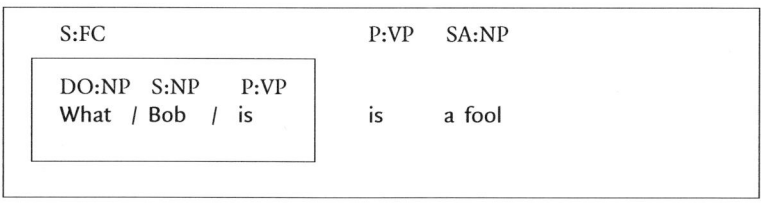

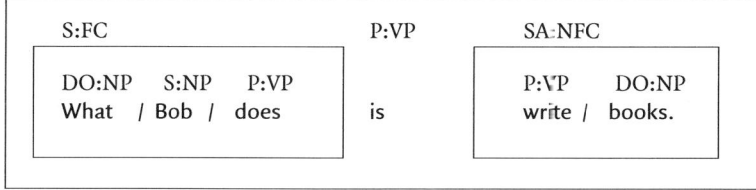

EXERCISE 47   Identify the sentence type (normal, passive, existential, cleft, or extraposed) and analyze the sentences at sentence level naming functions and realizations of the constituents.

1   It is an unusual method to offer students a reading passage that is an almost literal word-for-word translation from French into English.
2   It is English words in French word order that make the text easy to understand.
3   I consider it helpful to quickly convey a sense of the overall patterns of French sentences.
4   In subsequent passages, there are common French words introduced into the reading materials, where they take the place of their English equivalents.
5   It is useful to start with a text that a monolingual English speaker can understand with no more than a minimum of explanation because the student is led, by gradual steps, to a text that is written in French.

7.5 Summary

In the introduction, we reviewed the differences between sentences, main clauses, dependent clauses, which may be finite or non-finite, and phrases. In Table 29, each is defined and characterized.

Table 29 Distinguishing sentences, clauses and phrases

Sentence
— It is a group of words that expresses a whole event or situation.
— It contains a subject and predicate.
— It must have a finite verb.

Clause

Independent
— It is a group of words that expresses a whole event or situation.
— It contains a subject and predicate.
— It must have a finite verb.
— It can stand by itself as a sentence or
— It can be the main part of a sentence.

Dependent

Finite
— It is a group of words that expresses a whole event or situation.
— It contains a subject and predicate.
— It must have a finite verb.
— It starts with a subordinator (but that may be understood).
— It cannot stand on its own, but functions as a clause or phrase constituent.

Non-finite
— It is a group of words that expresses a whole event or situation.
— It contains a predicate (the subject may be understood).
— It does not have a finite verb.
— It may or may not start with a subordinator.
— It cannot stand on its own, but functions as a clause or phrase constituent.

Phrase
— It is a group of related words that does not express a whole event or situation.
— It does not have both a subject and a predicate.
— It cannot stand on its own, but functions as a clause or phrase constituent.

In the remainder of the chapter, we discussed mainly the finite and non-finite clauses that may be used to realize subjects, objects, attributes, and adverbials. Finite and non-finite clauses may function as subject, direct object, subject attribute or object attribute. The subordinators in these finite clauses are *that*, *if* or *whether*, or an interrogative pronoun, depending on whether the clause is related to a statement, yes/no question, or WH-question. Non-finite noun clauses may have a *to* infinitive, an *-ing* form, or a plain infinitive, depending on the meaning of the lexical verb as used in the main clause.

Finite *that* clauses and non-finite *to* infinitive clauses functioning as subject (or object) may be extraposed. In such sentences, we have two subjects (or objects), a temporary *it* and the real subject.

Finite and non-finite clauses may also function as adverbial. Non-finite adverb clauses may have a *to* infinitive or an *-ing* form. A *to* infinitive usually expresses purpose. An *-ing* form at the beginning usually has a 'while' or 'because' sense; an *-ing* form at the end usually has a 'result' sense.

Finally, we looked at some non-canonical constructions, which may be difficult to analyze. The approach in this book has been to name constituents as much as possible according to their actual function in the construction. In passive sentences, the old object now functions as subject and the *by* phrase as adverbial. In extraposed sentences, we used the terms "temporary" subject or object for the dummy *it*. In the case of ellipsis, we just analyze the left-over sentence parts as they occur in the new construction. In the case of existential constructions, *there* is considered an adverb. However, when we analyze cleft-constructions and we try to name the parts as usual, the analyses are tenuous to say the least.

8 How to analyze sentences at all levels

8.1 Introduction

This book is meant to make students aware of different levels of analysis at the sentence, clause, and phrase level and familiarize students with terminology. We hope it gives not only a strong basis for further syntactic theory courses but also more practical ones in grammar and writing. The skills learned can also be applied to analyze style in literary works or even forensics. Finally, the terms and analyses can be used in tracing language development, even your own. Therefore, we offer this chapter to review all the steps needed to analyze sentences at ever deeper levels.

8.2 How to go about analyzing long and complex sentences

When sentences are rather short, it is usually rather easy to see how many clauses it has, which clause is the main one, and which clauses may be dependent. However, as you have seen in the exercises, many sentences consist of a variety of constructions and it is not always easy to determine at first sight which one is the main clause, which structures are dependent ones, and how the sentence should be analyzed.

Remember that a compound sentence is analyzed as separate sentences. If a sentence is complex, it is analyzed as one sentence with one or more dependent clauses functioning as sentence constituents. Therefore, before you start analyzing a sentence, it is important to find subjects and predicates first and then decide whether it is a simple, compound, complex, or compound-complex sentence. To help you determine the type of sentence, you can go through the following steps:

Step 1: Find finite verbs

First, it is important to identify main clauses and dependent clauses. As only finite clauses can be main clauses, you should first find *finite verbs*. At least one of the finite clauses is a main clause.

If there is more than one finite clause, you want to know if the sentence contains only one or two or more main clauses. If there is a semi-colon (or sometimes a colon), you can be almost sure you have a compound sentence, with a main clause on each side.

Step 2: Find coordinators and subordinators

Another way to see whether there are main clauses or dependent ones is to find *coordinators and subordinators*; these will also help you see where clauses begin (remember the subordinator *that* may be understood.) Clauses introduced by subordinators are always dependent clauses.

Step 3: Determine sentence type

Once you have identified main clauses and dependent clauses, you can classify the sentence type. If there is only one finite clause, it is a *simple sentence*. If there are two or more complete, independent clauses, each with its own subject and predicate, separated by a semi-colon (or sometimes even a colon) or connected by a coordinate conjunction or a correlative conjunction, it is a *compound sentence*. If there is an independent clause and one or more dependent clauses, it is a *complex sentence*. Finally, if the sentence has both independent and dependent clauses connected by coordinators and subordinators, it is a *compound-complex* sentence.*

---

*. Note that in determining sentence types, we ignore non-finite dependent clauses. If a sentence has only one finite clause (which has to be the main one) and one or more non-finite ones, we will consider it a simple one, mainly because English has so many non-finite clauses and verb forms used as adjectives, that it would be difficult to decide when a non-finite verb form is part of a non-finite clause or not.

EXERCISE 48   In the following passage from *Language: The Loaded Weapon* by Dwight Bolinger, underline finite verbs and circle subordinators and coordinators. Identify main clauses and dependent clauses, and then determine whether the following sentences are simple, compound, complex, or compound-complex.

1. Every act that every human adult performs communicates.

2. Within hours of birth, a human infant is already responding to the rhythms of the mother's speech, in 'a dance-like sharing of microbody motion.'

3. Even involuntary acts communicate, they are symptoms, and they are modified in significant ways; a sneeze may be unavoidable, but the manner of it betrays attitudes of hygiene, courtesy, or self-restraint.

4. When the act exists because it communicates, it becomes symbolic: a handshake is for friendship or frankness, a bow for deference or submission, an affected sob to evoke sympathy or pity.

8.3 How to go about analyzing long and complex noun phrases

One particular difficulty in analyzing sentences is finding out where a sentence constituent begins and where it ends. Especially noun phrases may be troublesome as they may be preceded by determiners and premodifiers and followed by all kinds of modifiers — prepositional phrases, noun phrases, adjective phrases, adverb phrases, finite clauses, and non-finite clauses — all of which might also contain postmodifiers at ever deeper levels. To help you determine where a noun phrase begins and ends and to analyze it, you can go through the following steps

Step 1: Find the head

First, to analyze these noun phrases it is important to find the *head*. Remember, that the head of a noun phrase may be preceded by a determiner or premodifier, but not by a preposition. Any phrase starting with a preposition is a prepositional phrase. Remember also that the head of a noun phrase cannot be terribly far into the phrase, unless there happen to be a great many premodifiers, which is very seldom the case.

Step 2: Find the determiners

Once you have found the head, find the *determiner(s)*, which may include articles, pronouns, and numerals. Often there is only one article, pronoun, or numeral. However, sometimes there are two or three together. Remember that a *specifying genitive* (noun with 's), which indicates ownership, is also considered a determiner. When there is more than one determiner, it is usually quite difficult to argue which one is the more important, so if there is not clearly one word modifying another one, we will just analyze them as separate determiners.

For example, the phrase *all the men* can be analyzed as a noun phrase with two determiners: *all* and *the*. However, when we have a specifying genitive, the article in front of the genitive noun is usually the determiner of the genitive noun as in [[all] [the president's] men]. In this phrase, *the* does not tell which *men*, but which *president*. We would analyze this as follows: *all* is a determiner realized by an indefinite pronoun and *the president's* is a determiner realized by a specifying genitive (see Chapter 6, Section 2).

```
noun phrase
┌─────────────────────────────────────────────────────────┐
│   det:indef.pr.        det:spec. gen.                   │
│  ┌───────────┐       ┌──────────────────┐               │
│  │   all     │       │ the president's  │      men      │
│  └───────────┘       └──────────────────┘               │
└─────────────────────────────────────────────────────────┘
```

Step 3: Find premodifiers

Once you have found the determiner(s) (if there are any), find the *premodifier(s)* between the determiner(s) and the head. If there is more than one word, you must decide if they — together — form one modifier or if they form separate modifiers, in which case each separate one says something about the head noun. For example, in the phrase *their pinky-brown bodies*, we have to do with one premodifier *pinky-brown*, because *pinky* says something about the kind of brown, not the bodies. But in the phrase *their smooth brown bodies* we have to do with two separate premodifiers (both realized by adjective phrases) as both *smooth* and *brown* say something about *bodies*.

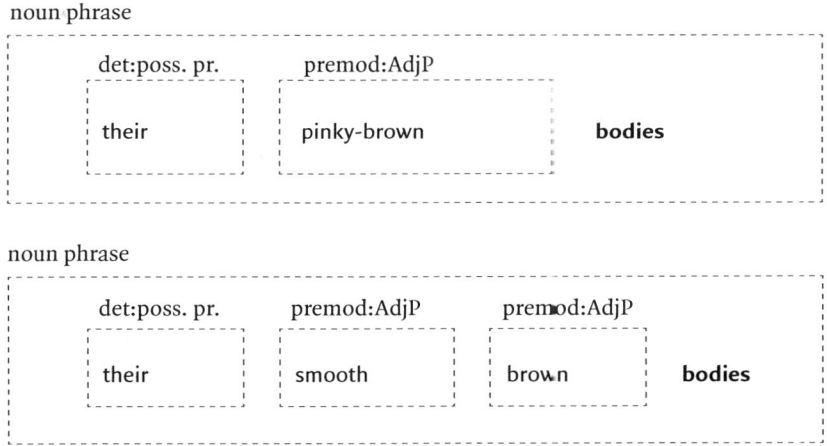

Finally, you may have noticed that sometimes one word like *smooth* is called an *adjective* and at other times an *adjective phrase*. It is called a *phrase* if it can potentially consist of more than one word as in *very smooth*. This is the case if you name the realization of a clause constituent or a modifier. For example, in the sentence *He is happy* the subject attribute is realized by an adjective phrase as it could potentially be something like *terribly happy*. When you analyze the adjective phrase, *happy* is the head, realized by an adjective.

Step 4: Find postmodifiers
Once you have found the determiner(s) and premodifier(s), you have to find the *postmodifier(s)*. Again, you have to ask yourself if there is one (perhaps with several dependent ones) or more than one. For example, in the phrase *the coat in the closet in the room upstairs*, there is only one postmodifier for the noun *coat* because the whole phrase says something about *coat*. The prepositional phrase *in the room upstairs* says something about *closet*, not *coat*. The noun *closet* also has only one postmodifier, as *upstairs* modifies only the noun *room*.

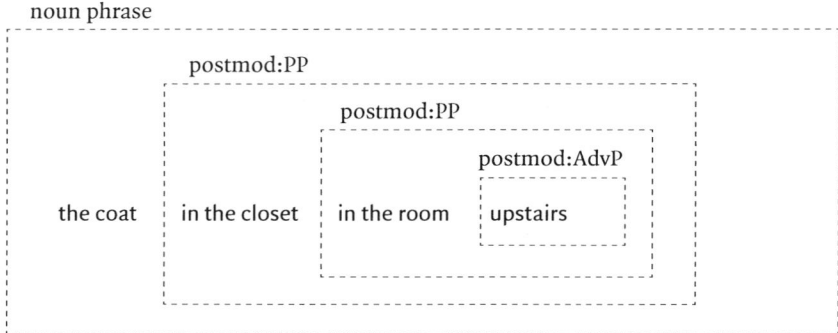

In contrast, the phrase *the coat in the closet that you wore last year* has two postmodifiers, the first one is realized by the prepositional phrase *in the closet* and the second one by the finite clause *that you wore last night*.

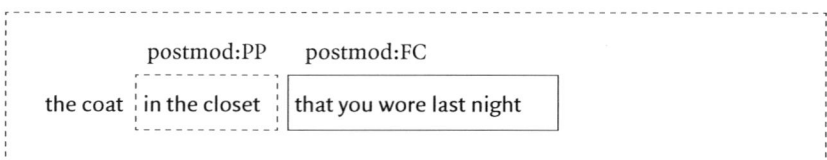

To determine whether a phrase or clause following a noun is part of the noun phrase or a separate constituent, try moving it. If it can easily be moved to another place in the sentence, then it is usually an adverbial. If it cannot be moved and the phrase or clause says something about only the noun in front of it, you can be sure it is a postmodifier of a noun.

EXERCISE 49   Analyze the following noun phrases into their constituents: determiner(s), premodifier(s), head, and postmodifier(s) and name their realizations. Do not analyze further. The first one has been done for you.

1   [the] rhythm [of the mother's speech]*

    the   det:article
    rhythms   head:noun
    of [...]speech postmodifier:PP

2   the mother's speech

3   our most complex system of signs

4   a structure of words and relationships that interpenetrates our world so thoroughly that nothing out there can be disentangled from it

5   a dance-like sharing of microbody motion

EXERCISE 50   In the following passage, also from *Language: The Loaded Weapon* by Dwight Bolinger, several nouns have been underlined. Indicate the beginning and the end of the phrase of which this noun is the head. If there is a postmodifier in the phrase, indicate how it is realized. The first one has been done for you.

                postmod:FC
[<u>Every act</u> that every human adult performs] communicates. Within <u>hours</u> of birth, a human infant is already responding to the <u>rhythms</u> of the mother's speech, in 'a dance-like <u>sharing</u> of microbody motion.' Even involuntary <u>acts</u> communicate. They are <u>symptoms</u>, modified in significant ways — a sneeze may be unavoidable,

---

* Note that *of the mother's speech* is a prepositional phrase. In this exercise you are asked not to analyze further, so all you have to do is identify it as postmodifier realized by a PP. However, the prepositional phrase consists of a preposition followed by a noun phrase. And if you are asked to analyze further, you can analyze the noun phrase, too, as in sentence 2 in this exercise.

8.3   How to go about analyzing long and complex noun phrases

but the <u>manner</u> of it betrays <u>attitudes</u> of hygiene, courtesy, or self-restraint. When the act exists because it communicates, it becomes symbolic — a <u>handshake</u> for friendship or frankness, a <u>bow</u> for deference or submission, an affected <u>sob</u> to evoke sympathy or pity. And when the symbol ceases to look or sound like what it symbolizes, it becomes a sign. Language is our most complex system of signs — an intricate <u>structure</u> of words and <u>relationships</u> that interpenetrates our world so thoroughly that nothing out there can be disentangled from it. To understand <u>language</u> as in large part the mirror of the world and the world as in large part the creature of language we must look at how this marvelous instrument is put together and how it works.

EXERCISE 51   The following sentence, from *The Catch* by Nadine Gordimer, contains a noun phrase with an unusual number of postmodifiers at ever deeper levels. To analyze this noun phrase step by step, answer the questions below the passage.

> After a few days, he began to say* good morning, and looking up they found his <u>face</u>, a long <u>head</u> with a shining dark dome surrounded with curly hair given a strong liveliness by the sharp coarse strokes of gray hairs, the beautiful curved nose handed out so impartially to Indians, dark eyes slightly bloodshot from the sun, a wide muscular mouth smiling on strong uneven teeth that projected slightly like the good useful teeth of an animal.

> * The verbs *began* and *to say* could be regarded as a V P and D O or as one V P, where *began* has the function of a semi-auxiliary of aspect. The latter analysis makes more sense if we look at meaning especially.

Step 1: How many separate postmodifiers does the noun *face* have? Set it/them off with square brackets.

Step 2: How many separate postmodifiers does the noun *head* have? Note that the preposition *with* has several complements.

Step 3: How many complements does the preposition *with* have? Set off each one with square brackets.

Step 4: In the following part of the sentence, several other nouns have been underlined. If the noun has a postmodifier, set it off with square brackets. Be sure to set off the complete modifier, which in turn may include another noun that has a postmodifier.

a long head with a shining dark <u>dome</u> surrounded with curly <u>hair</u> given a strong liveliness by the sharp coarse strokes of gray hairs, the beautiful curved <u>nose</u> handed out so impartially to Indians, dark <u>eyes</u> slightly bloodshot from the sun, a wide muscular <u>mouth</u> smiling on strong uneven <u>teeth</u> that projected slightly like the good useful teeth of an animal.

Step 5: To help you visualize the complexity of such a noun phrase with postmodifiers at different levels, you can write down each modifier separately and show lower levels by indenting further. Identify the realization of each postmodifier. The first two have been done for you.

> a long head
>> postmod: PP
>> with [...] animals.
>>> complement: NP
>>> a shining dark **dome**

> surrounded with curly **hair**
>> given a strong liveliness by the sharp coarse **strokes**
>> of gray hairs,
> the beautiful curved **nose**[*]
>> **handed out so impartially to Indians,**
> dark **eyes**
>> slightly bloodshot from the sun,
> a wide muscular **mouth**
>> smiling on strong uneven **teeth**
>>> that projected slightly like the good useful **teeth**
>>> of an animal.

8.4 How to go about analyzing sentences at different levels

Now that we have reviewed a few troublesome facts and made clear that even a noun phrase can be analyzed at ever deeper levels, we will take the following sentence, taken from a previous exercise as an example and analyze the whole sentence step by step until it cannot be analyzed any further.

> They did not know his name, and now, although they might have asked the first day and got away with it, it was suddenly impossible, because he didn't ask them theirs.

---

[*] The preposition *with* has been written down to show at what level these phrases occur, but even though the preposition *with* may be understood, you should analyze what you see. Therefore, this is a noun phrase.

Step 1: Find finite verbs
First find *finite verbs* to help you see how many finite clauses there are. The finite verbs are shown in bold.

> They **did** not know his name, and now, although they **might** have asked the first day and got away with it, it **was** suddenly impossible, because he **did**n't ask them theirs.

Step 2: Find coordinators and subordinators
There is no semi-colon, but there are several coordinators and subordinators. The subordinators and coordinators are shown in bold.

> They did not know his name, **and** now, **although** they might have asked the first day **and** got away with it, it was suddenly impossible, **because** he didn't ask them theirs.

To see if we have to analyze one or more main clauses, we focus on coordinate conjunctions first.

Step 3: Find parts with main clauses
There are two coordinate conjunctions, both are *and*. The first one connects two complete sentences: [*They did not know his name,*] and [*now, although [...] theirs.*].

The second *and* connects two predicates: *might have [asked the first day]* AND *(might have) [got away with it]*. We may conclude that this sentence is definitely compound as it consists of two main parts, each to be analyzed separately.

part 1	They did not know his name,
coord. conj.	and
part 2	now, although they might have asked the first day and got away with it, it was suddenly impossible, because he didn't ask them theirs.

Now each part of the compound sentence can be analyzed at Level 1 into *sentence constituents* (S, P, DO, IO, etc.). Below, the *function* and *realization* of each constituent at *sentence level* is named. The first part consists of only one clause.

[[They] [did [not] know] [his name,]]

Level 1: Part 1 into clause constituents

	Function:	Realization
They	S:	NP
did know	P:	VP
not	A:	AdvP
his name	DO:	NP

Each of the sentence constituents mentioned above consists of a phrase. Each of these can be analyzed at yet a second level, into *phrase constituents*.

Level 2: Constituents of Part 1 at phrase level

		Function:	Realization
They	NP	head:	pronoun
did know	VP	head:	lexical verb
		aux:	auxiliary verb
not	AdvP	head:	adverb
his name	NP	head:	noun
		det:	possessive pronoun

As none of these phrases contain any other phrases or clauses, we have finished analyzing Part 1 at all possible levels.

Now we will analyze Part 2 at Level 1 into sentence constituents. We have already gone through Steps 1 and 2 and know that there are two subordinators, *although* and *because*, which give clear indications that there are some dependent clauses functioning as adverbials. The easiest way to go about analyzing this part is to find the boundaries of the dependent clauses. Then we will have the main clause left over.

> now, [**although** they might have asked the first day and got away with it,] it was suddenly impossible, [**because** he didn't ask them theirs]

The part that is left over is *now it was suddenly impossible*, clearly the main clause, which should have its own subject and predicate. The whole part can now be analyzed into sentence constituents at Level 1 as follows:

> [[now], [although they might have asked the first day and got away with it,][it] [was] [suddenly] [impossible,] [because he didn't ask them theirs].]

Level 1: Part 2 into clause constituents

	Function:	Realization
now	A:	AdvP
although [...] it	A:	FC
it	S:	NP
was	P:	VP
suddenly	A:	AdvP
impossible	SA:	AdjP
because [...] theirs	A:	FC

Each of the sentence constituents mentioned above consists of either a phrase or a dependent clause. Each of these can be analyzed at Level 2, the phrases into phrase constituents and the clauses into clause constituents. First we will look at the constituents of the phrases then at those of the dependent clauses.

Level 2: Constituents of main clause in Part 2 at phrase level

		Function:	Realization
now	AdvP	head:	adverb
it	NP	head:	personal pronoun
was	VP	head:	lexical verb
suddenly	AdvP	head:	adverb
impossible	AdjP	head:	adjective

None of these phrases have any further phrases or clauses to be analyzed, so we have finished analyzing these. Now we will analyze the dependent clauses in Part 2:

(although) [they] [might have asked] [the first day] (and) [got away with][it]]

Level 2: Constituents of first dependent clause in Part 2 at clause level

	Function:	Realization
although	none	subordinate conjunction
they	S:	NP
might have asked	P:	VP
the first day	A:	NP
and	none	coordinate conjunction
got away with	P:	VP
it	DO:	NP

The constituents of the first dependent clause can be analyzed at level 3.

Level 3: Constituents of first dependent clause in Part 2 at phrase level

		Function:	Realization
they	NP	head:	personal pronoun
might have asked	VP	head:	lexical verb
		aux:	auxiliary verbs
the first day	NP	head:	noun
		det:	article
		det:	numeral
got away with	VP	head:	lexical verb

None of these phrases have any further phrases or clauses to be analyzed, so we have finished analyzing these. Now we will analyze the second dependent clauses at level 2:

[(because) [he] [did[n't] ask] [them] [theirs].

Level 2: Constituents of second dependent clause in Part 2 at clause level

	Function:	Realization
because	none	subordinate conjunction
he	S:	NP
did ask	P:	VP
not	A:	AdvP
them	IO:	NP
theirs	DO:	NP

The constituents of the second dependent clause can be analyzed at Level 3.

Level 3: Constituents of second dependent clause in Part 2 at phrase level

		Function:	Realization
he	NP	head:	personal pronoun
did ask	VP	head:	lexical verb
		aux:	auxiliary verb
not	AdvP	head:	adverb
them	NP	head:	personal pronoun
theirs	NP	head:	possessive pronoun

We have now finished analyzing this sentence because none of the phrases analyzed contain further phrases or clauses to be analyzed; however, as you saw earlier, the levels within phrases and clauses can theoretically go further down indefinitely. A clause can contain further dependent clauses and a phrase can contain further phrases or dependent clauses. Of course, there is a practical limit. If sentences contain too many different levels, they become quite incomprehensible.

EXERCISE 52 Some of the postmodifiers in our previous exercise are non-finite clauses. Analyze each clause into its constituents. If the non-finite clause contains another clause, analyze it, too. Do not analyze further at the phrase level. The first one has been done for you.

       (a long head)
          P:VP   A:PP   P:VP

1   with a shining dark dome [surrounded / with curly hair [given /
      DO:NP   A:PP
   a strong liveliness / by the sharp coarse strokes of gray hairs,]]

2   (with) the beautiful curved nose [handed out so impartially to Indians],

3   (with) dark eyes [slightly bloodshot from the sun],

4   (with) a wide muscular mouth [smiling on strong uneven teeth that projected slightly like the good useful teeth of an animal].

8.5 Analyzing sentences at different levels on your own

In the previous section, we have shown how a sentence can be analyzed step by step. In the remainder of this section, you are guided through each step again, but now you will be asked to fill in the relevant details.

You will be analyzing a short passage (from *Miles City, Montana* by Alice Munro) at sentence and clause levels. Read the passage below and answer the questions pertaining to it:

> (a) I don't think so. (b) I don't think I really saw all this. (c) Perhaps I saw my father carrying him and the other men following along, and the dogs, but I would not have been allowed to get close enough to see something like mud in his nostril. (d) I must have heard someone talking about that and imagined that I saw it. (e) I see his face unaltered except for the mud — Steve Gauley's familiar, sharp-honed sneaky looking face — and it wouldn't have been like that; it would have been bloated and changed and perhaps muddied all over after so many hours in the water.

EXERCISE 53   Answer the following questions and fill in the blanks where necessary.

1. In the passage above, there is only one simple sentence. Which one is it?
2. Analyze sentence (b) by filling in the blanks below:

    I don't think I really saw all this,

Step 1: Find finite verbs

There are two _____ verbs, namely _____ and _____, so we can conclude we have at least _____ clauses.

Step 2: Find coordinators and subordinators

To see if we have a compound or _____ sentence we have to find coordinators and subordinators. There is no _____ or correlative conjunction, but the word _____ is understood after the verb _____. The understood *that* is here a _____; therefore, we know this clause is a _____ one, and the sentence is a _____ one. The dependent clause functions as _____ of the sentence.

We can now finish analyzing this sentence at different levels. Put the function and realization above each sentence and clause constituent at Level 1 and 2 in the next schema. We will not worry about analyzing at phrase level, since all of them are rather simple.

| I / do [n't] think | I / really / saw / all this |

3. Analyze sentence (c):

   Perhaps I saw my father carrying him and the other men following along, and the dogs, but I would not have been allowed to get close enough to see something like mud in his nostril by filling in the blanks.

Step 1: Find finite verbs

There are several clauses, some finite and some _____. For main clauses, the verb must always be _____. The finite verbs in this sentence are _____ and _____. There are quite a few non-finite verbs like _____ and _____, but we will ignore those for the time being as they are always part of a _____ clause.

Step 2: Find coordinators and subordinators

For now, we want to see if we have to do with one or more independent sentence parts. To do so, we have to find coordinators. There are _____ of them. They are _____, _____, and _____. Only one of these, _____, connects two independent sentence parts. We can conclude we have a _____ sentence and we have to analyze it as _____ separate sentences.

We can now proceed with the analysis of Part 1 of this sentence:

Perhaps I saw my father carrying him and the other men following along, and the dogs.

The subject is _____ and the predicator is _____. The next questions is 'what' did I see. Actually, I saw _____ things: *my father carrying him, the* _____, *and the* _____. So this sentence has three _____. The one sentence constituent we have not named yet is *perhaps*, which functions as _____.

Let's look further at the direct objects. Two of them are _____ clauses, each of which can be analyzed at Level 2. In the first non-finite clause, the subject is _____, realized by a _____, the predicator is _____, realized by a _____, and the direct object is _____, realized by a _____.

The second non-finite clause has as its subject _____, realized by a _____, and the predicator is *following along*, which happens to be a _____ verb.

The third direct object is realized by a _____. We have now finished the analysis at clause levels of Part 1 of this sentence. Put the function and realization above each sentence and clause constituent in the next schema.

```
Perhaps / I / saw /   | my father / carrying / him |

(and) | the other men / following along, |

(and) / the dogs
```

We can now proceed with the analysis of Part 2 of the sentence:

> but I would not have been allowed to get close enough to see something like mud in his nostril.

This sentence part has quite a few verbs, but there is only one finite one, which is _____. We may safely assume that this sentence part is simple even though we are likely to find one or more _____ clauses. We will first find the main part of this clause, which must center around *would*, as it is the only finite verb.

This sentence is difficult to analyze because it has a very complex verb phrase. What verbs are part of the first verb phrase? There are two ways we can answer this, both of which are correct: *would have been allowed* or *would have been allowed to get*, depending on whether we regard *to be allowed* as an _____ verb or a lexical verb. For example, in a sentence like 'I allowed John to go' the verb *allow* is clearly a _____ verb, but in its very frequently used passive counterpart, *He is allowed to go* the whole phrase *is allowed to* could be substituted with the modal auxiliary _____ and therefore *to be allowed to* can be regarded as a semi-modal. We will go further with the second analysis, mainly because it will provide the simplest solution for the remainder of the sentence.

Now that we have found the predicator, we will have to decide what the function of the remainder of the clause is. *Close enough to see something like mud in his nostril* answers the question '*where* is he allowed to *get*.' Therefore, we may conclude that this part functions as _____. The main word (head) in this adverbial is _____, which is an _____, so the adverbial is realized as an _____. But, *close* is followed by *enough to see something like mud in his nostril*. The main part of this postmodifier is the word _____,

195   8.5   Analyzing sentences at different levels on your own

so the postmodifier of *close* is realized by an _____ phrase. The adverb *enough* is in turn postmodified by *to see something like mud in his nostril*, which is a _____ clause. In this clause, we have the verb phrase _____ and a direct object _____.

Finally, there is one word left in the sentence, namely _____, which is a _____ conjunction and does not have a function in the clause.

We have now finished with the analysis of Part 2, including the analysis at phrase level of the *close* phrase. Put the function and realization of each constituent at the different levels shown in the schema.

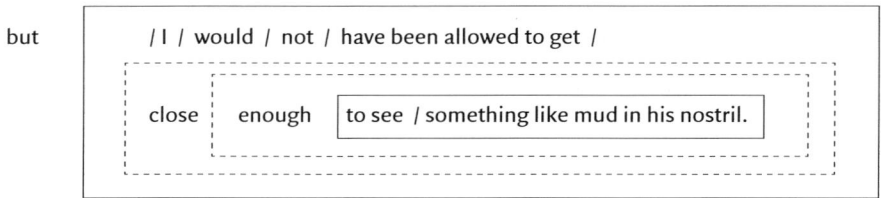

4. Analyze the two following sentences (d and e) at sentence and clause levels, first into sentence constituents and then each dependent clause into clause constituents.

(d) I must have heard someone talking about that and imagined that I saw it.

(e) I see his face unaltered except for the mud — Steve Gauley's familiar, sharp-honed sneaky looking face — and it wouldn't have been like that; it would have been bloated and changed and perhaps muddied all over after so many hours in the water.

8.6 Summary

In this chapter you have seen how a sentence may be analyzed at ever deeper levels. First, you should find finite verbs, coordinators, and subordinators to help you identify main clauses versus dependent clauses

Each main or dependent (finite or non-finite) clause should be analyzed into sentence or clause constituents (S, P, DO, and so on). These constituents are realized by phrases or dependent clauses. A noun phrase can be analyzed further into determiner(s), premodifier(s), heads, and postmodifier(s). Premodifiers are always realized by phrases and postmodifiers by either phrases or clauses. These can be analyzed further, too, until there are no more phrases or clauses to be analyzed. Adjective and adverb phrases may also have premodifiers and postmodifiers. The postmodifiers of adjectives and adverbs can also be phrases or clauses.

When there are several premodifiers or postmodifiers in a phrase, it is important to see at what levels these modifiers function. Are they part of one phrase with several dependent ones inside it or are they phrases modifying the head separately.

By going through the steps as outlined in this chapter, you should be able to analyze any English sentence, no matter how complex it is, unless of course a writer doesn't "play by the rules"! And indeed sometimes there may be good (stylistic) reasons not to.

9 How to apply sentence construction knowledge to writing

9.1 Introduction

This book has dealt with sentence constructions at all levels, from single words and phrases to the most complex sentences in English. Most texts in the exercises were based on excerpts from well-known short stories by famous authors. These authors probably did not know the names of all the types of constructions, but they used their intuition and sense of linguistic rhythm to make sure that every word, every sentence construction, and every punctuation mark was as effective as it could be. Unlike these talented writers, novice writers may not have that intuition yet and may need some guidance. This chapter will deal with common problems that novice writers — both native and non-native speakers of English — may have, especially in more academic writing.

First of all, if you want to write effectively, you have to keep many things in mind. Of course, the most important is keeping your audience in mind (what type of writing do you need: formal, informal, creative, academic, for young or adult readers, and so on) and then focusing on the actual content, organization, and coherence. Good writers tend to write and rewrite their texts numerous times, trying to find the right words and phrases to express what they want. They usually do not worry about grammar or punctuation until they are at the final proofreading stage. At that final point in the writing process, it is time to look at your sentence constructions to make sure your reader can fully understand your message. This chapter focuses on the analytical skills you have gained in this book and translates it to the actual writing context. It can help you proofread your writing in the final proofreading stage to avoid common writing problems.

9.2 How to avoid sentence and clause errors

In English formal writing (e.g. in newspapers, business communication, academic papers, essays, and so on) it is important to write complete sentences. Remember: a complete sentence requires a subject and a finite verb; it expresses a complete thought, also known as a main clause. In many English university courses in the US, students may actually get a "fail" if they inadvertently produce one of the following sentence errors: *fragment* (=incomplete sentences), *run-on sentence*, and/or a *comma splices* (not properly punctuated sentences). These sentence errors are explained in more detail below.

1 Fragment

A fragment is an incomplete sentence. The following example is a clause starting with the subordinating conjunction (*now*) *when*, making the clause a dependent one. There is no main clause. It can be corrected by adding a main clause or taking off the subordinating conjunction.

*Now when I had mastered the language of this water.	Fragment. This is not a full sentence, but an isolated dependent clause.
Now when I had mastered the language of this water, I had come to know every trifling feature that bordered the great river.	Complete sentence. It has a dependent clause and a main clause.
Now I had mastered the language of this water.	Complete Sentence. This is now a main clause because the subordinate *when* is omitted.

2 Run-on sentence

A run-on sentence is the result of two complete sentences being joined together without any punctuation mark to separate them. In the following example, there are two main clauses [I had lost...something] and [it...lived]. These should be separated with a period, a semi-colon, or even a colon here. It could also be connected with a coordinate conjunction such as *and*. Please note that a simple comma may not be used, as this would result in a comma splice (see below).

*I had lost something it could never be restored to me while I lived.	Run-on sentence
I had lost something; it could never be restored to me while I lived.	Two complete sentences separated with a semi-colon
I had lost something, and it could never be restored to me while I lived.	Two complete sentences joined with a coordinator

3   Comma splice

To mark the end of a complete sentence, you need a period, an exclamation mark, or a question mark. When two complete sentences are somewhat logically related in meaning, they may be separated by means of a semi-colon or a colon or joined with a coordinator. However, they may not be separated with only a comma. Two complete sentences separated by only a comma results in a sentence error called a comma splice. A comma is simply not strong enough to join complete sentences. In the following example there are two main clauses [I had lost...lived] and [all the grace... river] separated only by a comma. In the sentences underneath it, the comma splice is repaired (by means of a semi-colon, colon, or coordinator, respectively)

*I had lost something which could never be restored to me while I lived, all the grace and beauty had gone out of the majestic river.	Comma splice
I had lost something which could never be restored to me while I lived; all the grace and beauty had gone out of the majestic river.	Two complete sentences separated with a semi-colon
I had lost something which could never be restored to me while I lived: all the grace and beauty had gone out of the majestic river.	Two complete sentences separated with a colon
I had lost something which could never be restored to me while I lived, and all the grace and beauty had gone out of the majestic river.	Two complete sentences joined with a coordinator, which is preceded by a comma

A comma splice very often occurs when a conjunctive adverb, like *therefore*, is used. A conjunctive adverb may sound like a conjunction because it expresses a logical relationship between two thoughts. However, grammatically it is an adverb as it can be moved around in the sentence. In the following example, there are two main clauses [I…water] and [I…river] logically connected with therefore, but separated by a comma without some type of conjunction. The sentence can be corrected by using either a period or semi-colon after the first complete sentence.

*I had mastered the language of this water, therefore, I had come to know every trifling feature that bordered the great river.	Comma splice
I had mastered the language of this water; therefore, I had come to know every trifling feature that bordered the great river.	Two complete sentences separated with a semi-colon

4   **Dangling modifier**

A dangling modifier is also an error, but at the phrase level, not the sentence level. It is a phrase or non-finite clause that is not clearly and logically related to the word or words it modifies (i.e. is placed next to) often because the understood subject of the modifier is not the same as the subject in the main clause. It usually occurs at the beginning of a sentence, but may also be at the end.

*After reading the original study, the article remains unconvincing.	Dangling modifier (the understood subject of reading is not "the article", the subject of the main clause)
After reading the original study, I find the article unconvincing.	Logical modifier (the understood subject of reading is "I", the subject of the main clause)
*Relieved of your responsibilities at your job, your home should be a place to relax.	Dangling modifier (the understood subject of relieved is not "your home", the subject of the main clause)

Relieved of your responsibilities at your job, you should be able to relax at home.	Logical modifier (the understood subject of relieved is "you", the subject of the main clause)
*The experiment was a failure, not having studied the lab manual carefully.	Dangling modifier (the understood subject of not having is not "the experiment", the subject of the main clause)
They failed the experiment, not having studied the lab manual carefully.	Logical modifier (the understood subject of not having is not "they", the subject of the main clause)

EXERCISE 54 Identify the following sentences adapted from *Life on the Mississippi* by Mark Twain as either a *complete sentence, fragment, run-on sentence,* or *comma splice* and make corrections if needed.

1 Now I had mastered the language of this water.

2 I had come to know every trifling feature that bordered the great river.

3 As familiarly as I knew the letters of the alphabet.

4 I had made a valuable acquisition I had lost something too.

5 I had lost something, it could never be restored to me while I lived.

6 All the grace, the beauty, the poetry having gone out of the majestic river.

EXERCISE 55 Combining information from the sentences in Exercise 54, create two pairs of sentences, one with a dangling modifier and one with a logical modifier. An example is given below.

Dangling modifier: Having mastered the language of this water, every trifling feature was known to me.

Logical modifier: Having mastered the language of this water, I knew every trifling feature.

9.3 How to use commas

Within complete sentences, commas can help the reader find and predict relevant sentence parts within a sentence. Moreover, as the texts of many of the exercises in this book have shown, good writers intuitively know that the right punctuation can make or break the rhythm of a single sentence. Actually, English punctuation conventions are quite regular, logical, and easy to apply, especially if you know how to analyze a sentence into its constituents. Novice writers, however, tend to use too many commas, or use only one comma when two are needed.

To avoid overusing commas, you should be aware of the following rule: the obligatory basic constituents of a sentence or clause — the subject, predicator, and its complement — are never separated by commas. Therefore, there is no comma after a subject or before an object or attribute, even if the object or complement is a dependent clause. The only exception is a direct quote.

*She heard, that he would have the day off.	No comma should be used before a direct object.
She heard that he would have the day off.	No comma should be used before a direct object.
She said, "I'll be darned if I give him the day off."	A comma should be used before a direct object if it is a direct quotation.

Still there are a few cases in which commas are required or needed for readability. These are explained below.

1 Adverbials

The only constituent that is often not obligatory in a sentence is an adverbial. If adverbials occur in their 'normal' place, after the subject, predicate, and complement, and continue the train of thought, they are usually not set off with a comma. However, long adverbials at the beginning of a sentence are set off with a comma as it helps the reader locate the subject more easily. In other words, commas after long sentence-initial adverbials can help readers find their way in the sentence. Commas may be used when adverbials interrupt the main flow of a sentence or if they express a strong contrast with the ideas in the main clause or express some afterthought or comment on the main clause.

She called him **because she wanted to know what the assignment was.**	No comma for an adverbial at the end of a sentence.
Because she wanted to know what the assignment was, she called him.	A comma to set off a long adverbial at the beginning of a sentence.
She called him, **although she knew exactly what the assignment was.**	A comma to set off an adverbial at the end that expresses a strong concession or contrast.
She called him, **not because she wanted to know what the assignment was**, but because she wanted to hear his voice.	A comma to set off an interrupting adverbial.
She called him because she wanted to hear his voice, **in my opinion.**	A comma to set off an afterthought.

2 Restrictive and non-restrictive elements

In Chapter 6 we discussed restrictive and non-restrictive postmodifiers of nouns in detail. They can be phrases, non-finite clauses, or finite clauses. Restrictive elements are those that are needed to identify the noun that is modified and are pronounced with a rising intonation. No commas should be used with restrictive elements.

Non-restrictive elements, on the other hand, are not needed to identify the noun but add extra information. The whole element is usually pronounced with falling intonation. As a non-restrictive element interrupts the flow of the sentence, it must be set off on both sides with commas (neutral), dashes (gives more emphasis to the non-restrictive element) or parentheses (gives less emphasis to the non-restrictive element).

At home her landlady, **Mrs. Crompton,** was feeling unwell.	A non-restrictive postmodifier of *landlady* set off with commas
She cooked her a meal **that she would be able to digest easily.**	A restrictive postmodifier of *meal* without commas
The meal that **she cooked the night before***, would be easily digestible	*That she cooked the night before* is a restrictive modifier and should not be followed by a comma.

EXERCISE 56   In the following section from *Boys and Girls* by Alice Munro, the author used commas to set off the first non-restrictive element, but the second one is set off with dashes. Why do you think the author chose to set off the second element with dashes? What is so special about it?

> Along the streets of this town were arranged large, sturdy pens. Each of them had a real door that a man could go through, <u>a wooden ramp along the wire</u>, for the foxes to run up and down on, and a kennel — <u>sometimes like a clothes chest with airholes</u> — where they slept and stayed in winter and had their young.

EXERCISE 57   In the following passage from *A Course of English Studies* by Ruth Prawer Jhabvala, use slashes to set off sentence and clause constituents in the way you have been taught to do in the book. Then add commas where necessary. Explain your choices. The number of commas used in the original passage are given in parentheses. Since punctuation is also a matter of personal style, you may prefer to use more or fewer commas. Discuss the different possibilities and their stylistic effects.

1   The next Saturday / it / was raining // but / nevertheless / Nalini stood and waited / for him / outside his house. (1)

In this sentence, a comma could be used after *the next Saturday* (a longer adverbial at the beginning of the sentence), before *but* (which connects two complete main clauses) and before and after *nevertheless* (interrupting adverbial). The author chose to put a comma only before *but*, probably because the adverbials are short, the sentence can be processed easily without the commas, and commas would have interrupted the flow and rhythm of the sentence too much.

2   At first he did not seem to be very pleased to see her and it was only when they had walked away from the house for some distance that he made her sit on the cross-bar of his bicycle. (2)

3   They rode like that together through the rain. (0)

4   It was like a dream she in his arms and feeling his breath on her face and everything around them the trees and the sky and the tops of the houses melting away into mist and soft rain. (4)

5   They went to the same shop and bought almost the same things but this time when they came out and she already saw the smile of farewell forming on his lips she quickly said 'Can't we have coffee somewhere?' (4)

6   They went to a shop which served home-made rock cakes and had copper urns for decoration. (0)

7   It was full of housewives having their coffee break so the only table available was one by the coat rack which was rather uncomfortable because of all the dripping coats and umbrellas. (2)

8   Nalini didn't mind but Dr. Greaves sat hunched together and looking miserable. (1)

9   His thin hair was all wet and stuck to his head and sometimes a drop came dripping down his face. (0)

10 Nalini looked at him: 'Cold?' she asked with tender concern. (1)

3   Coordinate constructions

As in many other languages, in English the goal is to eliminate repetition of sentence parts that can be clearly understood from previous sentences. Often coordinators are used to connect the left-over sentence parts. These coordinators are not preceded by a comma if they connect two sentence parts.

> The servants [got the hampers ready] **and** ~~the servants~~ [packed them in the back of the car.]

In the following example, you can see how three sentences may be combined by leaving out the repeated parts. Note that in the combined sentence the first coordinator *and* is also omitted as it is also clearly understood. In the resulting sentence, there are three items in a series, with just a comma between item 1 and 2 and the coordinator (with a comma) between item 2 and 3.

> She told Norman [how marvelous the picnics were they had at home],
> ~~She told Norman~~ [how the servants got the hampers ready and packed them in the back of the car]
> ~~She told Norman~~ [how they then drove off to some lovely spot].
> She told Norman [how marvelous the picnics were they had at home], **and** [how the servants got the hampers ready and packed them in the back of the car], **and** [how they then drove off to some lovely spot].
> It might be in [a deserted palace], ~~or it might be in~~ [an amphitheater], **or** it might be in [a summer tank], always some romantic ruin overgrown with creepers and flowers.

It is also possible to combine two complete sentences, each with their own finite verb phrase, with a coordinator. In that case, there is usually a comma before the coordinator.

> The next Sunday it was raining, **but** Nalini stood and waited for him outside his house.

Finally, two or more adjectives can modify a noun. These adjectives may be coordinate in that they both describe the noun equally (and their order can be reversed) or cumulative, in that one adjective describes a more inherent quality of the noun (and their order cannot be reversed). In the case of premodifiers, either a comma or a coordinate conjunction can be used between the adjectives. If there are more than two, commas are preferred.

> Lyka is a happy and enthusiastic dog. (premodifying)
> Lyka is a happy, enthusiastic dog. (premodifying)
> Lyka is a happy, enthusiastic **and** loving dog. (premodifying)
> Lyka is a happy, enthusiastic, **and** loving dog. (premodifying)

Note the comma before *and* is really optional and often called an "Oxford comma".

> What a creative **and** generous gift!
> What a creative, generous gift!

In the case of modifiers in a complement, there is usually an *and* between the coordinate adjectives.

> Melissa is so smart **and** thoughtful. (coordinate adjectives in the complement)

In the case of cumulative adjectives, there is usually no comma between the adjectives. Note that the order cannot be reversed to stray/vicious.

> Have you seen those vicious stray dogs?

A final note about coordinate constructions is that the commas are helpful in reading longer parts that are connected, but leaving them off is not an error. In fact, they are very often left off in creative writing. Note this sentence from *The Catch* by Nadine Gordimer.

His <u>thin strong bony</u> legs passed by at eye level every morning as they lay, stranded on the <u>hard smooth</u> sand.

EXERCISE 58 The following section from *Miles City, Montana* by Alice Munro is punctuated by a creative writer, who probably used their feeling for style rather than standard rules to put punctuation marks. In most cases the author followed 'the rules' given above, but in some cases used punctuation marks for effect. For each underlined set of items, identify the punctuation 'rule'. If it does not clearly fit a rule, try to explain why the author did or did not use a punctuation mark to separate the items.

> My father came across the (1) <u>field carrying</u> the body of the (2) <u>boy who</u> had been drowned. There were several men (3a) <u>together, returning</u> from the (3b) <u>search, but</u> he was the (4) <u>one carrying</u> the body. The men were muddy and (5) <u>exhausted, and</u> walked with their heads (6) <u>down, as</u> if they were ashamed. Even the dogs were (7) <u>dispirited, dripping</u> from the cold river. When they all set (8) <u>out, hours before, the</u> dogs were nervy and (9) <u>yelping, the men</u> tense and (10) <u>determined, and there</u> was a (11) <u>constrained, unspeakable</u> excitement about the whole scene. It was (12) <u>understood that t</u>hey might find something horrible.

EXERCISE 59 In the following stream of words (adapted from *Life on the Mississippi* by Mark Twain), set off complete sentences with a period and add commas where needed.

> now when I had mastered the language of this water and had come to know every trifling feature that bordered the great river as familiarly as I knew the letters of the alphabet I had made a valuable acquisition but I had lost something too I had lost something which could never be restored to me while I lived all the grace the beauty the poetry had gone out of the majestic river

9.4 How to make sure each sentence is effective

When you proofread, you should make sure your sentence constructions fit not only your own writing style but also the target audience. They need to be able to understand your message without having to read sentences two or three times. For example, long sentences or overly complex sentences do not necessarily make good sentence writing. Sometimes a simple sentence is the more powerful as it makes a point stand out. A passive construction may be needed in some genres, but they are often more difficult to process, so they should be used sparingly. It is also important to eliminate unnecessary words as they may blur the actual message.

1 Use simple sentences effectively

In creative writing, the rhythm of a sentence is important. In the following passage from *A Farm at Raraba* by Ernst Havemann, the author used some longer, more rambling sentences but there are three simple, short sentences. Examine each simple sentence and try to explain why the writer used it as he did.

> <u>My late dad was a magnificent shot</u>. One time when we were hunting in the Low Veld and had paused for a smoke, there was the yelp of a wild dog, and a troop of impala came bounding over the tall grass. Opposite us, three hundred yards off, was a stony ridge like a wall, six feet high. You would think those buck would avoid it, but no, they went straight at it. One after the other, without pausing or swerving, they leapt over it. <u>They cleared it by three feet</u>. I tell you, friend, it was a beautiful sight. <u>You can't beat Nature for beauty, eh.</u>

2 Avoid redundancy

Creative writers, whose texts we have used in the exercises in this book, may write and rewrite almost every word or sentence until they are sure every word is effectively used, no more and no less than needed. Novice writers, on the other hand, tend to use too many words to say what they need to say. The effect is that the reader needs to process all this information, which may be redundant, and therefore do not understand the message right away. Below are some examples of student work.

First, an example of a sentence with a lot of redundancy:

> *Pragmatics* is concerned with the search for a coherent general framework for the discussion and comparison of results of the fundamental research, in various disciplines, carried out by those dealing with aspects of language use or the functionality of language.

To avoid redundancy in your own sentences, you can identify really meaningful keywords in the context such as lexical verbs and nouns. Then you can see if you really need the remaining words and if not, you can delete or rephrase them.

> ***Pragmatics*** is concerned with the search for **a coherent general framework** for the **discussion** and **comparison** of **results** of the fundamental research, in various disciplines, carried out by those dealing with aspects of **language use** or **the functionality of language**.

> Pragmatics ~~is concerned with~~ concerns ~~the search for~~ a coherent general framework ~~for the discussion~~ to discuss and compare ~~comparison of results of the fundamental research~~ findings from ~~, in~~ various disciplines ~~, carried out by those~~ dealing with aspects of language use or the functionality of language.

> Pragmatics concerns a coherent general framework to discuss and compare findings from various disciplines dealing with aspects of language use or the functionality of language.

3   Avoid front-weighted sentences

Novice writers, especially second language writers, may tend to overload the subject by putting too much information in it and consequently making it very long. This is also called 'front-weighting', since the 'heaviest' load of information is placed at the beginning of the sentence or clause. To read and process an English text as efficiently as possible, the proficient reader usually tries to segment the sentence in its main parts: the subject, the predicator, and the remainder of the sentence. It helps the reader if the predicator comes soon; therefore, front-weighted sentences with very long subjects should be avoided.

Here's an example of front-weighted sentence:

> <u>That it would be read not only by pragmaticians and students of language, but also by everyone who could benefit from more insights into problems of language use</u> was one of the aims of the journal.

Although the example sentence is syntactically correct, it is rather awkward and difficult to read. We can improve the sentence by shifting the 'weight' towards the end, i.e. by creating an end-weighted sentence:

> One of the aims of the journal was <u>that it would be read not only by pragmaticians and students of language, but also by everyone who could benefit from more insights into problems of language use.</u>

EXERCISE 60 An experienced language editor has rewritten some of the sentences from the same student, trying to make the language more concise and to eliminate redundant information. Compare the sentences and try to explain the editor's choices.

1. The most important factors affecting learning a second language (be it English, French or Macedonian) are motivation and attitude.

    The most important factors affecting learning a second language (be it English, French or Macedonian) are motivation and attitude.

2. Students who are motivated and who have a positive attitude towards the concerning language and its speakers, are mostly more willing to learn that language and therefore most of them will usually obtain higher marks than other students.

    Motivated students with a positive attitude towards the language and its speakers are usually more willing to learn that language and will obtain higher marks than other students.

3   One study on second language learning conducted by Lambert and Gardner (1972) clearly shows this relationship between motivation and attitude on the one hand and obtaining high marks on the other hand. In their study about high school students in Louisiana and their French language skills, it turned out that students who were motivated to do well obtained higher marks than their less motivated or unmotivated colleagues.

For example, Lambert and Gardner (1972) studied high school students in Louisiana learning French, and students who were more motivated obtained higher marks than their less motivated peers.

4   The results also showed that students with a positive attitude towards French-speaking people and their ways of life were more likely to obtain higher marks than students who were prejudiced towards French-speaking people and who denigrated the French way of life.

The results also showed that students with a positive attitude towards French-speaking people and their ways of life were more likely to obtain higher marks than students who were prejudiced towards French-speaking people and denigrated the French way of life.

4   **Avoid awkward and vague passive constructions**

The passive voice is a very useful construction if it is just not relevant who does what. It is needed if the "agent" of an act is not known, not so important, or irrelevant. Moreover, in some academic genres such as scientific reports, especially in the methods section, the passive voice is preferred as the writer otherwise needs to refer to themselves too many times. A passive construction is also quite common and useful in ellipted postmodifiers (see Chapter 7).

However, novice writers tend to overuse the passive voice because they feel it makes them sound more academic, but in effect, an overuse of passives may create wordy sentences and blurs who does what.

EXERCISE 61   Read the same excerpt again (from *Farm at Raraba* by Ernst Havemann) and compare it with our (very poorly) rewritten version. Are the passive constructions less effective? If so, why?

> My late dad was a magnificent shot. One time when we were hunting in the Low Veld and had paused for a smoke, there was the yelp of a wild dog, and a troop of impala came bounding over the tall grass. Opposite us, three hundred yards off, was a stony ridge like a wall, six feet high. You would think those buck would avoid it, but no, they went straight at it. One after the other, without pausing or swerving, they leapt over it. They cleared it by three feet. I tell you, friend, it was a beautiful sight. You can't beat Nature for beauty, eh.
>
> My late dad was a magnificent shot. One time when we were hunting in the Low Veld and had paused for a smoke, <u>the yelp of a wild dog was heard</u>, and <u>a troop of impala bounding over the tall grass was seen</u>. Opposite us, three hundred yards off, was a stony ridge like a wall, six feet high. You would think that <u>it could be avoided by those buck</u>, but no, they went straight at it. One after the other, without pausing or swerving, they leapt over it. They cleared it by three feet. I tell you, friend, it was a beautiful sight. You can't beat Nature for beauty, eh.

5   **Make sure constructions are parallel**
In general, proficient readers do not read every word separately, but they read whole phrases at the time and they make predictions about the rest of the sentence to process its meaning. As a writer you can help the reader by using predictable constructions. Sentences are easier and more pleasant to read or listen to if there is an agreement in their grammatical structure, particularly when it comes to lists. This principle is known as parallelism, parallel structure, or parallel construction.

Parallelism is used often by good speakers (and writers) as it not only helps create a good rhythm, which is pleasant to the ear, but also helps the listener to process the information more efficiently. The following sentence is from a speech by John F. Kennedy addressed to the Irish Parliament in 1963. Note that there are six verbs all used in parallel after *you have*. They are all past participles of lexical verbs.

> You have <u>modernized your economy</u>, <u>harnessed your rivers</u>, <u>diversified your industry</u>, <u>liberalized your trade</u>, <u>electrified your farms</u>, <u>accelerated your rate growth</u>, and <u>improved the living standard of your people.</u>

EXERCISE 62   The following excerpt from an academic abstract has several parallel constructions. Underline the constructions and explain what makes the constructions parallel.

> They indicated challenges in global aspects of writing a research article, especially writing various text types, linking ideas smoothly and coherently, structuring the text, citing academic sources, summarizing and or paraphrasing academic sources, elaborating and supporting ideas in each paragraph, and organizing ideas clearly and logically.

9.5 How to create coherence with sentence constructions

English word order is quite predictable (Subject, Predicator, Complement) and correct punctuation marks help the reader find the relevant parts easily. Another feature of English academic writing is that information is presented in predictable parts. For example, in English essay writing or paragraph writing, the topic and the direction in which it is developed is given first so that the reader can easily follow the train of thought. The same applies to English sentences. To maintain the flow, a sentence starts with 'old' information (i.e. something the reader already knows, often from the preceding sentence) and ends with new information. This is often called the 'end focus' principle.

This principle also applies to connections between paragraphs. For good coherence, the first part of the first sentence should refer to or remind the reader of something that was said at the very end of the preceding paragraph.

Here is an example of coherence achieved with the end focus principle:

> The most important factors affecting learning a second language (be it English, French or Macedonian) are **motivation and attitude**. **Motivated students with a positive attitude** towards the language and its speakers are usually more willing to learn that language and will obtain higher marks than other students.

Here is an example of weak coherence because the end-focus principle is flaunted:

> The most important factors affecting learning a second language (be it English, French or Macedonian) are **motivation and attitude**. Students who are more willing to learn a language and will obtain higher marks than other students are **motivated students with a positive attitude** towards the language and its speakers.

EXERCISE 63   The following passage is an abstract written for a conference paper. The first sentence is the original first sentence. The remaining sentences have been put in random order. Rearrange these sentences in the right order so that the text adheres most clearly to the end focus principle, then underline the parts of each sentence that establish their end focus. The first two sentences have been done for you.

1   Academic writing (AW) in English remains problematic for students at the highest academic levels as students have to write various types of texts to pass their courses and publish articles in journals. After a literature review and a needs analysis was conducted, the authors piloted <u>a genre-based AW course</u> and evaluated it.

2. <u>This paper reports on the course</u>, the survey the students took before the course and the evaluation after the course.

3. Finally, the students recommended that Academic Writing should be a required course during the first year of their study.

4. In addition, the course materials, observations of classroom practices and reflections of individual feedback sessions were included in the data.

5. In addition, they indicated that they would like personal feedback in the process of writing from their tutors for other courses.

6. Results (understood of the data) indicated that most participants had not had AW training before they entered the doctoral program.

7. The most positive comments were on the personal feedback sessions.

8. They indicated challenges in global aspects of writing a research article, especially writing various text types, linking ideas smoothly and coherently, structuring the text, citing academic sources, summarizing and or paraphrasing academic sources, elaborating and supporting ideas in each paragraph, and organizing ideas clearly and logically.

9. This paper reports on the course, the survey the students took before the course and the evaluation after the course.

9.6 Summary

In this chapter, we looked at how to use your knowledge of constructions to punctuate sentences correctly. There are few absolute rules in punctuation; however, in formal writing complete sentences need to end with a period, question mark, or exclamation mark. A semi-colon or colon may also indicate the end of a complete sentence if the following complete sentence is logically related.

Failing to set off a sentence with the correct punctuation results in one of the following three sentence errors:

> Fragment: incomplete sentence ending with a sentence punctuation mark
> Comma splice: two complete sentences separated with a comma
> Run-on sentence: two complete sentences not separated with a punctuation mark

Commas should be used as sparingly as possible. A default sentence (subject, predicator, and remainder) in a normal word order should not have any commas. Only non-restrictive elements must be set off with commas on both sides. Further commas are often optional, but can be used to help the reader process the information more efficiently. Commas may be used to set off long introductory elements, interrupting elements or elements that interrupt the normal flow of the sentence in that they are contrastive or more of an afterthought.

Also in compound constructions, there is a great deal of leeway for the writer and commas should be used mainly to help readers segment the sentences easily. Commas may be used between two complete sentences joined with a coordinator and may take the place of an understood coordinator.

Finally, well-written sentences should not contain redundant parts or words, including wordy passive constructions, and where possible contain parallel constructions. Also, for coherence, the word order should be arranged in such a way that the beginning of a sentence joins the idea of the last part of the preceding one.

Key to the exercises

EXERCISE 3   Identify the functions of those constituents.

The waitresses **S** / are basking **P** / in the sun **A** / like a herd of skinned seals, their pinky-brown bodies shining with oil. They **S** / are wearing **P** / their bathing suits **DO** / because it's the afternoon **A**. / In the early dawn and the dusk **A** / they **S** / sometimes **A** / go skinny-dipping, which makes this itchy crouching in the mosquito-infested bushes across from their small private dock a great deal more worthwhile.
    Donny **S** / has **P** / the binoculars, which are not his own but Monty's **DO**. / Monty's dad **S** / gave **P** / them **DO** / to him **IO** / for bird-watching **A** / but Monty **S** / isn't interested in birds. He **S** / has found **P** / a better use for the binoculars **DO** /: he **S** / rents / them **DO** / out to the other boys, five minutes maximum, a nickel a look or else a chocolate bar from the tuck shop, though he prefers the money.

EXERCISE 4   Name the function of the sentence constituents separated with slashes. Then indicate which pattern the sentence has.

1. Last week **A** / Michael **S** / showed **P** / us **IO** / how to prepare a 'fruit leather' **DO**. (*giving* pattern)
2. He **S** / told **P** / us **IO** / to buy over ripe and bruised fruit on sale **DO**. (*giving* pattern)
3. We **S** / bought **P** / him **BO** / peaches, apricots, and strawberries **DO**. (*buying* pattern)
4. He **S** / showed **P** / us **IO** / how to cut up the fruit **DO**. (*giving* pattern)
5. He **S** / put **P** / the fruit **DO** / through a food mill **A**. (*doing* pattern)
6. Then **A** / he **S** / put **P** / the fruit **DO** / in a large pot **A**. (*doing* pattern)
7. He **S** / told **P** / me **IO** / to add one tablespoon of honey per pound of fruit **DO**. (*giving* pattern)
8. He **S** / heated **P** / the mixture **DO**. (*doing* pattern)
9. He **S** / stirred **P** / it **DO** / until it boiled **A**. (*doing* pattern)
10. He **S** / cooked **P** / the mixture **DO** / for three minutes **A**. (*doing* pattern)

11 He **S** / prepared **P** / paper plates **DO** / to dry the fruit **A**. (*doing* pattern)
12 He **S** / used **P** / plastic wrap **DO** / to cover the plates **A**. (*doing* pattern)
13 After stretching the plastic around the plate **A**, / we **S** / taped **P** / it **DO** / to the back **A**. (*doing* pattern)
14 The plastic **S** / had to be **P** / tight and flat **SA**. (*being* pattern)
15 We **S** / spread **P** / a thin layer of fruit **DO** / on each plate **A**. (*doing* pattern)
16 We **S** / placed **P** / the plates, covered with cheesecloth **DO**, / in a shadow box **A** / to dry in the sun **A**. (*doing* pattern)
17 We **S** / brought **P** / the plates **DO** / inside **A** / at night **A**. (*doing* pattern)
18 In about two days **A** / the fruit **S** / was **P** / dry **SA**. (*being* pattern)
19 After three days **A**, / he **S** / brought **P** / us **IO** / the dried fruit leather **DO**. (*giving* pattern)
20 We **S** / considered **P** / this snack **DO** / a real treat **OA**. (*considering* pattern)

EXERCISE 5
1 A sentence can only have one S.
2 A sentence can only have one DO.
3 Direct object, because IO or BO cannot occur in a sentence without a DO. (unless the sentence is a passive one, which will be discussed later.)
4 No, there is either an SA or a DO.
5 Yes, a sentence can have an unlimited number of adverbials.
6 Possible combinations:
S — P — A
S — P — DO — A
S — P — DO — OA
S — P

EXERCISE 6 Create two different sentences, (a) one with two main clauses and (b) one with a main clause and a dependent clause. The connector you may use has been given.

1 a. The human liver weighs three to four pounds, **so** it is the heaviest organ in the human body.
  b. The human liver, **which** is the heaviest organ in the human body, weighs three to four pounds.
2 a. In 1858, the first mechanical washing machine was invented by Hamilton E. Smith, **but** it was a hand-cranked affair.

b. In 1858, the first mechanical washing machine, **which** was a hand-cranked affair, was invented by Hamilton E. Smith. / In 1858, the first mechanical washing machine, **which** was invented by Hamilton E. Smith, was a hand-cranked affair.

3 a. The aroma of coffee is not produced by the caffeine is contains, **for** caffeine imparts neither color nor favor.
   b. The aroma of coffee is not produced by the caffeine is contains **because** caffeine imparts neither color nor flavor.

EXERCISE 7   Underline each dependent clause. Then, set off sentence constituents with slashes and identify each constituent as S, P, SA, DO, IO/BO, OA, A.

1 Thomas A. Edison **S** / [did (not **A**) make **P** / the first electric light bulb **DO** / <u>as it is popularly believed</u> **A**.
2 Cherrapunji, India, <u>which has an average annual rainfall of 427 inches</u>, **S** / is **P** / the wettest place on earth **SA**.
3 A state of intoxication **S** / is **P** / a condition <u>in which there is recognizable disturbance of intellect, movement and coordination</u> **SA**.
4 The largest fish <u>anyone has ever caught</u> **S** / was **P** / a white shark <u>that weighed 2,176 pounds</u> **SA**.
5 Only five percent of the people of the United States **S** / say **P** / <u>that they dream in color</u> **DO**.

EXERCISE 8   Set off sentences with a period. How many sentences does Exercise 8 contain?

Exercise 8 contains three sentences:
1 Now ... too.
2 I ... lived.
3 All ... river.

Key to the exercises

EXERCISE 9　　In each sentence from Exercise 8, circle all subordinators (here in **boldface**) and underline main clauses. What types of sentences are these?

[[Now **when** I had mastered the language of this water] and [had come to know every trifling feature [**that** bordered the great river] **as** familiarly **as** I knew the letters of the alphabet]] <u>I had made a valuable acquisition</u> [but <u>I had lost something too</u>]. (This sentence is **compound-complex**. It contains two main clauses and several dependent ones.)

<u>I had lost something</u> [**which** could never be restored to me [**while** I lived]].

(This sentence is **complex**. It contains dependent clauses.)

<u>All the grace, the beauty, the poetry had gone out of the majestic river</u>.

(This sentence is **simple**. It contains one main clause.)

EXERCISE 10　　Underline coordinators and subordinators and set off dependent clauses with square brackets and sentence constituents (subject, predicator, etc.) with slashes. Then name the function of the sentence constituents.

I **S** / had lost **P** / something [<u>which</u> could never be restored to me [<u>while</u> I lived]] **DO**.
All the grace, the beauty, the poetry **S** / had gone **P** / out of the majestic river **A**.

EXERCISE 11　　Underline all verb phrases and indicate whether they are simple or complex.

My father <u>came</u> (simple) across the field <u>carrying</u> (simple) the body of the boy who <u>had been drowned</u> (complex). There <u>were</u> (simple) several men together, <u>returning</u> (simple) from the search, but he <u>was</u> (simple) the one <u>carrying</u> (simple) the body. The men <u>were</u> (simple) muddy and exhausted, and <u>walked</u> (simple) with their heads down, as if they <u>were</u> (simple) ashamed.
　　Even the dogs <u>were</u> (simple) dispirited, (and they were) <u>dripping</u> (simple) from the cold river. When they all <u>set out</u> (simple), hours before, the dogs <u>were</u> (simple) nervy and <u>(were) yelping</u> (complex), the men tense and determined, and there <u>was</u> (simple) a constrained, unspeakable excetement about the whole scene. It <u>was understood</u> (complex) that they <u>might find</u> (complex) something horrible.

EXERCISE 12 Go back to the extract in Exercise 11 and identify each verb as *lexical* or *auxiliary*.

came (lexical)	was (lexical)	set out (lexical)
carrying (lexical)	carrying (lexical)	were (lexical)
had (auxiliary)	were (lexical)	(were) (auxiliary) yelping (lexical)
been (auxiliary)	walked (lexical)	was (lexical)
drowned (lexical)	were (lexical)	was (auxiliary) understood (lexical)
were (lexical)	were (lexical)	might (auxiliary) find (lexical)
returning (lexical)	dripping (lexical)	

EXERCISE 13 Indicate whether the underlined verbs are finite or not.

Next morning shortly after sunrise, just as the light <u>was</u> (finite) <u>beginning</u> (non-finite) <u>to come</u> (non-finite) <u>streaming</u> (non-finite) through the trees, while I <u>lay</u> (finite) <u>leaning</u> (non-finite) on my elbow <u>taking</u> (non-finite) my bread and tea, and <u>looking</u> (non-finite) across the canyon, <u>tracing</u> (non-finite) the dip of the granite headlands, and <u>trying</u> (non-finite) <u>to plan</u> (non-finite) a way to the river at a point likely <u>to be</u> (non-finite) fordable, suddenly I <u>caught</u> (finite) the big bright eyes of a deer <u>gazing</u> (non-finite) at me through the garden hedge. She <u>continued</u> (finite) <u>to gaze</u> (non-finite), while I <u>gazed</u> (finite) back with equal steadiness, motionless as a rock. In a few minutes she <u>ventured</u> (finite) forward a step, <u>exposing</u> (non-finite) the fine arching neck and forelegs, then <u>snorted</u> (finite) and <u>withdrew</u> (finite).

EXERCISE 14 In the passage in Exercise 13, identify all the non-finite forms as plain infinitive, to infinitive, present participle, or past participle. Which two non-finite forms do not occur in this passage?

beginning (present participle)	trying (present participle)
to come (to infinitive)	to plan (to infinitive)
streaming (present participle)	to be (to infinitive)
leaning (present participle)	gazing (present participle)
taking (present participle)	to gaze (to infinitive)
looking (present participle)	exposing (present participle)
tracing (present participle)	

Note: the plain infinitive and the past participle do not occur in this passage.

EXERCISE 15 Identify the form of each verb (present finite, past finite, plain infinitive, to infinitive, present participle, or past participle)

came (past finite)
carrying (present participle)
had (past finite)
been (past participle)
drowned (past participle)
were (past finite)
returning (present participle)
was (past finite)
carrying (present participle)
were (past finite)
walked (past finite)

were (past finite)
were (past finite)
dripping (present participle)
set out (past finite)
were (past finite)
yelping (present participle)
was (past finite)
was (past finite)
understood (past participle)
might (past finite)
find (plain infinitive)

EXERCISE 16 In the following short sentences, identify the type of verb (lexical verb, modal auxiliary, auxiliary of perfect aspect, progressive aspect, or passive voice or *do*) and identify the form of the verb.

1 Mary writes (lexical verb — present finite) a letter every day.
2 Mary wrote (lexical verb — past finite) a letter yesterday.
3 She will (auxiliary verb of mood — present finite) write (lexical verb — plain infinitive) a great deal more in the next few years.
4 Mary has (auxiliary verb of perfect aspect — present finite) been (auxiliary verb of progressive aspect — past participle) writing (lexical verb — present participle) many letters.
5 Mary had (auxiliary verb of perfect aspect — past finite) been (auxiliary verb of progressive aspect — past participle) writing (lexical verb — present participle) many letters.
6 Mary is (auxiliary verb of progressive aspect — present finite) writing (lexical verb — present participle) now.
7 Mary was (auxiliary verb of progressive aspect — past finite) writing (lexical verb — present participle) yesterday.
8 She could (auxiliary verb of mood — past finite) be (auxiliary verb of progressive aspect — plain infinitive) writing (lexical verb — present participle) a letter to her grandmother.

9. She <u>need</u> (auxiliary verb of mood — present finite) not <u>write</u> (lexical verb — plain infinitive) to her sister.
10. She <u>is able</u> (auxiliary verb of mood — present finite) <u>to write</u> (lexical verb — to infinitive) a letter in about one minute.
11. An average letter <u>is</u> (auxiliary verb of passive voice — present finite) <u>written</u> (lexical verb — past participle) in about 30 minutes.
12. One letter <u>was</u> (auxiliary verb of passive voice — past finite) <u>written</u> (lexical verb — past participle) in 10 minutes.
13. The next letter to her boyfriend <u>will</u> (auxiliary verb of mood — present finite) <u>be</u> (auxiliary verb of passive voice — plain infinitive) <u>written</u> (lexical verb — past participle) in 5 minutes.
14. Half of her letters <u>have</u> (auxiliary verb of perfect aspect — present finite) <u>been</u> (auxiliary verb of passive voice — past participle) <u>written</u> (lexical verb — past participle) by hand.
15. Many of her letters <u>had</u> (auxiliary verb of perfect aspect — past finite) <u>been</u> (auxiliary verb of passive voice — past participle) <u>written</u> (lexical verb — past participle) in pencil.
16. By next year all her letters <u>will</u> (auxiliary verb of mood — present finite) <u>have</u> (auxiliary verb of perfect aspect — plain infinitive) <u>been</u> (auxiliary verb of passive voice — past participle) <u>written</u> (lexical verb — past participle) on a word processor.

EXERCISE 17   In the following sentences, fill in the blank with the correct form of a verb. Even though you will probably intuitively know which form to use, explain your choice by referring to the order and form rules.

1. Mary <u>read</u> a book yesterday. (This sentence needs a lexical verb because there isn't one. This verb must have a finite form because it is the only one. It must be the past finite form because of *yesterday*.)
2. She <u>is</u> reading now. (Sentence needs a finite form because it is the first verb in the verb phrase; it must be a form of progressive *be* because the next verb has a present participle form; and it must be present because of the word *now*)
3. She <u>will</u> (*could, should,* etc.) read a great deal more in the next few years. (Sentence needs a finite form because it is the first verb in the verb phrase; it must be a central modal because the next verb has a plain infinitive form; it doesn't matter if it is present or past because almost all central modals have a future meaning.)

4 Mary has <u>been</u> reading a lot recently. (Sentence needs a form of progressive *be* because the next verb has a present participle form; *be* must have the past participle form because it comes after perfect *have*.)

5 Mary <u>could</u> have read more if she had had more time. (Sentence needs a finite form because it is the first verb in the verb phrase; it must be a central modal because the next verb has a plain infinitive form; here it must be the modal *could* because the verb phrase refers to a past situation.)

EXERCISE 18   Identify the function of each underlined *be* verb.

It <u>was</u> (lexical verb) in Burma, a sodden morning of the rains. A sickly light, like yellow tinfoil, <u>was</u> (auxiliary verb of progressive aspect) slanting over the high walls into the jail yard. We <u>were</u> (auxiliary verb of progressive aspect) waiting outside the condemned cells, a row of sheds fronted with double bars, like small animal cages. Each cell measured about ten feet by ten and <u>was</u> (lexical verb) quite bare within except for a plank bed and a pot of drinking water. In some of them brown silent men <u>were</u> (auxiliary verb of progressive aspects) squatting at the inner bars, with their blankets draped round them. These <u>were</u> (lexical verb) the condemned men, due <u>to be</u> (auxiliary verb of passive voice) hanged within the next week or two.

EXERCISE 19   In the following passage (adapted from *A Hanging* by George Orwell), sentence constituents have been set off with slashes. First name each sentence constituent. Then identify the type of lexical verb (*intransitive*, *copula*, or *transitive*) in the verb phrase, which has been underlined.

1 One prisoner **S** / had been <u>brought</u> **P** (transitive) / out of his cell **A**.
2 He **S** / <u>was</u> **P** (copula) / a Hindu, a puny wisp of a man, with a shaven head and vague liquid eyes **SA**.
3 He **S** / <u>had</u> **P** (transitive) / a thick, sprouting moustache, absurdly too big for his body, rather like the moustache of a comic man on the films **DO**.
4 Six tall Indian warders **S** / were <u>guarding</u> **P** (transitive) / him **DO** (and) / <u>getting</u> **P** (transitive) / him **DO** / ready for the gallows **OA**.
5 Two of them **S** / <u>stood by</u> **P** (intransitive) / with rifles and fixed bayonets **A**;
6 the others **S** / <u>handcuffed</u> **P** (transitive) / him **DO**,

7   passed **P** (transitive) / a chain **DO** / through his handcuffs **A** (and) fixed **P** (transitive) / it **DO** / to their belts **A**,

8   (and) / lashed **P** (transitive) / his arms **DO** / tight to his sides **A**.

9   They **S** / crowded **P** (intransitive) / very close about him **A**, / with their hands always on him in a careful, caressing grip, as though all the while feeling him to make sure he was there **A**.

10   It **S** / was **P** (copula) / like men handling a fish which is still alive and may jump back into the water **SA**.*

11   (But) he **S** / stood **P** (intransitive verb or copula verb) / quite unresisting, yielding his arms limply to the ropes **A**, / as though he hardly noticed what was happening **A**.

EXERCISE 20   Name each sentence constituent (set off with slashes) and identify the type of lexical verb.

1. Here **A** / I **S** / will describe **P** (monotransitive) / an unconventional method that I have been using to help people learn to read French **DO**.
2. I **S** / begin **P** (intransitive) / by offering students a reading passage that is an almost literal word-for-word translation from French into English **A**.
3. It **S** / has **P** (monotransitive) / English words **DO** / in French word order **A**.
4. A text of this sort **S** / quickly **A** / conveys **P** (monotransitive) / a sense of the overall patterns of French sentences **DO**.
5. In subsequent passages **A** / the most common French words **S** / are introduced **P** (monotransitive — passive sentence) / into the reading materials, where they take the place of their English equivalents **A**.
6. Step by step **A** / an ever larger portion of French words **S** / appears **P** (intransitive) / in the reading passages **A** / (and) the text **S** / progressively **A** / changes **P** (intransitive) / into French **A**.
7. Starting with a text that a monolingual English speaker can understand with no more than a minimum of explanation **A** /, the student **S** / is led **P** (monotransitive — passive sentence) /, by gradual steps **A** /, to a text that is written in French **A**.
8. In other words **A** / I **S** / offer **P** (ditransitive) / students **IO** / a reading passage that is an almost literal word-for-word translation from French into English **DO**.

* Even though the part after the *be* verb starts with a preposition (*like*), this part is felt to be a S A rather than an A because it could be easily substituted with an adjective like *soft* or *gentle*.

9 English words in French word order **S** / <u>make</u> **P** (complex transitive) / the text **DO** / easy to understand **OA**.

10 I **S** / <u>consider</u> **P** (complex transitive) / such a text **DO** / a helpful one in quickly conveying a sense of the overall patterns of French sentences **OA**.

11 In subsequent passages **A**, / common French words **S** / are <u>introduced</u> **P** <u>(monotransitive)</u>/ into the reading materials, where they take the place of their English equivalents **A**.

12 Starting with a text that a monolingual English speaker can understand with no more than a minimum of explanation **S** / <u>is</u> **P** (copula) / useful **SA** / because the student is led, by gradual steps, to a text that is written in French **A**.

EXERCISE 21   Create sentences with different types of direct objects: (a) single word, (b) phrase, (c) finite clause, and (d) non-finite clause. Answers may vary. Here are a few possible answers:*

see
(a) I see you.
(b) I saw a red cat.
(c) I see (that) you want to tell me something.
(d) I saw them reading the newspaper.

order
(a) I ordered coffee.
(b) I usually order a cup of tea.
(c) She ordered that he stay in bed.*
(d) He ordered me to bring him a cup of tea.

ask
(a) I asked her.
(b) She asked her mother.
(c) He has asked me if I could help him.
(d) I will ask him to join me.

* In a clause after a verb like *order*, the finite verb is in the subjunctive mood, which has no -s ending for the third person singular.

EXERCISE 22 Name each sentence constituent (set off with slashes) and identify the type of transitive verb. Then change the active sentence into a passive one.

1 Everyone **S** / must have <u>admired</u> **P** (monotransitive) / him **DO**.
He must have been admired (by everyone).
2 Students **S** / must <u>pay attention to</u> **P** (monotransitive) / the teacher **DO**.
The teacher must be paid attention to (by students).
3 My brother **S** / has <u>given</u> **P** (ditransitive) / me **IO** / some bookcases **DO**.
Some book cases have been given to me (by my brother).
I have been given some bookcases (by my brother).
4 They **S** / <u>made</u> **P** (monotransitive) / me leave immediately **DO**.
I was made to leave immediately (by them).
5 We **S** / <u>believe</u> **P** (monotransitive) / him to be honest **DO**.
He is believed to be honest (by us).
6 We **S** / are <u>electing</u> **P** (complex transitive) / her **DO** / chair **OA**.
She is being elected chair (by us.)

EXERCISE 23 Identify the underlined past participle forms. Which ones are used as adjectives?

My father came across the field carrying the body of the boy who had been <u>drowned</u> (part of passive verb phrase) The men were muddy and <u>exhausted</u> (adjective) as if they were <u>ashamed</u> (adjective). Even the dogs were <u>dispirited</u> (adjective) the men tense and <u>determined</u> (adjective) It was <u>understood</u> (part of passive verb phrase)

EXERCISE 24 Identify each underlined verb as auxiliary (aux.) of mood, perfect aspect, progressive aspect, or passive voice or lexical (lex.), i.e. intransitive, copula, monotransitive, ditransitive, or complex transitive. If necessary, create a short sentence to help you identify the type of lexical verb.

Between two oval hills of pink granite there<u>'s</u> (lex.: copula) a small crescent of beach. The boys, <u>wearing</u> (lex.: monotransitive [*they wear their bathing suits*]) their bathing suits (as they never <u>do</u> (lex.: intransitive) on canoe trips but only around the camp where they <u>might</u> (aux.: of mood) <u>be</u> (aux.: of passive voice) <u>seen</u> (lex.: monotransitive [*girls see them*]) by girls), <u>are</u> (aux.: of progressive aspect) <u>doing</u> (lex.: monotransitive) their laundry, <u>standing up</u> (lex.: intransitive) to their knees and <u>swabbing</u> (lex.: monotransitive) their wet T-shirts and underpants with yellow bars of Sunlight soap. This only <u>happens</u> (lex.: intransitive) when they <u>run out of</u> (lex.: monotransitive) clothes, or when the stench of dirty socks in the cabin <u>becomes</u> (lex.: copula) too overpowering. Darce, the counselor <u>is</u> (aux.: of progressive aspect) <u>supervising</u> (lex.: intransitive), <u>stretched out</u> (lex.: monotransitive [*he stretches himself out*]) on a rock, <u>taking</u> (lex.: monotransitive) the sun on his already tanned torso and <u>smoking</u> (lex.: monotransitive) a fag. It'<u>s</u> (aux.: of passive voice) <u>forbidden</u> (lex.: monotransitive [*someone forbids something*]) <u>to smoke</u> (lex.:intransitive) in front of the campers but he <u>knows</u> (lex.:monotransitive [*he knows something*]) this bunch <u>won</u>'t (aux.: of mood [*will*]) <u>tell</u> (lex.:intransitive). <u>To be</u> (lex.: copula) on the safe side he'<u>s</u> (lex.: copula) furtive about it, <u>holding</u> (lex.: monotransitive) the cigarette down close to the rock and <u>sneaking</u> (lex.: monotransitive) quick puffs.

EXERCISE 25   For the following expressions, first create a meaningful sentence. Then indicate the function of the verb (transitive or intransitive) and the type of multi-word verb. Answers may vary. Here are a few possible answers:

How did that <u>come about</u> (= happen)? (intransitive — phrasal)
I <u>came across</u> (= discovered) *a beautiful book.* (transitive — prepositional)
We <u>came by</u> (= passed) *your house last night.* (transitive — prepositional)
Please <u>come down</u> (= descend) *fast.* (intransitive — phrasal)
He <u>came in for</u> (= experienced) *a big surprise.* (transitive — phrasal-prepositional)
Please <u>come off</u> your high horse. (= don't be so conceited) (transitive — prepositional)
He <u>came on</u> very strong. (= He flirted very much with me) (intransitive — phrasal)
He <u>came out</u>. (= He told people that he is gay) (intransitive — phrasal)
He <u>came up with</u> (= thought of) *a good idea.* (transitive — phrasal prepositional)
I am sure he will <u>come round to</u> (= eventually accept) *my way of thinking.* (transitive — phrasal prepositional)

EXERCISE 26   Underline all nouns and identify whether it is (a) proper or common, and (b) count or non-count.

dad (common, count)
shot (common, count)
time (common, count)
Low Veld (proper, non-count)
smoke (common, count)
yelp (common, count)
dog (common, count)
troop (common, count)
impala (common, count)
grass (common, non-count)
yards (common, count)
ridge (common, count)
wall (common, count)
feet (common, count)
buck* (common, count)
pausing (common, non-count)
swerving (common, non-count)
feet (common, count)
friend (common count)
sight (common, count)
Nature (proper, non-count)
beauty (common, non-count)

EXERCISE 27   Identify all words used as adjectives and adverbs.

His <u>thin strong bony</u> legs passed by at <u>eye</u> level every morning as they lay, <u>stranded</u> on the <u>hard smooth</u> sand. Washed up <u>thankfully</u> out of the swirl and buffet of the city, they were <u>happy</u> to lie <u>there</u>, but because they were accustomed to telling the time by their nerves'** response to the <u>different</u> tensions of the city, children crying in flats, lorries going <u>heavily</u> and bicycles jangling for <u>early</u> morning, skid of tyres, sound of frying and the <u>human insect</u> noise of thousands talking and walking and eating at midday — the <u>tensionless</u> shore keyed <u>only</u> to the tide gave them a sense of timelessness that, <u>however</u>*** much they rejoiced <u>mentally</u>, troubled their <u>habit-impressed</u> bodies with a lack of pressure. So the sound of his feet, thudding <u>nearer</u> over the sand, passing their heads with the <u>deep</u> sound of a man breathing in the heat above the <u>rolled up, faded</u> trousers, passing <u>away</u> up the beach and shrinking into the figure of an <u>Indian</u> fisherman, began to be something to be waited for. His coming and going divided the morning into three; the <u>short early</u> time before he passed, the time when he was <u>actually</u> passing and the <u>largish</u> chunk of <u>warm</u> midday that followed when he had gone.

* *Buck* is an unusual noun in that it is count, but does not get an -s to signal the plural (in South African English). Other such nouns are *sheep* and *fish*.

** This is a specifying genitive, which should not be regarded as an adjective. See section 6.2.

*** *However*, is often used as sentence adverb. Here though it modifies the word *much*.

EXERCISE 28   Identify the word class of all underlined words and indicate whether they are used dependently or independently.

His (possessive pronoun — dependent)
they (personal pronoun — independent)
the (article — dependent)
they (personal pronoun — independent)
their (possessive pronoun — dependent)
thousands (numeral — independent)

them (personal pronoun — independent)
that (relative pronoun — independent)
his (possessive pronoun — dependent)
a (article — dependent)
His (possessive pronoun — dependent)
that (relative pronoun — independent)

EXERCISE 29   Underline all words used as coordinators. Set off the parts that they introduce or connect with square brackets. Has this author kept the structures connected with a coordinator parallel?

His thin strong bony legs passed by at eye level every morning as they lay, stranded on the hard smooth sand. [Washed up thankfully out of the [swirl] <u>and</u> [buffet] of the city, they were happy to lie there], <u>but</u> [because they were accustomed to telling the time by their nerves' response to the different tensions of the city — [children crying in flats], [lorries going heavily] <u>and</u> [bicycles jangling for early morning], [skid of tyres], [sound of frying] <u>and</u> [the human insect noise of thousands [talking] <u>and</u> [walking] <u>and</u> [eating] at midday] — the tensionless shore keyed only to the tide gave them a sense of timelessness that, however much they rejoiced mentally, troubled their habit-impressed bodies with a lack of pressure]. <u>So</u>* the sound of his feet, thudding nearer over the sand, passing their heads with the deep sound of a man breathing in the heat above the rolled-up, faded trousers, [passing away up the beach] <u>and</u> [shrinking into the figure of an Indian fisherman], began to be something to be waited for. His [coming] <u>and</u> [going] divided the morning into three; [the short early time before he passed], [the time when he was actually passing] <u>and</u> [the largish chunk of warm midday that followed when he had gone].

In this passage, the author has kept all items parallel. A few examples are given here:

[swirl] <u>and</u> [buffet]: two nouns

---

* *So* is a coordinate conjunction linking two independent sentences. They have not been set off with square brackets here.

[Washed up …there], but [because they …at midday]: two main clauses, each starting with an adverbial

[children crying in flats], [lorries going heavily] and [bicycles jangling for early morning]: three non-finite -*ing* clauses, each with its own subject.

[skid of tyres], [sound of frying] and [the human insect noise of thousands talking and walking and eating at midday]: three nouns, each followed by an *of* phrase.

[talking] and [walking] and [eating]: three non-finite verb.

EXERCISE 30   Underline all words used as subordinator. Set off the parts that they introduce with square brackets. Identify the subordinator as subordinating conjunction (SC), relative pronoun (RP) or relative adverb (RA), or as interrogative pronoun (IP) or interrogative adverb (IA).

His thin strong bony legs passed by at eye level every morning [as (SC) they lay, stranded on the hard smooth sand]. Washed up thankfully out of the swirl and buffet of the city, they were happy to lie there, but [because (SC) they were accustomed to telling the time by their nerves' response to the different tensions of the city, children crying in flats, lorries going heavily and bicycles jangling for early morning, skid of tyres, sound of frying and the human insect noise of thousands talking and walking and eating at midday] — the tensionless shore keyed only to the tide gave them a sense of timelessness [that (RP), [however much (SC) they rejoiced mentally], troubled their habit-impressed bodies with a lack of pressure]. So the sound of his feet, thudding nearer over the sand, passing their heads with the deep sound of a man breathing in the heat above the rolled-up, faded trousers, passing away up the beach and shrinking into the figure of an Indian fisherman, began to be something to be waited for. His coming and going divided the morning into three; the short early time [before (SC) he passed] the time [when (RA) he was actually passing and the largish chunk of warm midday [that (RP) followed [when (SC) he had gone]]].

233   Key to the exercises

EXERCISE 31 Underline all words used as prepositions. Set off the parts that they introduce with square brackets.

His thin strong bony legs passed by [at eye level] every morning as they lay, stranded [on the hard smooth sand]. Washed up thankfully [out of the swirl and buffet] [of the city], they were happy to* lie there, but because they were accustomed to [telling the time] [by their nerves' response [to the different tensions [of the city]]], children crying [in flats], lorries going heavily and bicycles jangling [for early morning], skid [of tyres], sound [of frying] and the human insect noise [of thousands] talking and walking and eating [at midday] — the tensionless shore keyed only [to the tide] gave them a sense [of timelessness that, however much they rejoiced mentally, troubled their habit-impressed bodies [with a lack [of pressure]]]. So the sound [of his feet], thudding nearer [over the sand], passing their heads [with the deep sound [of a man breathing [in the heat [above the rolled-up, faded trousers]]]], passing away [up the beach] and shrinking [into the figure [of an Indian fisherman]], began to be [*something*] to be waited [for]. His coming and going divided the morning [into three]; the short early time [before he passed], the time when he was actually passing and the largish chunk [of warm midday] that followed when he had gone.

EXERCISE 32 Identify the word class of each word.

My (possessive pronoun) late (adjective) dad (noun) was (lexical verb) a (article) magnificent (adjective) shot (noun). One (cardinal numeral) time (noun) when (relative adverb) we (personal pronoun) were (auxiliary verb) hunting (lexical verb) in (preposition) the (article) Low Veld (noun) and (coordinate conjunction) had (auxiliary verb) paused (lexical verb) for (preposition) a (article) smoke (noun), there (adverb) was (lexical verb) the (article) yelp (noun) of (preposition) a (article) wild (adjective) dog (noun), and (coordinate conjunction) a (article) troop (noun) of (preposition) impala (noun) came (here used as auxiliary verb) bounding (lexical verb) over (preposition) the (article) tall (adjective) grass (noun). Opposite (preposition) us (personal pronoun), three hundred (cardinal numeral) yards (noun) off (adverb), was (lexical verb) a (article) stony (adjective) ridge (noun) like (preposition) a (article) wall (noun), six (cardinal numeral) feet (noun) high (adjective). You (personal pronoun) would (auxiliary verb) think (lexical verb) those (demonstrative pronoun) buck (noun) would (auxiliary verb) avoid (lexical verb) it (personal pronoun), but (coordinate conjunction) no (interjection), they (personal pronoun)

* *To* as part of a *to* infinitive is not considered a preposition. It is considered part of the verb, like *-ing* would be part of a verb like *walking*.

went (lexical verb) straight (adverb) at (preposition) it (personal pronoun). One (cardinal numeral) after (preposition) the (article) other (indefinite pronoun), without (preposition) pausing (noun) or (coordinate conjunction) swerving (noun), they (personal pronoun) leapt (lexical verb) over (preposition) it (personal pronoun). They (personal pronoun) cleared (lexical verb) it (personal pronoun) by (preposition) three (cardinal numeral) feet (noun). I (personal pronoun) tell (lexical verb) you (personal pronoun), friend (noun),␣t (personal pronoun) was (lexical verb) a (article) beautiful (adjective) sight (noun). You (personal pronoun) can (auxiliary verb) not (adverb) beat (lexical verb) Nature (noun) for (preposition) beauty (noun), eh (interjection).

EXERCISE 33   Identify the underlined phrases.

After a few days (PP)
good morning (NP)
looking up (VP)
shining (AdjP)
so impartially (AdvP)

slightly bloodshot from the sun (AdjP)
slightly (AdvP)
like the good useful teeth of an animal (PP)
taut (AdjP)
control (VP)

EXERCISE 34   Several nouns, functioning as heads of noun phrases, have been underlined. Indicate with square brackets the beginning and end of the noun phrase and analyze the phrase further as has been done in the examples above.

[a few (det:indefinite pronoun) days (head:noun)]
[a (det:art) shining (premod:AdjP) dark (premod:AdjP) dome (head:noun) surrounded with curly hair given a strong liveliness by the sharp coarse strokes of gray hairs (postmod:NFC)]
[the (det:art) beautiful (premod:AdjP) curved (premod:AdjP) nose (head:noun) handed out so impartially to Indians (postmod:NFC)]
[dark (premod:AdjP) eyes (head:noun) slightly bloodshot from the sun (postmod:AdjP)] [strong (premod:AdjP) uneven (premod:AdjP) teeth (head:noun) that projected slightly like the good useful teeth of an animal (postmod:FC)].
[his (det:possessive pronoun) legs (head:noun)]
[the (det:article) dark (premod:AdjP), dull-skinned (premod:AdjP) feet (head:noun) with the few black hairs on the big toe (postmod:PP)]
[the (det:art) long (premod:AdjP) hard (premod:AdjP) shaft (head:noun) of the shin tightly covered with [smooth (premod:AdjP) shiny (premod:AdjP) skin (head:noun)] (postmod:PP)]

[the (det:art) pull (head:noun) of the tendons at his ankle like the taut ropes that control the sail of a ship (postmod:PP)].
[his (det:possessive pronoun) fisherman's (premod:AdjP (classifying genitive)) life (head:noun)]
[their (det:possessive pronoun) holiday (premod:AdjP) freedom (head:noun)].

EXERCISE 35   In the following sentences noun phrases are underlined and any postmodifying clause or phrase has been put between parentheses. Identify the PostMod (a) as finite clause, non-finite clause, or phrase and (b) as restrictive or non-restrictive. The first one has been done for you.

1   Lincoln, (who was one of the truly great men of all time) (FC, non-restrictive), led the US during the Civil War.
2   Lincoln once said that his wife had got a notion (that he would be assassinated) (FC, restrictive).
3   His attempt (to reassure her) (NFC, restrictive) was to carry a cane on his nightly walks to the War Department.
4   Any person (plotting to kill him) (NFC, restrictive) was going to find a way (to do it anyway),(NFC, restrictive) he believed.
5   Lincoln, (a very public figure) (NP, non-restrictive), simply was not willing to live in fear despite this ever present threat.
6   The fact (that Lincoln was assassinated) (FC, non-restrictive), / now / seems to take on* / an ironic meaning.
7   The stories (concerning** President Lincoln's courage and humor) (PP, restrictive) / have made / him / a legend.

EXERCISE 36   Underline all finite relative clauses. Double underline the head noun, circle the relative pronoun (in **boldface** here), or indicate where the pronoun *that* could occur, and identify the function the relative pronoun has within the clause that it introduces.

Until they became ordinary, dull grown men, **who** S drank beer and made babies, the little village boys were a special set all on their own. They were kings **whom DO** no one ruled. They wandered where they willed from dawn to dusk and only condescended to come home at dusk because they were afraid of the horrible things in the dark **that S** might pounce on them. Unlike

* *Seems to take on* is regarded as one VP.

** As you saw in Section 5.4 *concerning* can be used as preposition.

the little (girls) <u>**who** S adored household chores and drawing water</u>, it was only now and then that the boys showed themselves as useful attachments to any household. When the first hard rains of summer fell, small dark (shapes), <u>**which** S were quite naked except for their loin-cloths</u>, sped out of the village into the bush. [...] They knew it had struggled to emerge from its (burrow), <u>**which** S had been flooded by the sudden rush of storm water</u> and as they pulled out the animal they would say, pityingly: 'Birds have more sense than rabbits, moles and porcupines. They build their homes in trees.'

EXERCISE 37

Underline all phrases and finite and non-finite clauses that function as postmodifiers of nouns. Circle the noun that is modified (in **boldface** here). Identify how it is realized and whether it is restrictive or non-restrictive.

In the **summer** of 1859, (PP — restrictive) a French **acrobat** called Blondin (NFC — restrictive) strung a rope across the **gorge** just below Niagara Falls (PP — restrictive). On June 30, he was ready to walk from the United States to Canada across that **rope**, which was more than 150 feet above Niagara's violent waters (FC — non-restrictive).

Blondin, sitting down on the rope halfway across (NFC — non-restrictive), scared the crowd as he lowered a string to a **boat** below (AdvP — restrictive), pulled up a bottle and took a drink. Then he continued his terrifying walk. Eighteen minutes after he began his stroll, he was greeted by a **crowd** cheering tremendously as he stepped on the Canadian side (NFC — restrictive). In less than seven minutes he completed his **trip** back to the United States (AdvP — restrictive).

People coming to the Falls that summer to see what the acrobat would do next (NFC — restrictive) were never disappointed by **Blondin**, who always thought of different tricks (FC — non-restrictive). He walked across with a **sack** over his head (PP — restrictive)! He pushed a wheelbarrow across! He did a headstand on the rope! And once **Blondin**, ready for a snack (AdjP — non-restrictive), took a table, chair and stove with him to the **middle** of the rope (PP — restrictive) and fixed an omelet!

One time, he convinced his **manager**, Harry Colcord (NP — non-restrictive), to ride across on his back; however, he did not try that **stunt**, a near disaster (NP — non-restrictive), again. A support wire snapped and jerked the main rope sideways. Finally, **Blondin**, managing to keep himself and his manager from falling (NFC — non-restrictive), was able to land safely on the other side after forty-five agonizing minutes.

EXERCISE 38   Underline each finite and non-finite verb phrase and identify whether it is finite (F) or no-finite (NF).

After a few days, he <u>began to say</u> (F) good morning, and <u>looking up</u> (NF) they <u>found</u> (F) his face, a long head with a shining dark dome <u>surrounded</u> (NF) with curly hair <u>given</u> (NF) a strong liveliness by the sharp coarse strokes of grey hairs, the beautiful curved nose <u>handed out</u> (NF) so impartially to Indians, dark eyes slightly bloodshot from the sun, a wide muscular mouth <u>smiling</u> (NF) on strong uneven teeth that <u>projected</u> (F) slightly like the good useful teeth of an animal. But it <u>was</u> (F) by his legs they <u>would have known</u> (F) him; the dark, dull-skinned feet with the few black hairs on the big toe, the long hard shaft of the shin tightly <u>covered</u> (NF) with smooth shiny skin, the pull of the tendons at his ankle like the taut ropes that <u>control</u> (F) the sail of a ship.

EXERCISE 39   Underline each adjective, and indicate with brackets the beginning and end of the phrase of which it is the head.

After a few days, he began to say [<u>good</u>] morning, and looking up they found his face, a [<u>long</u>] head with a [<u>shining</u>] [<u>dark</u>] dome surrounded with [<u>curly</u>] hair given a [<u>strong</u>] liveliness by the [<u>sharp</u>] [<u>coarse</u>] strokes of [<u>gray</u>] hairs, the [<u>beautiful</u>] [<u>curved</u>]nose handed out so impartially to Indians, [<u>dark</u>] eyes [slightly <u>bloodshot</u> from the sun], a [<u>wide</u>] [<u>muscular</u>] mouth smiling on [<u>strong</u>] [<u>uneven</u>] teeth that projected slightly like the [<u>good</u>] [<u>useful</u>] teeth of an animal. But it was by his legs they would have known him; the [<u>dark</u>], [<u>dull-skinned</u>] feet with the few [<u>black</u>] hairs on the [<u>big</u>] toe, the [<u>long</u>] [<u>hard</u>] shaft of the shin tightly covered with [<u>smooth</u>] [<u>shiny</u>] skin, the pull of the tendons at his ankle like the [<u>taut</u>] ropes that control the sail of a ship.

EXERCISE 40   Underline each adverb, and with square brackets indicate the beginning and end of the phrase of which it is the head.

They [<u>idly</u>] watched him go, not because they were so envious of his fisherman's life that they would [<u>really</u>] have liked to live it themselves, but because it had about it the frame of their holiday freedom. They looked at him [<u>enough</u> to think that they should have respect for one who has put a little space between himself and the rest of the world]. It's a good life said the young man, the words [not <u>quite</u>] hitting the nail of this respect. "I can [<u>just</u>] see you…' said the girl, smiling. She saw him in his blue creased suit, carrying a bottle of gin wrapped in brown paper, a packet of banana and the evening paper.

EXERCISE 41   Underline each preposition and indicate with square brackets the beginning and end of the phrase of which it is the head.

[After a few days], he began to say good morning, and looking up they found his face, a long head [with a shining dark dome surrounded [with curly hair given a strong liveliness [by the sharp coarse strokes [of grey hairs]]], the beautiful curved nose handed out so impartially [to Indians], dark eyes slightly bloodshot [from the sun], a wide muscular mouth smiling [on strong uneven teeth that projected slightly [like the good useful teeth [of an animal]]]. But it was [by his legs] they would have known him; the dark, dull-skinned feet [with the few black hairs [on the big toe]], the long hard shaft [of the shin tightly covered [with smooth shiny skin]], the pull [of the tendons] [at his ankle] [like the taut ropes that control the sail [of a ship]].

EXERCISE 42   The constituents at sentence level have been set off with slashes. For each constituent, identify its function and its realization.

They **S:NP** / did (not **A:AdvP**) know **P:VP** / his name **DO:NP**, / and / now **A:AdvP**, / although they might have asked the first day and got away with it, **A:FC** / it **S:NP** / was **P:VP** / suddenly **A:AdvP** / impossible **SA:AdjP** / because he didn't ask them theirs **A:FC**. / So / their you's and he's and I's **S:NP** / took on **P:VP** / the positiveness of names **DO:NP**, / and / yet **A:AdvP** / they **S:NP** / seemed to deepen **P:VP** / their sense of communication **DO:NP** / by the fact that they introduced none of the objectivity that names must always bring **A:PP**. / He **S:NP** / spoke (to them **IO:PP**) (quite a lot **A:AdvP**) about **P:VP** / Johannesburg, to which he assumed they must belong, as that was his generalization of city life **DO:NP**, / and / he **S:NP** / knew **P:VP**, / sympathetically **A:AdvP** / that they were city people **DO:FC** /. And / although they didn't live there, but somewhere near on a smaller pattern **A:FC**, / they **S:NP** / answered **P:VP** / as if they did **A:FC**. / They **S:NP** / also **A:AdvP** / talked (a little **A:NP**) of **P:VP** / his life, or rather (of) the processes of the sugar refinery from which his life depended **DO:NP**. / They **S:NP** / found **P:VP** / it **DO:NP** / fascinating **OA:AdjP** /.

EXERCISE 43   Analyze each sentence at sentence level, naming the function and realization of sentence constituents. Do not analyze the constituents further.

At a hearing of a Senate committee investigating working conditions in New York City in 1883 **A:PP** /, Conrad Carl, a tailor **S:NP** /, testified **P:VP** / that before the Civil War his had been "a very still business, very quiet **DO:FC**." / Then **A:AdvP** / the sewing machine **S:NP** / appeared **P:VP**. / We **S:NP** / admit **P:VP** / it stitched very nicely, nicer than the tailor could do **DO:FC**. / And / the

239   Key to the exercises

bosses **S:NP** / said **P:VP** /: 'We want you to use the sewing machine …' **DO:FC** / Then **A:AdvP** / he **S:NP** / was asked **P:VP** / how this innovation affected the tailors **DO:FC**. / Carl **S:NP** / replied **P:VP** /: " We work now in excitement — in a hurry **DO:FC**. / It **S:NP** / is **P:VP** / hunting **SA:NP** /; it **S:NP** / is **P:VP** / not **A:AdvP** / work **SA:NP** / at all **A:PP** ; it **S:NP** / is **P:VP** / a hunt **SA:NP**."

EXERCISE 44 Several non-finite clauses have been underlined. Which ones are used as direct objects of a sentence or a clause?

to come home at dusk (used as DO) to fall (**not** used as DO)
to encounter (**not** used as DO) peeping out (**not** used as DO)
doing household chores (used as DO) to emerge from its burrow (**not** used as DO)
drawing water (used as DO)

EXERCISE 45 Analyze the following sentences into sentence constituents and name their realizations. Then state in your own words what the logical relationship between the non-finite adverbial clause and the main clause is.

1 Running down the street **A:NFC**, / he **S:NP** / fell down **P:VP**.
   Running down the street expresses a 'while' or 'because' meaning.
2 They **S:NP** / ran **P:VP** / down the street **A:PP** /, stumbling over every thing that was in their way **A:NFC**.
   Stumbling over … their way expresses a 'while' meaning.
3 He **S:NP** / went **P:VP** / to the store **A:PP** / to buy some groceries **A:NFC**.
   To buy some groceries expresses a 'purpose' meaning.
4 To think that she had so much homework **A:NFC** /, it **TempS:NP** / surprises **P:VP** / me **DO:NP** / she went out last night **S:FC**.
   To think that he had so much homework expresses a 'hypothesis' meaning.

EXERCISE 46 Analyze each sentence at sentence level by inserting slashes to set off sentence constituents. Then give the function and realization of each sentence constituent. Do not analyze any further.

1 Until they became ordinary, dull grown men, who drank beer and made babies, **A:FC** / the little village boys **S:NP** / were **P:VP** / a special set all on their own **SA:NP**.

2 They **S:NP** / were **P:VP** / kings whom no one ruled **SA:NP**.
3 They **S:NP** / wandered **P:VP** / where they willed **A:FC** / from dawn to dusk **A:PP** / and **(no function)** / only **A:AdvP** / condescended **P:VP** / to come home at dusk **DO:NFC** / because they were afraid to encounter the horrible things in the dark that might pounce on them **A:FC**.
4 Unlike the little girls who adored doing household chores and drawing water, **A:PP** / it **TempS:NP** / was **P: VP** / only now and then **A:AdvP** / that the boys showed themselves as useful attachments to any household **S: FC**.
5 When the first hard rains of summer had started to fall, **A:FC** / small dark shapes, quite naked except for their loin-cloths, **S:NP** / sped out **P:VP** / of the village **A:PP** / into the bush **A:PP**.
6 They **S:NP** / knew **P:VP** / that the first downpour had drowned all the wild rabbits, moles and porcupines in their burrows in the earth **DO:FC**.
7 As they crouched down near the entrances to the burrows, **A:FC** / they **S:NP** / would see **P:VP** / a small drowned nose of an animal peeping out; **DO:NP** / they **S:NP** / knew **P:VP** / it had struggled to emerge from its burrow, flooded by the sudden rush of storm water **DO:FC** / and **(no function)** / as they pulled out the animal **A:FC** / they **S:NP** / would say **P:VP** /, pityingly: **A:AdvP** / 'Birds have more sense than rabbits, moles and porcupines. They build their homes in trees' **DO:FC**.

EXERCISE 47 Identify the sentence type (normal, passive, existential, cleft, or extraposed) and analyze the sentences at sentence levd=el naming functions and ralizations of the constituents.

1 It **tempS:NP** / is **P:VP** / an unusual method **SA:NP** / to offer students a reading passage that is an almost literal word-for-word translation from French into English **S:NFC**. (extraposed sentence type)
2 It **S:NP** / is **P:VP** / English words in French word order that make the text easy to understand **SA:NP**. (cleft sentence type)
3 I **S:NP** / consider **P:VP** / it **tempDO:NP** / helpful **OA:AdjP** / to quickly convey a sense of the overall patterns of French sentences **DO:NFC**. (extraposed sentence type)
4 In subsequent passages **A:PP**, / there **A:AdvP** / are **P:VP** / common French words introduced into the reading materials, where they take the place of their English equivalents **S:NP**. (existential sentence type)

5 It **tempS:NP** / is **P:VP** / useful **SA:AdjP** / to start with a text that a monolingual English speaker can understand with no more than a minimum of explanation **S:FC** / because the student is led, by gradual steps, to a text that is written in French **A:NFC**. (extraposed sentence type)

EXERCISE 48   Underline finite verbs and circle subordinators and coordinators (in **boldface** here). Identify main clauses and dependent clauses (here in *italics*), and then determine whether the following sentences are simple, compound, complex or compound-complex.

1 Every act **that** *every human adult performs* communicates. (complex)
2 Within hours of birth, a human infant is already responding to the rhythms of the mother's speech, in 'a dance-like sharing of microbody motion.' (simple)
3 Even involuntary acts communicate, / they are symptoms, / **and** they are modified in significant ways; (compound first part)
/ a sneeze may be unavoidable, / **but** the manner of it betrays attitudes of hygiene, courtesy, **or** self-restraint. (compound second part)
(compound whole sentence)
4 **When** *the act exists because it communicates*, / it becomes symbolic: a handshake is for friendship or frankness, a bow for deference or submission, an affected sob to evoke sympathy or pity. (compound-complex)

EXERCISE 49   Analyze the following noun phrases into its constituents: determiners, premodifiers, head and postmodifiers and name their realizations. Do not analyze further.

1 the / rhythms / of the mother's speech
    the   det:article
    rhythms   head:noun
    of ... speech   postmodifier:PP
2 the mother's / speech
    the mother's   det: specifying genitive
    speech   head:noun

3   our / most complex / system / of signs
    our   det:poss. pronoun
    most complex   premodifier:AdjP
    system   head:noun
    of signs   postmodifier:PP
4   a / structure / of words and relationships / that interpenetrates our world so thoroughly that nothing out there can be disentangled from it
    a   det:article
    structure   head:noun
    of ... rel.ships postmodifier:PP
    that ... it   postmodifier:FC
5   a / dance-like / sharing / of microbody motion
    a   det:article
    dance-like   premodifier:AdjP
    sharing   head:noun
    of ... motion   postmodifier:PP

EXERCISE 50   Indicate the beginning and the end of the phrase of which the noun is the head. If there is a postmodifier in the phrase, indicate how it is realized.

[Every act / that every human adult performs **postmod:FC**]
[hours / of birth **postmod:PP**]
[the / rhythms / of the mother's speech **postmod:PP**]
['a dance-like sharing / of microbody motion' **postmod:PP**]
[involuntary acts]
[symptoms, / modified in significant ways — a sneeze may be unavoidable **postmod:NFC**]
[the / manner / of it **postmod:PP**]
[attitudes / of hygiene, courtesy, or self-restraint **postmod:PP**]
[a handshake] (remember *for friendship or frankness* is considered an SA)
[a bow] (remember *for deference or submission* is considered an SA)
[an / affected / sob] (remember *to evoke sympathy or pity* is considered an SA)
[an / intricate / structure / of words and [relationships / that interpenetrates our world so thoroughly that nothing out there can be disentangled from it **postmod:FC**] **postmod:PP** (of *structure*)]
[language]

243   Key to the exercises

EXERCISE 51

1. How many separate postmodifiers does the noun *face* have? Set it/them off with square brackets.
The noun <u>face</u> has only <u>one</u> postmodifier.

After a few days, he began to say good morning, and looking up they found his <u>face</u>, [a long <u>head</u> ... animal].

2. How many separate postmodifiers does the noun *head* have? Set each one off with square brackets.
The noun <u>head</u> has only one postmodifier.

a long <u>head</u> [with ...animal]

3. How many complements does the preposition *with* have? Set each one off with square brackets.
The preposition *with* has four complements.

with [a shining ... grey hairs], [the beautiful curved nose ... Indians], [dark eyes ... the sun], [a wide muscular mouth ... animal].

4. In the following part of the sentence, several other nouns have been underlined. If the underlined noun has a postmodifier, set it off with square brackets. Be sure to set off the complete modifier, which in turn may include another noun that has a postmodifier.

a long head with a shining dark <u>dome</u> [surrounded with curly <u>hair</u> (given a strong liveliness by the sharp coarse strokes of grey hairs)], the beautiful curved <u>nose</u> [handed out so impartially to Indians], dark <u>eyes</u> [slightly bloodshot from the sun], a wide muscular <u>mouth</u> [smiling on strong uneven <u>teeth</u> [that projected slightly like the good useful teeth of an animal]].

5   Identify the realization of each postmodifier.

NP
a long **head**
   postmod: PP
   with ... animals.
      complement: NP
      a shining dark **dome**
         postmod:NFC
         surrounded with curly **hair**
            postmod:NFC
            given a strong liveliness by the sharp coarse **strokes**
               postmod:PP
               of gray hairs,

NP
the beautiful curved **nose***
   postmod:NFC
   handed out so impartially to **Indians**,

NP
dark **eyes**
   postmod:AdjP
   slightly bloodshot from the sun,

NP
a wide muscular **mouth**
   postmod:NFC
   smiling on strong uneven **teeth**
      postmod:FC
      that projected slightly like the good useful **teeth**
         postmod PP
         of an animal.

*   The preposition *with* has been written down to show at what level these phrases occur, but even though the preposition *with* may be understood, you should analyze what you see. Therefore, this is a noun phrase.

EXERCISE 52   Analyze each clause set off with brackets into its constituents. If the non-finite clause contains another clause, analyze it, too. Do not analyze further at the phrase level.

(a long head)

1   with a shining dark dome [surrounded **P:VP** / with curly hair **A:PP** [given **P:VP** / a strong liveliness **DO:NP** / by the sharp coarse strokes of grey hairs **A:PP**,]]
2   (with) the beautiful curved nose [handed out **P:VP** / so impartially **A:AdjP** / to Indians **IO:PP**,]
3   (with) dark eyes [slightly bloodshot **SA:AdjP** / from the sun **A:PP**],
4   (with) a wide muscular mouth [smiling **SA:NFC** / on strong uneven teeth **A:PP** [that **S:NP** / projected **P:VP** / slightly like the good useful teeth of an animal **A:AdvP**]].

EXERCISE 53   Answer the following questions and fill in the blanks where necessary

1   There is only one simple sentence. Which one is it? *(a) I don't think so.*

2   Analyze sentence (b) *I don't think I really saw all this*, by filling in the blanks:

There are two *finite* verbs, namely <u>do</u> and <u>saw</u>, so we can conclude we have at least <u>two</u> clauses. To see if we have a compound or <u>complex</u> sentence we have to find coordinators and subordinators. There is no <u>coordinate conjunction</u> or correlative conjunction, but the word *that* is understood after the verb <u>think</u>. The understood *that* is here a <u>subordinator</u>; therefore, we know this clause is a <u>dependent</u> one, and the sentence is a <u>complex</u> one. The dependent clause functions as the direct <u>object</u> of the sentence.

I **S:NP** / *do* **P:VP** *(n't* **A:AdvP**) *think* **P(cont)** [*I* **S:NP** / *really* **A:AdvP** / *saw* **P:VP** / *all this* **DO:NP**] **DO:FC**

3   Analyze sentence (c) *Perhaps I saw my father carrying him and the other men following along, and the dogs, but I would not have been allowed to get close enough to see something like mud in his nostril* by filling in the blanks.

There are several clauses, some finite and some <u>non-finite</u>. For main clauses, the verb must always be <u>finite</u>. The finite verbs in this sentence are <u>saw</u> and <u>would</u>. There are quite a few non-finite verbs like <u>carrying</u> and <u>following</u>, but we will ignore those for the time being as they are always part of a non-finite clause.

For now, we want to see if we have to do with one or more independent sentence parts. To do so, we have to find coordinators. There are three of them. They are and, and and but. Only one of these, but, connects two independent sentence parts. We can conclude we have a compound sentence and we have to analyze it as two separate sentences.

Part 1: Perhaps I saw my father carrying him and the other men following along, and the dogs

The subject is I and the predicator is saw. The next question is 'what' did I see? Actually, I saw three things: *my father carrying him*, *the other men following him*, and *the dogs*. So this sentence has three direct objects. The one sentence constituent we have not named yet is *perhaps*, which functions as adverbial.

Let's look further at the direct objects. Two of them are non-finite clauses, each of which can be analyzed at Level 2. In the first non-finite clause, the subject is *my father*, realized by a noun phrase, the predicator is *carrying*, realized by a verb phrase, and the direct object is *him*, realized by a noun phrase.

The second non-finite clause has as its subject *the other men*, realized by a noun phrase, and the predicator is *following along*, which happens to be a phrasal verb.

The third direct object is realized by a noun phrase. We have now finished the analysis at clause levels of Part 1 of this sentence. Put the function and realization above each sentence and clause constituent in the next schema.

Level 1: *Perhaps* **A:AdvP** / *I* **S:NP** / *saw* **P:VP** / *my father carrying him* **DO¹:NFC** /(and) / *the other men following along,* **DO²:NFC** / (and) / *the dogs* **DO³:NP**

Level 2: *my father* **S:NP** / *carrying* **P:VP** / *him* **DO:NP**; *the other men* **S:NP** / *following along* **P:VP**

Part 2: but I would not have been allowed to get close enough to see something like mud in his nostril.

This sentence part has quite a few verbs, but there is only one finite one, which is would. We may safely assume that this sentence event though we are likely to find one or more non-finite clauses. [...] There are two ways we can answer this, both of which are correct: *would have been allowed* or *would have been allowed to get*, depending on whether we regard *to be allowed* as an auxiliary verb or a lexical verb. For example, in a sentence like 'I allowed John to go' the verb allow is clearly a <u>lexical</u> verb, but in its very frequently used passive counterpart, *He is allowed to go* the whole phrase *is allowed to* could be substituted with the modal auxiliary <u>may</u> and therefore *to be allowed to* can be regarded as a semi-modal [...]

Close enough to see something like mud in his nostril answers the question '<u>where</u> *is he allowed to get.*' Therefore, we may conclude that this part functions as <u>adverbial</u>. The main word (head) in this adverbial is <u>close</u>, which is an <u>adverb</u>, so the adverbial is realized as an <u>adverb phrase</u>. But, *close* is followed by *enough to see something like mud in his nostril*. The main part of this postmodifier is the word <u>enough</u>, so the postmodifier is realized by an <u>adverb phrase</u>. The adverb *enough* is in turn postmodified by *to see something like mud in his nostril*, which is a <u>non-finite</u> clause. In this clause, we have the verb phrase <u>to see</u> and a direct object <u>something like mud in his nostril</u>.

Finally, there is one word left in the sentence, namely <u>but</u>, which is a <u>coordinate</u> conjunction and does not have a function in the clause.

but / I **S:NP** / would **P:VP** / not **A:AdvP** / have been allowed to get **(P cont.)** / [close (enough ((to see **P:VP** / something like mud in his nostril **DO:NFC**) **Postmod:NFC**) **A:AdvP**) **A:AdvP**]

4 Analyze the two following sentences at sentence and clause levels, first into sentence constituents and then each dependent clause into clause constituents.

d. I **S:NP** / must have heard **P:VP** / someone talking about that **DO:NP** / and / imagined **P:VP** / that I saw it **DO:FC**. someone **S:NP** / talking about **P:VP** / that **DO:NP**. that / I **S:NP** / saw **P:VP** / it **DO:NP**.

e. I **S:NP** / see **P:VP** / his face unaltered except for the mud — Steve Gauley's familiar, sharp-honed sneaky looking face — **DO:NP** / and / it **S:NP** / wouldn't have been **P:VP** / like that **SA:PP**; / it **S:NP** / would have been bloated* **P:VP** / and / changed **P:VP** / and / perhaps **A:AdvP** / muddied **P:VP** / all over **A:AdvP** / after so many hours in the water **A:PP**.

* It could be argued that *bloated, changed* and *muddied* function as SA. We opted for regarding it as part of the VP, because the phrase *after so many nouns in the water* highlights a 'process' rather than a 'state'.

EXERCISE 54   Identify the following sentences as either a complete sentence, fragment, run-on sentence, or comma splice and make corrections if needed.

1   Now I had mastered the language of this water.
    Complete sentence; no correction needed
2   I had come to know every trifling feature that bordered the great river.
    Complete sentence; no correction needed
3   As familiarly as I knew the letters of the alphabet.
    Fragment; possible correction: <u>I knew [something]</u> as familiarly as I knew the letters of the alphabet.
4   I had made a valuable acquisition I had lost something too.
    Run on; correction: I had made a valuable acquisition, <u>but</u> I had lost something too.
5   I had lost something, it could never be restored to me while I lived.
    Comma splice; possible correction: I had lost something. It could never be restored to me while I lived.
6   All the grace, the beauty, the poetry having gone out of the majestic river.
    Fragment; possible correction: All the grace, the beauty, the poetry <u>had</u> gone out of the majestic river.

EXERCISE 55   Using information in the sentences in Exercise 54, create two pairs of sentences, one with a dangling modifier and one with a logical modifier. Answers may vary. Several possible sentences are given below.

1   Dangling modifier: Having mastered the language of this water, every trifling feature was known to me.
    Logical modifier: Having mastered the language of this water, I knew every trifling feature.
2   Dangling modifier: A valuable acquisition made, I had lost something too.
    Logical modifier: Having made a valuable acquisition, I had lost something too.
3   Dangling modifier: Having lost something, it could never be restored to me while I lived.
    Logical modifier: Having lost something, I would never be able to restore it while I lived.
4   Dangling modifier: Having all gone out of the majestic river, the grace, the beauty, the poetry could never be restored to me anymore while I lived.
    Logical modifier: Having all gone out of the majestic river, I could never restore the grace, the beauty, the poetry anymore while I lived.

EXERCISE 56   In the following section from *Boys and Girls* by Alice Munro, the author used commas to set off the first non-restrictive element, but the second one is set off with dashes. Why do you think the author chose to set off the second element with dashes? What is so special about it?

Along the streets of this town were arranged large, sturdy pens. Each of them had a real door that a man could go through, <u>a wooden ramp along the wire</u>, for the foxes to run up and down on, and a kennel — <u>sometimes like a clothes chest with airholes</u> — where they slept and stayed in winter and had their young. A restrictive postmodifier of kennel set off with dashes

The stylistic difference here highlights the restrictive postmodifier of kennel, which is set off with dashes.

EXERCISE 57   Set off sentence and clause constituents with slashes. Then add commas where necessary. Explain your choice.

1   The next Saturday / it / was raining, / (but) / nevertheless / Nalini / stood / and / waited for / him / outside his house. (1)

In this sentence, a comma could be used after *the next Saturday* (a longer adverbial at the beginning of the sentence), before but (which connects two complete main clauses) and before and after *nevertheless* (interrupting adverbial). The author chose to put a comma only before *but*, probably because the adverbials are short, the sentence can be processed easily without the commas, and commas would have interrupted the flow and rhythm of the sentence too much.

2   At first / he / did [not] seem to be / very pleased to see her /, (and) it / was / only / when they had walked away from the house for some distance, / that he made her sit on the cross-bar of his bicycle. (2)

The first comma is needed to separate two main clauses. The second comma is needed to set off the adverbial *when* clause. Note that this second main clause has an extraposed construction and the *when* clause comes before the real subject.

3   They rode like that together through the rain. (0)

No comma is needed because the sentence has regular word order without interrupting elements.

4   It / was / like a dream, [she in his arms and feeling his breath on her face], and [everything around them, [the trees] and [the sky] and [the tops of the houses], melting away into mist and soft rain]. (4)

This is really a simple sentence as it has only one finite verb. There is a comma after *dream* to set off a non-restrictive postmodifier, which goes from [*she ... rain*]. This postmodifier, in turn, consists of two main parts [*she ... face*] and [*everything ... rain*]. These main parts, even though they are not full finite clauses are separated with a comma to help the reader recognize them as main parts. After *everything around them* there are three non-restrictive postmodifiers, *the trees* and *the sky* and *the tops of the houses*, in a series. Since the author used *and* between these three items, no comma is needed. A comma is needed after this series to show that the non-restrictive postmodifier of *everything* has ended.

5   They / went / to the same shop (and) / bought / almost the same things /, (but) this time, when they came out and she already saw the smile of farewell forming on his lips, / she / quickly / said, 'Can't we have coffee somewhere?'. (4)

There is no comma before the first *and* because it connects only two predicates (not full clauses). A comma is used before *but* because it connects two full main clauses. Commas are needed to set off *when...lips* because it is a non-restrictive postmodifier of *this time*. Finally, a comma is needed after *said* because the direct object is a direct quotation.

6   They / went / to a shop which served home-made rock cakes (and) had copper urns for decoration. (0)

No commas are needed because there is regular word order, the *which* clause is restrictive, and the conjunction *and* connects only predicates.

7   It / was / full of housewives having their coffee break/, (so) the only table available / was / one by the coat rack, which was rather uncomfortable because of all the dripping coats and umbrellas. (2)

A comma is needed before the coordinating conjunction *so* because it connects two complete main clauses. A comma is needed to set off the non-restrictive *which* clause after the phrase *one by the coat rack*.

8   Nalini / did [n't] mind/, (but) / Dr. Greaves / sat / hunched together (and) looking miserable. (1)

A comma is needed before the coordinating conjunction *but* to set off the two main clauses. No comma is needed before *and* because it connects predicates.

9   His thin hair / was / all wet (and) stuck / to his head (and) sometimes / a drop / came dripping / down his face. (0)

In this sentence, a comma could be placed before the second *and* as it connects two complete main clauses. However, the author probably decided not to use one because the clauses are rather short and simple.

10   Nalini looked at him: 'Cold?', she asked with tender concern. (1)

The colon is used to show that the first clause expresses some type of announcement. The comma is used after *cold* to set off a direct quote; note that the order of the second clause is unusual. The direct quotation is a direct object.

EXERCISE 58   The following section from *Miles City, Montana* by Alice Munro is punctuated by a creative writer, who probably used their feeling for style rather than standard rules to put punctuation marks. In most cases the author followed "the rules" given above, but in some cases he used punctuation marks for effect. For each underlined set of items, identify the punctuation "rule". If it does not clearly fit a rule, try to explain why the writer did or did not use a punctuation mark to separate the items.

1   *carrying* starts off adverbial clause, but because it is at the end of the sentence, no comma is needed]
2   *who* is a relative pronoun that introduces a restrictive relative clause (*who had been drowned*), so no comma should be used.
3   a+b: *who were* is ellipted between *together* and *returning*, making this a non-restrictive relative clause, which needs to be set off with commas.
4   *one* and *carrying* are both part of the same restrictive relative clause *the one [who was] carrying the body*, in which *who was* has been ellipted, and in which no commas should be used.

5   this comma is a stylistic choice. The independent clause introduced by *and* lacks a subject (e.g. *and [they] walked with their heads down*) and is therefore not entirely complete. According to 'the rules' there should therefore be no comma in front of *and*, but many writers still use a comma in these constructions. In this case, the author seems to really want a pause. *as if* introduces an adverbial that expresses an afterthought, which may be set off with a comma.

6   *dripping* introduces an adverbial non-finite dependent clause that tells the reader when the dogs were dispirited, i.e. *[while] dripping from the cold river*.

7   This sentence could have read: *hours before, when they all set out, [...]* and the *when* clause would have been non-restrictive, which would have needed a comma. In the order it is written now, the emphasis is more on the time that has gone by. *the men* introduces the second finite clause in a summation that starts with *the dogs were nervy and yelping* as the first part of that summation, so a comma should be used here.

8   *and there was* introduces the third and final finite clause in the summation, so a comma should be used here.

9   this comma separates two adjective phrases that independently modify the same noun: *excitement*, so a comma should be used here.

10 *that* functions as a subordinator that introduces a direct object preceded by the predicator of the sentence, i.e.: *It* **S** / *was understood* **P** / *that they might find something horrible* **DO**. Since main sentence constituents should not, as a general rule, be separated by commas, and because there are no other constructions that require commas, a comma should not be used here.

EXERCISE 59   In the following stream of words (adapted from *Life on the Mississippi* by Mark Twain), set off complete sentences with a period and add commas where needed.

Now when I had mastered the language of this water and had come to know every trifling feature that bordered the great river as familiarly as I knew the letters of the alphabet, I had made a valuable acquisition, but I had lost something too. I had lost something which could never be restored to me while I lived. All the grace, the beauty, the poetry had gone out of the majestic river.

EXERCISE 60   Read the sentences (from the same student) and try to determine redundant parts. Then compare with the rewritten version. Comment on the differences. Are there other ways to reduce redundancy?

1   The most important factors affecting learning a second language (be it English, French or Macedonian) are motivation and attitude.

The most important factors affecting learning a second language (be it English, French or Macedonian) are motivation and attitude.

Explanation: This sentence does not have redundant information and is concise enough.

2   Students who are motivated and who have a positive attitude towards the concerning language and its speakers, are mostly more willing to learn that language and therefore most of them will usually obtain higher marks than other students.

Motivated students with a positive attitude towards the language and its speakers are usually more willing to learn that language and will obtain higher marks than other students.

Explanation: The two relative clauses (*who are [...] and who have [...]*) have been rephrased more concisely. *Concerning* is redundant. The part after the comma (comma is incorrect) contains two parts of relevant information: *more willing to learn that language* and wanting to *obtain higher marks*. All irrelevant words have been taken out and the editor has made sure the parts remain parallel in structure with finite clauses (*are usually [...] and will obtain*)

3   One study on second language learning conducted by Lambert and Gardner (1972) clearly shows this relationship between motivation and attitude on the one hand and obtaining high marks on the other hand. In their study about high school students in Louisiana and their French language skills, it turned out that students who were motivated to do well obtained higher marks than their less motivated or unmotivated colleagues.

For example, Lambert and Gardner (1972) studied high school students in Louisiana learning French, and students who were more motivated obtained higher marks than their less motivated peers.

Explanation: In academic writing it is sufficient to mention the authors and the date; the reader then knows it is a reference to an academic study. The preceding sentence (2) already gave information about motivated students who are more willing to learn a language and obtain higher marks. Therefore, Lambert and Gardner (1972) is an example to support the statement in (2). This link is established with the use of *for example*. The editor removed the first sentence and rewrote the remainder much more concisely.

4   The results also showed that students with a positive attitude towards French-speaking people and their ways of life were more likely to obtain higher marks than students who were prejudiced towards French-speaking people and who denigrated the French way of life.

The results also showed that students with a positive attitude towards French-speaking people and their ways of life were more likely to obtain higher marks than students who were prejudiced towards French-speaking people and denigrated the French way of life.

Explanation: This sentence contains rather new information and cannot be changed much. Only the second *who* was taken out.

EXERCISE 61   Read the same excerpt again (from *Farm at Raraba* by Ernst Havemann) and compare it with our (poorly) rewritten version. Are the passive constructions less effective? If so, why?

My late dad was a magnificent shot. One time when we were hunting in the Low Veld and had paused for a smoke, there was the yelp of a wild dog, and a troop of impala came bounding over the tall grass. Opposite us, three hundred yards off, was a stony ridge like a wall, six feet high. You would think those buck would avoid it, but no, they went straight at it. One after the other, without pausing or swerving, they leapt over it. They cleared it by three feet. I tell you, friend, it was a beautiful sight. You can't beat Nature for beauty, eh.

My late dad was a magnificent shot. One time when we were hunting in the Low Veld and had paused for a smoke, the yelp of a wild dog was heard, and a troop of impala bounding over the tall grass was seen. Opposite us, three hundred yards off, was a stony ridge like a wall, six feet high. You would think that it could be avoided by those buck, but no, they went straight at it. One after the other, without pausing or swerving, they leapt over it. They cleared it by three feet. I tell you, friend, it was a beautiful sight. You can't beat Nature for beauty, eh.

1   *there was the yelp of a wild dog* — versus — the yelp of a wild dog was heard

In this clause *there* has the key function of creating an existential space (where the men were) in which something occurred in the background. If we make this clause passive, the *yelp* (new subject) would be much more foregrounded and draw too much of the readers' attention.

2   *a troop of impala came bounding over the tall grass* — versus — <u>a troop of impala bounding over the tall grass was seen</u>

In this sentence, the active voice creates an image in the readers' mind with the impala actually bounding. The passive voice is totally unnecessary and takes away from that clear imagery (e.g. by implying another observer).

3   *those buck would avoid it* — versus — <u>it could be avoided by those buck</u>

In this construction, the active voice gives *those buck* a mind of their own. The passive counterpart would make the reader focus more on the ridge and again the imagery of the buck leaping of their own free will be diminished.

EXERCISE 62   The following excerpt from an academic abstract has several parallel constructions. Underline the constructions and explain what makes the constructions parallel.

They indicated challenges in global aspects of writing a research article, especially writing various text types, linking ideas smoothly and coherently, structuring the text, citing academic sources, summarizing and or paraphrasing academic sources, elaborating and supporting ideas in each paragraph, and organizing ideas clearly and logically.

There are 9 verbs in the present participle form, each with direct objects. There are also parallel constructions with adverbs (smoothly-coherently; clearly-logically).

They indicated challenges in global aspects of writing a research article, especially <u>writing</u> various text types, <u>linking</u> ideas <u>smoothly</u> and <u>coherently,</u> <u>structuring</u> the text, <u>citing</u> academic sources, <u>summarizing</u> and or <u>paraphrasing</u> academic sources, <u>elaborating</u> and <u>supporting</u> ideas in each paragraph, and <u>organizing</u> ideas <u>clearly</u> and <u>logically</u>.

EXERCISE 63

The following passage is an abstract written for a conference paper. The first sentence is the original first sentence. The remaining sentences have been put in random order. Rearrange these sentences in the right order so that the text adheres most clearly to the end focus principle, then underline the parts of each sentence that establish their end focus. The first two sentences have been done for you.

1. Academic writing (AW) in English remains problematic for students at the highest academic levels as students have to write various types of texts to pass their courses and publish articles in journals. After a literature review and a needs analysis was conducted, the authors piloted <u>a genre-based AW course</u> and evaluated it.

2. <u>This paper reports on the course</u>, the survey the students took before the course and the evaluation after the course.

3. In addition, <u>the course materials</u>, observations of classroom practices and reflections of individual feedback sessions were included in <u>the data</u>.

4. <u>Results</u> [understood of the data] indicated that most participants had not had AW training before <u>they</u> entered the doctoral program

5. <u>They</u> indicated challenges in global aspects of writing a research article, especially <u>writing various text types, linking ideas smoothly and coherently, structuring the text, citing academic sources, summarizing and or paraphrasing academic sources, elaborating and supporting ideas in each paragraph, and organizing ideas clearly and logically.</u>

6. <u>All these aspects</u> were dealt with in the course and received <u>positive evaluations.</u>

7. <u>The most positive comments</u> were on the personal feedback sessions

8. Finally, <u>the students</u> recommended that *Academic Writing* should be a required course during the first year of their study.

9. In addition, they indicated that <u>they</u> would like personal feedback in the process of writing from their tutors for other courses.

257 Key to the exercises

Index

-ed form   50
-ing form   50, 91, 155, 158

A
a few   99
a great deal of   99
a great many   99
a lot of   99
abstract noun   89
active sentence   56, 72, 74
active voice   56
actor   72
adjective   77, 92, 183
adjective clause subordinator   105
adjective clause   38, 105
adjective phrase   118, 119, 136, 137, 179
adverb   92, 94
adverb clause subordinator   106
adverb in multi-word verb   81
adverb phrase   118, 138, 147, 161
adverbial   20, 30, 162
agent   64, 72, 213
appear   25
article   99, 114
assume   27
attribute   18, 20

aux   135
auxiliary verb   47

B
base form   51, 61
basic verb forms   50, 51
be   24, 53, 60, 61
become   25
being pattern   24
believe   75
benefactive object   20, 25

C
call   27
can   55, 62
cardinal numeral   99
central modal   55, 62
certify   27
classifying genitive   122
clause   33, 151
cleft constructions   170
closed word class   88
coherence   215
come   62
comma   102, 126, 203
comma splice   102, 200
common noun   89
communicative function   16

comparative form   92
complement   23
complement of preposition   140
complex sentence   36, 176, 210
complex transitive verb   27, 67, 73, 83, 165
complex verb phrase   46
compound object   101
compound sentence   34, 101, 176
compound subject   101
compound-complex sentence   41, 176
concerning   115, 140
concrete noun   89
conjunction   101
conjunctive adverb   36, 93, 102, 115, 201
connectors   101, 114
consider   27
constituent   20, 22, 45
conventionalized passive construction   77, 84, 165
coordinate conjunction   35, 101, 199
coordinator   35, 101, 176, 200
copula verb   25, 65
correlative conjunction   35, 101
could   55, 62

count noun 89
crown 27

D
dangling modifier 201
dare 55, 62
declarative 15
declare 27
deem 27
demonstrative pronoun 97
dependent clause 36, 151
dependent pronoun 95, 121
determiner 96, 100, 121, 122, 178
direct object 20, 69
direct quotation 154
direct quotation as direct object 154
discontinuous modifier of adjectives 136
discontinuous modifier of adverb 138
ditransitive verb 25, 67, 73, 165
do 57, 60, 62
doing/seeing pattern 25, 65

E
each other 98
elect 27
ellipsis 167
ellipsis in relative clauses 132
end focus principle 215
end weighted sentence 212
exclamatory 15
existential construction 169

extraposed construction 160, 166
extraposed object 160
extraposed subject 160
extraposition 160, 166

F
feel 25, 157
finite adverb clause 162
finite clause 69, 153
finite dependent clause 153
finite verb 48, 152, 176, 185
finite verb forms 48
force 70
fragment 199
front-weighted sentence 212
function 20, 45, 87, 117
functions of phrases 142

G
get 62
giving/buying pattern 25
go 62
grow 25

H
have 54, 60, 62, 157
head 117, 178
hear 157
help 157
helping verb 47
how(ever) 154

I
idiomatic noun preposition verb 81
imperative 16
indefinite pronoun 98
independent clause 35, 151
independent pronoun 129
indirect object 20, 26
indirect quotation 154
indirect quotation as direct object 154
interjection 111
interrogative 16
interrogative adverb 92, 104, 114
interrogative pronoun 97, 113, 173
intransitive verb 24, 65, 83
irregular verb 51
it's/its 96

K
keep on 62

L
let 157
lexical verb 47, 64
look 25

M
main clause 34, 150, 173
main verb 47
make 25, 27, 157
making/considering pattern 27, 67
many a 99

marginal modal   55
mass noun   89
may   55, 62
might   55, 62
modal auxiliary   55
modals   55, 62
modify   92
monotransitive verb   25, 67, 73
mood (grammatical)   56, 60, 62
multi-word verb   80
multi-word preposition   109
must   55, 62

N

name   27
need   55, 62
non-canonical construction   150
non-count noun   89
non-finite clause(s)   70, 74, 91, 155
non-finite adverb clause   162
non-finite dependent clause   176
non-finite noun clause   153
non-finite verb   50
non-restrictive postmodifiers   125
notice   157
noun clause   153
noun clause subordinator   104
noun phrase   119
nouns   88
number (grammatical)   49
numeral   99, 113

O

object attribute   20
observe   157
one another   98
open word class   112
order   71
ordering of auxiliary verbs   58
ordinal numeral   99
ought to   55, 62

P

parallel structures   102, 214
participants   17
passive auxiliary   72
passive *be*   56, 63
passive construction   72, 164
passive sentence   57, 165
passive voice   57
past participle   50
past participle as adjective   77
past tense   48
patient   72
perfect *have*   54, 59
person (grammatical)   48
personal pronoun   96
phrasal prepositional verb   81
phrasal verb   81
phrase   43, 69, 86, 117, 152, 13
phrase constituents   142
plain infinitive   50, 157
possessive pronoun   96
postmodifiers of nouns   119, 124, 180
predicate   22
predicator   23

premodifier   179
premodifiers of nouns   119, 179
preposition in multi-word verb   81
prepositional phrase   118, 141
prepositional verb   81
preposition   108, 115
present participle   50, 53, 61
present tense   48
process   18
progressive *be*   53, 59
pronoun   95, 113
proper noun   89
prototypical sentence patterns   23
prove   25, 27
pseudo-cleft construction   171
punctuation of compound structures   203, 207
punctuation of dependent structures   203
punctuation of sentence/clause constituents   203
punctuation of postmodifiers   204

Q

quantifier   98

R

realization   45, 87, 118
reciprocal pronoun   98
redundancy   210
reflexive pronoun   98
regard   27

regular verb   51
relative adverb   93, 105
relative clause subordinator   105
relative clause   38, 105, 151
relative pronoun   96, 105, 129
remain   25
restrictive postmodifier   125
run-on sentence   199
running pattern   24

S

see   75, 157
seem   25
semi-colon   35, 199
semi-modal   56, 76
sentence   33, 150, 173
sentence adverbs   93
sentence constituents   31
setting   18, 20
shall   55, 62
should   55, 62
simple sentence   34, 176
simple verb phrase   46
smell   25
so   99
sound   25
specifying genitive   122, 178
specifying modifier   125
start   62
statement   153
subject   20, 45

subject attribute   20, 24, 45
subordinate clause   34
subordinating conjunction   104, 105
subordinator   36, 97, 104, 154, 176
supposed to   76, 112

T

taste   25
tell   71
temporary object   166
temporary subject   160
tensed verb   48
that   96, 151, 153
there   169
to be   74
to be able to   56, 62
to be allowed to   56, 62, 76
to be believed to   62
to be forced to   62
to have to   56, 62
to infinitive   50, 155, 157
to seem to   62
to want to   56, 62
transitive verb   65, 164
transitive verbs and passive sentences   73, 164
turn   25

U

used to   55, 62

V

varieties   15
verb phrase   45, 118, 135
verbs   91

W

what(ever)   154
when(ever)   154
where(ever)   154
which   96
which clause as adverbial   161
which(ever)   154
who   96
who(ever)   154
whom   96
whose   96, 129
wh-question   154
will   55, 62
wipe   68
word class   86, 112
word order   29
would   55, 62

Y

yes/no question   154